RURAL WOMEN WORKERS IN NINETEENTH-CENTURY ENGLAND

RURAL WOMEN WORKERS IN NINETEENTH-CENTURY ENGLAND

GENDER, WORK AND WAGES

Nicola Verdon

THE BOYDELL PRESS

© Nicola Verdon 2002

All Rights Reserved. Except as permitted under current legislation no part of this work may be photocopied, stored in a retrieval system, published, performed in public, adapted, broadcast, transmitted, recorded or reproduced in any form or by any means, without the prior permission of the copyright owner

The right of Nicola Verdon to be identified as the author of this work has been asserted in accordance with sections 77 and 78 of the Copyright, Designs and Patents Act 1988

First published 2002
The Boydell Press, Woodbridge

ISBN 978-0-85115-906-5

Transferred to digital printing

The Boydell Press is an imprint of Boydell & Brewer Ltd
PO Box 9, Woodbridge, Suffolk IP12 3DF, UK
and of Boydell & Brewer Inc.
668 Mt. Hope Avenue, Rochester NY 14620, USA
website: www.boydellandbrewer.com

A CIP record for this title is available
from the British Library

This publication is printed on acid-free paper

Contents

Acknowledgements	vi
List of illustrations	vii
Introduction Rural women workers: the forgotten labour force	1
1 Women, work and wages in historical perspective	7
2 Differing views of rural women's work in documentary material: an overview of printed sources	40
3 Women in the agricultural labour market: female farm servants	77
4 Women in the agricultural labour market: female day labourers	98
5 Alternative employment opportunities: domestic industries	132
6 Survival strategies: women, work and the informal economy	164
Conclusion Assessing women's work	196
Bibliography	201
Index	229

Acknowledgements

I have incurred many debts whilst writing this book and would like to take this opportunity to express my gratitude. The study began as a PhD thesis funded by University College, Northampton, and I would like to thank colleagues there, and more recently at Harlaxton College and the Rural History Centre, University of Reading, who have offered advice and assistance throughout the project. Special thanks go to my two supervisors, Pete King at Northampton and Alun Howkins at Sussex, who imparted – and continue to provide – invaluable guidance, insight and inspiration. Audiences at several conferences, notably those run by the Agricultural History Society in 1997 and 2000, the Social History Society in 1998, and the Economic History Society in 2000, and university seminar series (Northampton in 1996, Nottingham Trent and Sussex in 1998) have helped shape my ideas. I would also particularly like to thank Helen Speechley who generously provided me with earlier versions of her research. Staff at the British Library, Leicester and Reading University libraries, Norfolk, East Yorkshire and Bedford record offices and local studies libraries assisted in the research for the thesis and book. Several others have (sometimes unwittingly) helped in many different ways over the past few years: Ed Bolt, Christine Garwood, Jennifer Hall, my parents and family deserve special mention.

Illustrations

Figures

2.1	Distribution and prevalence of women's and children's work in domestic industry in England in 1834	54
2.2	Contribution of men, women and children to annual family income in 1834	60
3.1	The movement in servants' wages at Driffield, 1870 to 1890	94
4.1	Days worked by male, female and child labourers on Earsham Home Farm, Norfolk in 1807	100
4.2	Days worked by male, female and child labourers on Earsham Home Farm in 1837	101
4.3	Days worked by male, female and child day labourers on Saltmarshe Home Farm, East Yorkshire in 1820	102
4.4	Days worked by male, female and child day labourers on Saltmarshe Home Farm in 1840	104
5.1	Numbers employed in lace-making and straw-plaiting in Bedfordshire, 1841 to 1901	153

Tables

2.1	Average annual earnings of men, women and children in the household accounts of Davies and Eden	44
2.2	Male and female agricultural day rates as recorded in the General Views	48
2.3	Wages of general male and female servants in first edition General Views	50
2.4	Wages of general male and female servants in second edition General Views	50
2.5	The incidence of women's and children's involvement in agricultural work in 1834	56
2.6	The incidence of women's and children's involvement in haymaking, weeding and harvest work as indicated in Question 11 of the 1834 Poor Law Report	58
2.7	Women's agricultural work and wages in 1843	65
2.8	Female agricultural work by county in 1867 to 1869	68
2.9	Weekly earnings of agricultural labourers in England, Michaelmas 1860	70

ILLUSTRATIONS

2.10	Number of agricultural labourers in England and Wales, 1841 to 1901	74
4.1	Days worked by women, men and children, 1861 to 1891, at Hoverton St Peter, Norfolk	115
4.2	Days worked by women, men and children on Sewerby Home Farm, East Yorkshire, between 1861 and 1891	116
4.3	Women workers on Laxton Manor Farm, May 1882 to April 1883 and their occupational designation in the 1881 census	118
4.4	Female day wage rates on selected farms in the nineteenth century	125
5.1	Annual farm expenditure on male, female and child labour in nineteenth-century Bedfordshire	142
5.2	Nineteenth-century weekly wages in lace-making, straw-plaiting and agriculture	143

Introduction

Rural women workers: the forgotten labour force

I have seen many a Poor woman go to the fields in bitter winter weather, cleaning turnips and beet for the sum of ten pence a day. They would come home up to there knees in mud and whet, and then they would have the housework to do, washing cooking mending, and all the other jobs which come along when there is a big famely to do for, and famelys mostely were big in them days.[1]

If life were hard for the men, it were harder still for the women. They often worked side by side with their menfolk in the fields all day, then went home and while their husbands fed the pig or fetched a yoke o'water, they'd get the meal going. But most men could rest a while after tea, at least in winter, but the mother had to set about preparing for the next day, getting the children washed and off to bed, and making and mending clothes and what bits o' furniture and linen they had in the house. Then they'd have to be up with the lark in the morning to sweep and clean the home afore it were time to go to work again.[2]

These two contemporary autobiographical accounts from the Fens offer us a rare glimpse into the reality of life for many women living in the English countryside in the second half of the nineteenth century. Those women who were married with a family were confronted with the familiar – and recognisably modern – dilemma of balancing domestic and childcare responsibilities with contributing financially towards the meagre household income. For many other groups of women – for example, those not yet married or those already widowed – the economic choices they encountered on a day-to-day basis could be even more stark. The ways women could earn a living in

---

[1] Lilias Rider Haggard, ed., '*I Walked by Night*': *By the King of the Norfolk Poachers*, 1st edn 1935 (Oxford, 1982), pp. 90–1.
[2] Sybil Marshall, *Fenland Chronicle: Recollections of William Henry and Kate Mary Edwards* (Cambridge, 1967), p. 216.

the nineteenth century clearly depended on many considerations: the area of the country in which they lived, their age and marital status, the number of children they had and local custom regarding female labour were especially significant. In addition, long-term changes in the agricultural and industrial sectors of the economy also profoundly affected women's movements in and out of the nineteenth-century rural labour market. What do we understand about the impact of these variables on the daily lives of rural women workers? Surprisingly little, despite the impressive ascent of both women's history and agrarian social history as established academic disciplines since the 1960s. The roles performed by women living and working in rural England still remain obscure. This book therefore aims to make a contribution towards filling a substantial and important gap in the history of the nineteenth-century English countryside.

My research on women's employment in the nineteenth-century rural economy does not stand alone. It has been guided and framed by a number of other scholars working in the field. Indeed, while acknowledging the relative dearth of studies on rural labouring women, this is not to deny that there has been a marked escalation of academic interest in the subject in the late 1980s and 1990s. In 1995 Pamela Sharpe called for historians of agricultural labour to

> Build up a corrective picture at the local level by developing new sources, in which, as far as is possible, we can discover the feminine aspect. What women actually did needs to be established from the bottom up, paying attention to localised differences and to such factors as seasonal change, age-specificity, and marital status.[3]

In many ways this plea has been heeded. Detailed studies of farm labour books and other archival sources by Joyce Burnette, Mary Bouquet, Judy Gielgud, Celia Miller, Pamela Sharpe and Helen Speechley on different English counties have begun to unravel the complex regional diversity in rural women's employment opportunities and wage-earning patterns in the period after 1700.[4] Such research has stimulated a more focused and perceptive

---

[3] Pamela Sharpe, 'Continuity and change: Women's history and economic history in Britain', *Economic History Review*, XLVIII (1995), pp. 353–69 (p. 357).

[4] Joyce Burnette, 'Labourers at the Oakes. Changes in the demand for female day-labourers at a farm near Sheffield during the Agricultural Revolution', *Journal of Economic History*, LIX (1999), pp. 41–67; Mary Bouquet, *Family, Servants and Visitors: The Farm Household in Nineteenth and Twentieth-Century Devon* (Norwich, 1985); Judy Gielgud, 'Nineteenth-century farm women in Northumberland and Cumbria: The neglected workforce' (D.Phil. thesis, University of Sussex, 1992); Celia Miller, 'The hidden workforce: Female fieldworkers in Gloucestershire, 1870–1901', *Southern History*, 6 (1984), pp. 139–61; Pamela Sharpe, *Adapting to Capitalism: Working Women in the English Economy, 1700–1850* (Basingstoke, 1996); Helen V. Speechley, 'Female and child agricultural day labourers in Somerset, c.1685–1870' (Ph.D. thesis, University of Exeter, 1999).

recognition of the impact of gender, age, locality and custom on the agrarian workforce in past centuries and they serve as examples on which to build. However, our knowledge of women's employment in the nineteenth-century countryside is still far from complete. As Sharpe has recently pointed out, 'we still have little idea of where and when women worked on farms' and 'only further local research, which considers both economic explanations and less quantifiable aspects of human experience in tandem, can take us beyond this necessarily sketchy picture'.[5]

My interest in the subject is underpinned by the belief that it is impossible to gain a complete understanding of the lives of poor labouring families without a full consideration of the economic contribution made by women to the rural household. While few historians today would deny this, there are still serious omissions within the current literature on women's work in nineteenth-century rural England which this book aims to rectify. On a simple level this study sets out to write women into the historical record of the English countryside: it is an empirical investigation into the types of labour rural women were employed to perform on a day-to-day basis. The practice of work – or lack of work – was one of the defining features of the lives of the rural labouring poor in nineteenth-century rural England, although the work of women is rarely seen in such terms and has too often been relegated to the sidelines of the male experience. While research on women's work – particularly agricultural work – has proved a relatively popular and fruitful avenue of investigation, no study has yet attempted a detailed analysis of the wide range of occupations rural labouring women participated in.[6] Therefore the main structure of this book is constructed around an examination of the key pursuits open to women in the formal rural labour market. Chapter 2 reappraises the usefulness of a range of contemporary printed material to the study of rural women's work. This provides an overview of the formal published account of female labour patterns in the nineteenth-century countryside. The remainder of the book offers a thematic discussion of certain productive activities: Chapter 3 looks at the incidence of female farm service, Chapter 4 focuses on women who worked as agricultural day labourers, and Chapter 5 is concerned with the involvement of women in rural domestic industries. However, it is now widely recognised that narrow econometric definitions of 'work', 'occupations' and 'earnings' significantly

---

[5] Pamela Sharpe, 'The female labour market in English agriculture during the Industrial Revolution: Expansion or contraction?', *Agricultural History Review*, 47 (1999), pp. 161–81 (pp. 161 and 181).

[6] The one exception to this is Pamela Horn's *Victorian Countrywomen* (Oxford, 1991). She looks at the occupations women from all classes participated in. While this book includes much interesting material, it lacks a detailed analytical and theoretical approach to the evidence.

affect the way we measure women's economic activities.⁷ Chapter 6 therefore highlights the more informal ways women contributed economically to rural labouring households. These included the exploitation of common rights such as gleaning, the cultivation of allotments and cottage gardens, taking in washing, rearing animals and nursing sick and elderly neighbours. Such an approach allows the interaction between the informal and formal economies – and the way women moved between them – to be more fully explored.

This methodology – writing a history of women's work to parallel those already completed for male rural workers – is entirely appropriate considering the paucity of published research on female labourers in the nineteenth-century countryside. However, in many respects the more important project is to conceptualise the nature of rural women's labour within the broader theoretical debates on women and work. How the processes of industrialisation and technical change in the late eighteenth and nineteenth centuries transformed patterns of female labour in urban, industrial enterprises has been extensively discussed. The consequences for female labourers of government legislation aimed specifically at containing their hours and places of work has also been analysed. The ways ideological constructs of working women altered over the period, and the extent these exerted influence on the types of work women sought, forms another major strand of research. Chapter 2 will explore these themes in more detail. So far, however, few of these theoretical arguments have been transferred to women employed in the rural labour market. Changing technology in nineteenth-century agricultural work – especially harvest work – and the subsequent impact on women's work has been examined.⁸ Recent research has also begun to explore the nature of the sexual division of agricultural labour, the male–female wage gap and continuities and changes in the utilisation of female workers across time and space. (The current state of scholarship on rural labouring women will also be appraised in Chapter 2.) Despite this, our comprehension of these issues is still in its infancy. A number of key questions will therefore be addressed throughout the following chapters.

First, the importance of region is central: what regional differences and similarities are discernible in women's work across rural England, and how can we account for these? The research for this book is based on detailed analysis of local archives from a limited number of English counties, mainly

---

⁷ See Edward Higgs, 'Women, occupations and work in the nineteenth-century censuses', *History Workshop Journal*, 23 (1987), pp. 59–82; Bridget Hill, 'Women, work and the census: A problem for historians of women', *History Workshop Journal*, 35 (1993), pp. 78–94; Sara Horrell and Jane Humphries, 'Women's labour force participation and the transition to the male breadwinner family', *Economic History Review*, XLVIII (1995), pp. 89–117.
⁸ K. D. M. Snell, *Annals of the Labouring Poor: Social Change and Agrarian England, 1660–1900* (Cambridge, 1985), ch.1; Michael Roberts, 'Sickles and scythes: Women's work and men's work at harvest time', *History Workshop Journal*, 7 (1979), pp. 3–28.

INTRODUCTION

East Yorkshire, Norfolk and Bedfordshire. In order to overcome this narrow concentration, other regional studies have been incorporated, where appropriate, to broaden the geographical scope of the book. This method enables a unique comparative overview of female labour patterns across the regions of England to be realised. The sexual division of labour in the nineteenth-century countryside forms the second major theoretical concern. Was there a rigid division between men's and women's work across rural England, or were boundaries more fluid and regionally specific? Was women's employment in rural England uniformally low paid and labelled as unskilled, or were there times when female labour was attractive and highly sought after? How much were women paid for their labour, and why was a male–female wage gap a persistent feature of the rural labour market? The issue of continuity and change in patterns of women's work is also significant: how did the types and amount of work women were engaged to perform change over the course of the century? Is the notion of a decline in women's economic participation applicable across all rural regions and occupations? This book is based on the period from the beginning of the Napoleonic Wars in the 1790s to the close of the agricultural depression in the 1890s. Thus, the broad impact of shifting economic forces and technological innovations over the course of the century will be detected.

Other themes have been incorporated. It is important to assess the influence that lifecycle variables had on women's work patterns: how far was women's labour dependent upon their marital and age specificity? What impact did children have on the family economy? While the labour of women forms the central axis of the book, the complex and changing relationship between male, female and child workers has to be considered and the importance of kinship networks – both in the formal and informal economies – discussed. Finally the role of ideology is assessed: how did attitudes towards female labourers change over the course of the nineteenth century, and in what ways did this affect women's access to employment? Were concepts such as separate spheres, domestic ideology and the family wage relevant to the everyday reality of rural labouring families?

I am conscious of the omissions in this book. A holistic and systematic analysis of the whole range of tasks undertaken by rural labouring women in the nineteenth century has not been possible. I have not looked at domestic service or at localised industrial employment opportunities. Nor have I examined the criminal activities of women which some historians would view as belonging to the legitimate economic activities of poor rural women in the past.[9] This book concentrates on certain regions of England: future analysis of local records from other counties may lead us to different conclusions.

---

[9] See e.g. Penelope Lane, 'Work on the margins: Poor women and the informal economy of eighteenth and early nineteenth-century Leicestershire', *Midland History*, 22 (1997), pp. 85–99.

However, these gaps should not detract from the primary concerns of the book. It is hoped that this study will bridge the divide between economic history, rural history and women's history, and rescue rural women from their relative invisibility in the historiography. The omissions leave plenty of scope for future studies.

1

Women, work and wages in historical perspective

The aim of this chapter is to present a historiographical account of research on women's employment in the nineteenth century. This will provide a framework for the following chapters. My approach is certainly not novel: many historians have furnished their accounts of gender, work and industrialisation with a similar grounding. However, it is worth reiterating the main stands of this historical debate in order to locate the subject of rural women's employment within the broader context of research on women and work in the nineteenth century. This chapter does not discuss the protracted and complex path taken by economic history towards becoming more sensitive to the implications of gender. Nor does it assess the subtle divisions between the approaches taken by women's history, gender history and feminist history. Katrina Honeyman has recently provided an excellent account of economic history's tendency to marginalise women and recent efforts to mainstream gender history within the context of industrialisation, as well as the broad developments in feminist history.[1] Instead, the following section appraises the key themes and debates that have resulted from scholarly research on women, work and industrialisation in the past thirty years or so. This will be followed by a consideration of the major arguments that have dominated recent agrarian history and a review of new endeavours designed to write women into the rural historiography. The chapter will close with an analysis of sources for the study of rural women's work, highlighting the uses and limitations of material on which the book is based. Overall it is my intention in this chapter to bring together the foremost scholarship on investigating and interpreting the economic position of nineteenth-century women in an accessible and informative forum.

---

[1] Katrina Honeyman, *Women, Gender and Industrialisation in England, 1700–1870* (Basingstoke, 2000): see ch. 1, 'Feminist history and the historiography of the industrial revolution'.

Women, work and industrialisation in England: the key debates

There is a general dearth of literature on the economic position of rural women in the nineteenth century. This contrasts with the interest shown in women who lived in industrial and urban areas of England.[2] Although it has been difficult to break down the gender blindness of some stands of economic history, the importance of gender to economic analyses is now generally recognised. This has resulted in a steady move away from studies that concentrate on the male experience of labour in the formal economy of paid work outside the home.[3] As Honeyman argues, research on the work of women (and children) has resulted in a revised perception of industrialisation, producing 'some of the most stimulating reinterpretations of the Industrial Revolution period'.[4]

The debates on the impact of industrialisation in late eighteenth- and nineteenth-century England are vast and complex. It is not within my scope to document them here. But if we concentrate on the specific issue of women's work and industrial change, it is possible to pinpoint the key theoretical controversies which have engendered debate.[5] First, the effects of

---

[2] The split between the rural and urban economy was not unequivocal however, particularly in the early phases of industrialisation when much industrial employment was situated in the countryside.

[3] Pat Hudson has shown how research on women and industrialisation has altered since the mid-1980s. Earlier accounts, she argues, were based on attempts to write a parallel history of women to match those of the male experience. These were concerned with the formal economy of waged work outside the home and produced a linear picture of radical change in women's lives. More recent histories have attempted to integrate women's experiences into mainstream accounts, and new themes and concerns have emerged as a result. Pat Hudson, 'Women and industrialisation', in June Purvis, ed., *Women's History: Britain, 1850–1945. An Introduction* (London, 1995), pp. 23–50 (pp. 25–6).

[4] Honeyman, *Women, Gender and Industrialisation*, p. 8.

[5] There are a large number of books and essays which seek to summarise the debates surrounding women's work and the process of industrialisation in the eighteenth and nineteenth centuries. Among the most useful include Harriet Bradley, *Men's Work, Women's Work: A Sociological History of the Sexual Division of Labour in Employment* (Cambridge, 1989); Pat Hudson and W. R. Lee, eds, *Women's Work and the Family Economy in Historical Perspective* (Manchester, 1990); Jane Humphries, '"Lurking in the wings...": Women in the historiography of the industrial revolution', *Business and Economic History*, 20 (1991), pp. 32–44; Angela V. John, ed., *Unequal Opportunities: Women's Employment in England, 1800–1918* (Oxford, 1986); Patrick Joyce, ed., *The Historical Meanings of Work* (Cambridge, 1987); R. E. Pahl, *Divisions of Labour* (Oxford, 1984); Purvis, ed., *Women's History*, esp. ch. 2 and ch. 4; Jane Rendall, *Women in an Industrialising Society: England, 1750–1880* (Oxford, 1990); Sonya Rose, '"Gender at work": Sex, class and industrial capitalism', *History Workshop Journal*, 21 (1986), pp. 113–31; Pamela Sharpe, 'Continuity and change: Women's history and economic history in Britain', *Economic History Review*, XLVIII (1995), pp. 353–69; Janet Thomas, 'Women and capitalism: Oppression or emancipation? A review article', *Comparative Studies in Society and History*, 30 (1988), pp. 534–49; Deborah Valenze, *The First Industrial Woman* (Oxford, 1995).

technological innovation and changes in the organisation and site of labour on female workers have been pivotal concerns. In relation to this, the questioning of the pervasiveness of the separation of home and workplace has been central. Second, historians have debated how various ideological constructs impacted on working women. These included not only the formal state-sanctioned legislation aimed at women in the workforce, but also the ubiquitous social definitions and images of womanhood and femininity that were reworked and repackaged in the nineteenth century. Another primary concern has been the processes by which notions such as skill, domestic ideology, patriarchy and male breadwinner were reformulated at this time. In addition, the wrangle over whether continuity or change best defines the working experiences of female labourers underpins much of the literature that is concerned with women's economic history.

In simplistic terms, historical assessments of the impact of industrialisation on women's employment patterns and standards of living are polarised: 'optimistic' or 'pessimistic', 'evolutionary' or 'revolutionary'.[6] With regard to female employment the 'optimistic' view argues that the industrial revolution presented women with wider job opportunities, leading eventually to their emancipation. R. M. Hartwell, Ivy Pinchbeck, Neil McKendrick and Edward Shorter have all been labelled as 'optimists'.[7] The 'pessimist' account suggests that industrial development reduced women's employment options, leaving them increasingly confined to a narrow range of low-paid and low-skilled jobs which, in turn, reinforced their dependency on men.[8]

---

[6] See David Cannadine, 'The past and the present in the English industrial revolution, 1880–1980', *Past and Present*, 103 (1984), pp. 149–58, for a review of the ways historians have conceptualised the industrial revolution in the past century.

[7] Hartwell writes, 'It was during the Industrial Revolution, and largely because of the economic opportunities it afforded to working-class women, that there was the beginnings of that most important and most beneficial of all social revolutions of the last two centuries, the emancipation of women'. R. M. Hartwell, *The Industrial Revolution and Economic Growth* (London, 1971), p. 343. Pinchbeck argues that the industrial revolution gave single women 'social and economic independence' while married women gained 'since it led to the assumption that men's wages should be paid on a family basis, and prepared the way for the more modern conception that in the rearing of children and in home-making, the married woman makes an adequate economic contribution'. Ivy Pinchbeck, *Women Workers and the Industrial Revolution, 1750–1850*, 1st edn 1930 (London, 1981), p. 313. McKendrick sees industrialisation as increasing women's earnings which became central to the domestic economy of nineteenth-century families. Neil McKendrick, 'Home demand and economic growth: A new view of the role of women and children in the industrial revolution', in Neil McKendrick, ed., *Historical Perspectives in English Thought and Society in Honour of J. H. Plumb* (London, 1974), pp. 152–210. Shorter meanwhile argues that individualism of the market place was transferred to family roles and structures during industrialisation, liberating women in the process. Edward Shorter, *The Making of the Modern Family* (London, 1976), pp. 255–6.

[8] Alice Clark is the most widely quoted proponent of the pessimist viewpoint. She argues that the great deterioration of women's position occurred in the seventeenth century as a

Sara Horrell and Jane Humphries have suggested that these disparate views can be reconciled if more attention is focused on the timing of industrialisation and a clear distinction drawn between the phases of proto-industry and factory production.[9] Maxine Berg and Pat Hudson have been especially successful at exposing the unique role performed by female workers during the early stages of industrialisation: they argue that most established histories have failed to acknowledge that economic change in the late eighteenth and early nineteenth centuries swelled opportunities for women's work in certain regions and sectors.[10] Proto-industry – the production of goods (mainly textiles) in cottage workshops by a cheap labour force supplying national and international markets – placed women's work at a premium. This phase saw the use of female and child labour in market-orientated production on a uniquely large scale compared with previous or subsequent developments.[11] Berg highlights how cheap women's labour was utilised in conjunction with technical and organisational innovation to yield higher profits than were possible under earlier manufacturing

---

result of the rise of capitalism. Alice Clark, *Working Life of Women in the Seventeenth Century*, 1st edn 1919 (London, 1982). Eric Richards also argues that before the industrial revolution there was substantial female participation in the economy which fell off as a result of industrialisation. Eric Richards, 'Women in the British economy since about 1700', *History*, 59 (1974), pp. 337–57. Marxist feminists also espouse a pessimistic view of industrialisation, arguing that the oppression of women was necessary for the operation of industrial capitalism. See Michele Barrett, *Women's Oppression Today* (London, 1980); Thomas, 'Women and capitalism', p. 536.

[9] Sara Horrell and Jane Humphries, 'Women's labour force participation and the transition to the male breadwinner family', *Economic History Review*, XLVIII (1995), pp. 89–117 (p. 94).

[10] Maxine Berg and Pat Hudson, 'Rehabilitating the industrial revolution', *Economic History Review*, XLV (1992), pp. 24–50.

[11] Maxine Berg, 'Women's work, mechanisation and the early phases of industrialisation in England', in Joyce, ed., *Historical Meanings of Work*, pp. 64–98. The concept of proto-industry is not without controversy and has also generated a large amount of literature. See Franklin F. Mendels, 'Proto-industrialisation: The first phase of the industrial process', *Journal of Economic History*, XXXII (1972), pp. 241–61, and a reply, D. C. Coleman, 'Proto-industrialisation: A concept too many', *Economic History Review*, XXXVI (1983), pp. 435–48. Good overviews of the uses and limitations of the concept are provided by Rab Houston and K. D. M. Snell, 'Proto-industrialisation? Cottage industry, social change and industrial revolution', *Historical Journal*, 27 (1984), pp. 473–92; L. A. Clarkson, *Proto-industrialisation: The First Phase of Industrialisation?* (London, 1985) and Wolfgang Mager, 'Proto-industrialisation and proto-industry: The uses and drawbacks of two concepts', *Continuity and Change*, 8 (1993), pp. 181–215. One of the most significant disadvantages of the concept is the fact that it is very restricted in the range of occupations it encompasses. Nearly all of them are drawn from the woollen, linen and cotton industries and other sectors are ignored because they do not fit into the dynamic model. See Clarkson, *Proto-industrialisation*, p. 54.

regimes.[12] Textiles, especially cotton, was a key sector in this process. When production was transferred to factory-based production in this industry, the central role of women continued.[13] By the mid-nineteenth century however, the integral role of female and child labour was beginning to decline: the proto-industries were collapsing in the face of heavy factory competition and women workers were absent from the radically transformed heavy industries such as shipbuilding, iron and steel. It was these heavy industries which became increasingly important to British manufacturing prosperity as the century wore on.[14] In this scenario then, the process of industrialisation first increased female opportunities only to shut them down at a later stage.

Under some conditions industrial capitalism did result in dramatic and visible changes in the type and processes of women's employment. However, while women's importance in the textiles sector is acknowledged, there are dangers in concentrating on this form of employment. Female textile workers in factories were untypical and unrepresentative of the nineteenth-century female workforce as a whole.[15] The vast majority of women continued to work in their homes, in small workshops, in the sweated trades and in domestic service. For these women, the technological advancements that underpinned the conversion of female labour in cotton textiles had little meaning. Horrell and Humphries, using a database of household budgets drawn from a cross-section of labouring families, argue that with the exception of factory families, women and children did not substantially increase their relative contribution to the household income in most occupational groups in the first half of the nineteenth century. 'If anything', they contend, 'there was a decline, with increasing dependence on male earnings'.[16] Moreover, although industrialisation generated significant growth in textile factory jobs for women, at the same time it destroyed a stable by-employment for women in the form of spinning.[17] This loss was devastating for rural women. In some regions it significantly curtailed their wage-earning potential

---

[12] Maxine Berg, *The Age of Manufactures, 1700–1820: Industry, Innovation and Work in Britain* (London, 1994), p. 142.
[13] Maxine Berg, 'What difference did women's work make to the industrial revolution?', *History Workshop Journal*, 35 (1993), pp. 22–44 (p. 27).
[14] Ellen Jordan, 'The exclusion of women from industry in nineteenth-century Britain', *Comparative Studies in Society and History*, 31 (1989), pp. 273–96; Berg and Hudson, 'Rehabilitating the industrial revolution', p. 37. This does, however, ignore the new service jobs for women which developed during the second half of the nineteenth century including domestic service, dressmaking and tailoring.
[15] Michael Fores argues that between only 10 and 12 per cent of the British population were employed in factories 'by the time the "revolution" was meant to be over'. Michael Fores, 'The myth of a British industrial revolution', *History*, 66 (1981), pp. 181–98 (p. 191).
[16] Horrell and Humphries, 'Women's labour force participation', p. 105.
[17] Humphries, '"Lurking in the wings . . ."', p. 40.

and the contraction of spinning work in the English countryside forms a dominant theme in much contemporary writing in the early nineteenth century. The significance of this decline will be explored further in Chapter 2.

A number of received wisdoms on the nature of female labour have come under attack. The once-dominant assumption of the increasing separation of home and family has been questioned by recent research. According to Leonore Davidoff and Catherine Hall, the period 1780 to 1850 witnessed the removal of middle-class women from active participation in business, withdrawing to the family-centred world of home.[18] However, this transition did not necessarily affect women of the working class in the same way. The continued interaction of employment and family in the nineteenth century in some regions and industries is now recognised. Similarly, the persistence of the household as a site for waged work into the twentieth century is generally acknowledged. Sally Alexander, for example, has shown how the high price of rent and fuel in London meant that the introduction of mechanised production in a factory-based system was not viable in the capital, and few trades were transformed in this way until the twentieth century. Instead, the supply of cheap female labour favoured the development of sweated outwork. Thus, the work women did, Alexander argues, was either transference of domestic skills to the formal labour market (for example, cooking and cleaning), or work that had traditionally been done by women as part of domestic manufacture.[19] Sonya Rose has shown how the requirement for women to do homework as seamers actually expanded during the transition to factory production in the Nottinghamshire framework knitting industry. This increased demand was a result of changes in the methods of manufacture.[20] Davidoff also highlights the interaction between home and work in the nineteenth century by looking at the case of women who took lodgers into their households.[21]

---

[18] Leonore Davidoff and Catherine Hall, *Family Fortunes: Men and Women of the English Middle Class, 1780–1850* (London, 1987). See also Catherine Hall, *White, Male and Middle Class: Explorations in Feminism and History* (Cambridge, 1992); Leonore Davidoff, *Worlds Between: Historical Perspectives on Gender and Class* (Cambridge, 1995).

[19] Sally Alexander, 'Women's work in nineteenth-century London: A study of the years 1820–1850', in Juliet Mitchell and Ann Oakley, eds, *The Rights and Wrongs of Women* (Harmondsworth, 1976), pp. 59–111. See also James A. Schmiechen, *Sweated Industries and Sweated Labour: The London Clothing Trades* (Urbana, 1984).

[20] Sonya Rose, 'Proto-industry, women's work and the household economy in the transition to industrial capitalism', *Journal of Family History*, 13 (1988), pp. 181–93.

[21] Leonore Davidoff, 'The separation of home and work? Landladies and lodgers in nineteenth and twentieth-century England', in Sandra Burman, ed., *Fit Work for Women* (London, 1979), pp. 64–97. Diana Gittins has also revealed the complex interaction between the three spheres of marriage, work and kinship in her essay 'Marital status, work and kinship, 1850–1930', in Jane Lewis, ed., *Labour and Love: Women's Experiences of Home and Family, 1850–1940* (Oxford, 1986), pp. 249–65.

Women's history has enhanced our understanding of the industrial revolution by inaugurating new ways of looking at the processes of industrialisation. As part of this shift it is now widely accepted that an assessment of the industrial revolution should not be confined entirely to the consideration of broad economic transformations and technological change. The conditions of women's work were not determined solely by economic factors but also by a complex mixture of wider social and cultural attitudes that placed certain prohibitions and proscriptions on female labour. Industrialisation did bring some widening of opportunities for women to work outside the home in certain regions and occupations, but it was accompanied by a reworking of the sexual division of labour, as well as the emergence of new outlooks and social constraints. The definition of skilled labour and the idea of patriarchal power were reconfigured in the new industrial environment, while concepts such as the family wage and male breadwinner, and opinions about the 'proper' place of women, were extended and popularised.

Although proto-industry relied heavily on female labour there is little evidence to suggest that it was accompanied by any wholesale change in the status or perception of women workers. Female labour was cheap, and remained so because women's work was seen as low status and supplemental to household income. Women were not released from traditional domestic roles and 'proto-industry added to the drudgery of female existence'.[22] Similarly, technological change in the later stages of industrialisation did not significantly affect the type or status of work performed by women. In theory, as Hudson argues, the deskilling of industry which was implicit in many forms of mechanisation may have been expected to create new openings for women in previously male dominated areas of work. This was because divisions based on physical labour became obsolete. However, the transition to factory production, technical change and the extensive subdivision of labour processes – where these occurred – were accompanied by 'a reworking of gender notions that served to retain the more prestigious and better-paid work for men'.[23] The meanings attached to the notion of 'skill' were ideologically constructed, and new types of skill networks and labour hierarchies emerged in factory settings.[24] Nancy Grey Osterud has analysed gender divisions in the Leicester hosiery industry during its transition from outwork to factory production in the nineteenth century. She argues that the gender division of labour was 'amplified' and 'sharpened', when production moved

---

[22] Pat Hudson, *The Industrial Revolution* (London, 1992), p. 227.
[23] Ibid., p. 229.
[24] Important discussions of skill and its meanings may be found in Anne Phillips and Barbara Taylor, 'Sex and skill: Notes towards a feminist economics', *Feminist Review*, 6 (1980), pp. 79–88; Cynthia Cockburn, *Brothers: Male Dominance and Technical Change* (London, 1983); William Lazonick, 'Industrial relations and technological change: The case of the self-acting mule', *Cambridge Journal of Economics*, 3 (1979), pp. 231–62.

outside the home into the factory. This move created gender-defined work which provided the basis for a customary woman's wage, paid at a lower rate than the male wage.²⁵ Hall's research also highlights how the sexual division of labour was reworked in cotton textiles as changes in technology and location of work occurred. Although women in the Lancashire cotton industry were better paid and shared more equality with men than women working in most other industries, men monopolised mule spinning in the factories and the newly formed male unions operated limitations on entry to the trade as a protective measure.²⁶

The concept of the family wage – whereby a male worker was paid a sufficient amount of money to be able to support his family without his wife having to work – legitimised the continuation of low female wage levels as women were seen as working only to augment the male wage.²⁷ The perception of 'work' as the occupation of a family shifted to 'work' as the waged labour of an individual in the nineteenth century. This had the effect of elevating and prioritising the male wage.²⁸ Women were viewed as depen-

---

[25] Nancy Grey Osterud, 'Gender divisions and the organisation of work in the Leicester hosiery industry', in John, ed., *Unequal Opportunities*, pp. 45–70 (p. 65). Osterud does show how the move from home to factory production was not fully completed until the 1870s however.

[26] Catherine Hall, 'The home turned upside down? The working class family in cotton textiles', in Elizabeth Whitelegg *et al.*, eds, *The Changing Experience of Women* (Oxford, 1982), pp. 17–29. Humphries has attempted a reinterpretation of the sexual division of labour which, she argues, was linked to the manipulation of female sexuality in order to control population growth in times of scarcity. Jane Humphries, '"... the most free from objection ..." The sexual division of labour and women's work in nineteenth-century England', *Journal of Economic History*, XLVII (1987), pp. 929–48 (p. 947).

[27] Humphries claims that the family wage was not a sexist device adopted by nineteenth-century working-class men, but a strategy adopted by men and women against the exploitative capitalist system. Jane Humphries, 'Protective legislation, the capitalist state and working class men: The case of the 1842 mines regulation act', *Feminist Review*, 7 (1981), pp. 1–33. This is criticised by Harold Benenson, who argues that female textile workers in Lancashire did not embrace the concept as it would have meant job losses. See Harold Benenson, 'The "family wage" and working women's consciousness in Britain, 1880–1914', *Politics and Society*, 19 (1991), pp. 71–108. Michele Barrett and Mary McIntosh, who contend that the concept enforced the oppression of women and increased dependency on men, also question Humphries' view. Michele Barrett and Mary McIntosh, 'The "family wage"', in Whitelegg *et al.*, eds, *Changing Experience of Women*, pp. 71–87. See also Hilary Land, 'The family wage', *Feminist Review*, 6 (1980), pp. 55–77; Wally Seccombe, 'Patriarchy stabilised: The construction of the male breadwinner wage norm in nineteenth-century Britain', *Social History*, 11 (1986), pp. 53–76; Sonya Rose, 'Gender antagonism and class conflict: Exclusionary strategies of male trade unions in nineteenth-century Britain', *Social History*, 13 (1988), pp. 191–208, and Anna Clark, *The Struggle for the Breeches: Gender and the Making of the British Working Class* (London, 1995), ch.7.

[28] For an interesting discussion of the evolution of the concept of the 'wage' see John Rule, *The Labouring Classes in Early Industrial England, 1750–1850* (London, 1986), ch.4.

dants, supported first by their fathers, and after marriage, by their husbands. Men largely retained their ability to define their superior social status through work, whereas women's standing in the labour market continued to be defined through their domestic and reproductive responsibilities. Moreover, protective legislation, introduced from the 1830s, defined women as a group requiring special protection, further reinforcing the belief that women's roles should be confined to the domestic sphere. This placed injunctions on when women could enter the workforce and the nature of the waged work they could perform.[29]

Notions such as the male breadwinner and the family wage became instruments of power in the nineteenth century. The impact these ideas had on most working-class families is debatable though. None the less, they remained important ideological tools, and they were sustained and endorsed by the growing strength of the domestic ideal for women. Put simply, this belief situated women in the private sphere of home, dependent on men who went out into the public sphere of work. Many of these ideological constructs were not unique to the nineteenth century.[30] However, as society became increasingly urbanised and class based, working women emerged as a 'problem' and a threat. It is within this context that especially elaborate expressions of women's 'proper' place were articulated. The domestic ideology affected many prevalent attitudes towards female work – and female workers – in the nineteenth century. Again, we have to question how far women themselves actually colluded with this outlook. Elizabeth Roberts has suggested that many working-class women expressed ambiguous attitudes towards their work. This meant that women tended to perceive their liberation in terms of a move back into the home, not into paid employment outside the household. We can comprehend this attitude, Roberts writes, 'when the strength of the domestic idyll is appreciated and the nature of the double burden of work carried by full-time working women is understood'.[31]

Historians such as Judith Bennett have employed the concept of patriarchy to explain women's subordinate position in the nineteenth-century labour

---

[29] Humphries, 'Protective legislation'. Angela V. John, *By the Sweat of their Brow: Women Workers at Victorian Coalmines* (London, 1980) traces the evolution of miners' resistance to women workers in the coal industry.
[30] Catherine Hall, 'The early formation of Victorian domestic ideology', in Burman, ed., *Fit Work for Women*, pp. 15–32. Hall argues that although many of the ideas propounded in the late eighteenth and early nineteenth centuries were formulated by Puritans a century earlier, they were reclaimed and strengthened by the new bourgeoisie who emerged as a result of industrialisation. See also Amanda Vickery, 'Golden age to separate spheres? A review of the categories and chronology of English women's history', *Historical Journal*, 36 (1993), pp. 383–414, which is a critical review of the two concepts.
[31] Elizabeth Roberts, *Women's Work, 1840–1940* (London, 1988), p. 16.

market.[32] Judith Lown describes patriarchy as a 'hierarchical system whereby adult male men occupy superordinate positions of power over women, children and younger men'. Paternalism, on the other hand, with its reliance on personal ties of dependency and deference, 'is one form of legitimisation that holders of patriarchal power adopt'.[33] Thus, scholars such as Lown claim that the action of patriarchy forms a 'central axis of historical and social change'.[34] In her work on the Courtauld silk factory in Halstead, Essex, Lown highlights how patriarchal family relations were reformulated in the factory setting. There, workplace supervision and hierarchies replicated the power structures of the family, with the employer as patriarch at the head of the system. She argues:

> In the social and economic transformation which was to alter the productive and reproductive arrangement of emergent capitalist societies, patriarchal interests were at the very centre of the struggles reshaping the class and gender hierarchies.[35]

Much of the literature on women's employment in the industrial era has been concerned with either the direction of change or the underlying continuities of work patterns. One of the ways scholars have approached this question is to analyse the broad trends in female participation rates in the workforce. This is not an easy undertaking. It is virtually impossible to be certain about eighteenth- and nineteenth-century female labour rates. Reliable statistics for the eighteenth century are uncommon and there are many drawbacks involved with using nineteenth-century census figures as confirmation of female occupational trends.[36] (These will be discussed later in this chapter.) While acknowledging the problems of the source, Roberts has used the census as a rough indicator of women's involvement in the labour force, and suggests that industrialisation had little impact on women's participation rates. These, she argues, remained static in the nineteenth century at around 30 per cent.[37] Roberts' arguments are framed by the earlier

---

[32] Judith Bennett, 'Women's history: A study in continuity and change', *Women's History Review*, 2 (1993), pp. 173–84. See Veronica Beechey, 'On patriarchy', *Feminist Review*, 3 (1979), pp. 66–82, for a discussion of the different approaches to the analysis of the concept of patriarchy.

[33] Judith Lown, 'Not much a factory, more a form of patriarchy: Gender and class during industrialisation', in Eva Gamarnikow et al., eds, *Gender, Class and Work* (London, 1983), pp. 28–45 (p. 29).

[34] Lown, 'Not much a factory', p. 35.

[35] Ibid., pp. 43–4. See also her book based on the Halstead silk factory, *Women and Industrialisation: Gender at Work in Nineteenth-Century England* (Oxford, 1990).

[36] However, there are two sets of pre-census listings for Cardington, Bedfordshire in 1782 and Corfe Castle, Dorset in 1790 that provide interesting information on occupational structures. See Osamu Saito, 'Who worked when: Life-time profiles of labour force participation in Cardington and Corfe Castle in the late eighteenth and mid nineteenth centuries', *Local Population Studies*, 22 (1979), pp. 14–29.

[37] Roberts, *Women's Work*, pp. 22.

work of Louise Tilly and Joan Scott. In their seminal text *Women, Work and Family*, Tilly and Scott contend that industrialisation did not change the type of work women did in any significant way, nor did it increase greatly the percentage of women in work over the course of the nineteenth century.[38] The lack of dependable statistics means that the overall effect of industrialisation on women's labour force participation remains unresolved.

The debate over continuity or change has recently re-emerged within the pages of *Women's History Review*. Bennett argues that continuity is the dominant theme when women's employment is placed in a long-term perspective and affirms the endurance of patriarchy across the centuries.[39] Bridget Hill meanwhile claims that those who argue for continuities ignore processes such as capitalism and industrialisation and deny that economic factors were crucial in shaping women's roles.[40] The issue is complicated still further by the fact that processes of industrialisation and the transition to new forms of work and workplaces were regionally and occupationally specific.[41] Such diversity of experience tends to be masked by studies that adopt a broad overview. The manifesto for selecting a regional and occupational approach to the study of gender, work and industrialisation has been outlined by Horrell and Humphries, who contend that

> accounts of women's and children's contributions to family incomes must be conditional on their occupational and regional identity, which limits 'grand theories' of the causes of women's marginalization. Theories that depict women, whatever their circumstances, as undifferentiated victims of allied economic and ideological forces must give way to detailed analysis of institutional changes at occupational and regional levels.[42]

It is through this more nuanced regional framework that future advances in the understanding of the changing nature of work and gender structures during industrialisation will come to fruition. In addition, it is evident that

---

[38] Louise Tilly and Joan Scott, *Women, Work and Family*, 1st edn 1978 (London, 1987), p. 77. Peter Earle's research on women's work in London also backs up this proposition. He shows that the general structure of female occupations in the seventeenth and eighteenth centuries was very similar to that in the 1851 census with women workers concentrated in a narrow range of occupations including domestic service, making and mending clothes, charring and laundry work and nursing. Thus, there is 'little evidence of a narrowing of women's employment opportunities as a result of the industrial revolution or Victorian mores'. Peter Earle, 'The female labour market in London in the late seventeenth and early eighteenth centuries', *Economic History Review*, XLII (1989), pp. 328–53 (p. 342).
[39] Bennett, 'Women's history'.
[40] Bridget Hill, 'Women's history: A study in change, continuity or standing still?', *Women's History Review*, 2 (1993), pp. 5–22.
[41] See e.g. Hudson, *Industrial Revolution*; Pat Hudson, ed., *Regions and Industries: A Perspective on the Industrial Revolution in Britain* (Cambridge, 1989).
[42] Horrell and Humphries, 'Women's labour force participation', p. 105.

social, cultural and ideological factors also have to be incorporated into the economic history of women in the eighteenth and nineteenth centuries to provide a clearer analysis. As Pamela Sharpe maintains, by doing this, 'we no longer need be hampered by overarching narratives of "continuity" versus "change", leading us to an understanding of individual experiences within the broad framework of the economic past'.[43]

Agrarian history and women's history: the debate on rural women's employment

Writing on rural England falls into two camps: that on the mechanics of farming, and other research on the wider social and cultural aspects of the countryside. One factor uniting the two groups is their gender blindness. As a result there has been relatively little written on the role of women workers in the nineteenth-century English countryside.

A dominant theme in agrarian history has been the timing of the 'agricultural revolution'. Early accounts stressed the influence of technological change and new crops in the century between 1750 and 1850, and the role of the 'Great Men' who enacted them. Lord Ernle is a leading pioneer of this view. Changes in the institutional structure of farming are seen as aiding the implementation of fresh products and processes. Thus parliamentary enclosure was pivotal to the success of agrarian changes as it swept away common property rights, an inhibitor to innovation and advancement.[44] This perspective remained the consensus opinion on the agricultural revolution until the 1960s when it was undermined by a wave of new scholarship. J. D. Chambers and Gordon Mingay led the way, arguing that eighteenth-century changes could be traced back to the seventeenth century and earlier, although they still placed the revolution in the century after 1750, and cited new fodder crops and rotations, convertible husbandry and parliamentary enclosure as its most significant factors.[45] Eric Kerridge pushed the parameters back further, situating the revolution between 1560 and 1673, while E. L. Jones contended that the period 1650 to 1750 witnessed the zenith of agricultural change.[46] Thus, by the 1970s, the period of the agricultural revolution had been stretched from the mid-sixteenth century to the mid-nineteenth century. However, the current consensus, based on fresh insights gained from new sources and innovative databases, has reinstated the

---

[43] Sharpe, 'Continuity and change', p. 364.
[44] Lord Ernle, *English Farming Past and Present*, 1st edn 1912 (London, 1961).
[45] J. D. Chambers and G. E. Mingay, *The Agricultural Revolution, 1750–1880* (London, 1966).
[46] Eric Kerridge, *The Agricultural Revolution* (London, 1967); E. L. Jones, *Agriculture and the Industrial Revolution* (London, 1974).

case for the agricultural revolution taking off in the period after 1750. Mark Overton argues that it was not until after 1750 that the dramatic and unprecedented improvements in output, land yield and labour productivity – along with equally dramatic changes in husbandry – were underway on a broad scale.[47] An analysis of over 300 farm records by Michael Turner, John Beckett and Bethanie Afton has resulted in similar confirmation. Farm records indicate that yields began to increase significantly in the first half of the nineteenth century, placing the location of the agricultural revolution 'firmly within the period from about 1800 to 1850'.[48]

What were the effects of these revolutionary processes on men and women who lived and worked in the countryside in the late eighteenth and nineteenth centuries? The first comprehensive attempt to trace the history of the agricultural worker was William Hasbach's *A History of the English Agricultural Labourer*. This book was published in English in 1908 and charts the progress of the labouring class from the Black Death to the end of the nineteenth century.[49] Hasbach argued that loss of common land during enclosure led to the demoralisation of rural labourers – whom he called the 'agricultural proletariat' – a situation they endeavoured to overturn during the remainder of the nineteenth century. J. L. and Barbara Hammond in *The Village Labourer*, carried this critique of agricultural improvement forward.[50] This book presents us with a picture of an efficient common land system that was destroyed by enclosure. Consequently the peasantry were driven from the land and the foundations of agrarian capitalism – dominated by a three-tier social structure of landlord, large tenant farmer and landless labourer – were laid. In the aftermath of this, the Hammonds claim, a bitter outburst of rioting – or the 'Last Labourers Revolt' – shook southern England in the early 1830s.[51]

A critique of the Hammonds' view of enclosure as a catastrophic event for the English countryside is central to Chambers and Mingay's account of

---

[47] Mark Overton, *Agricultural Revolution in England: The Transformation of the Agrarian Economy, 1500–1850* (Cambridge, 1996).
[48] M. E. Turner, J. V. Beckett and B. Afton, *Farm Production in England, 1700–1914* (Oxford, 2001), p. 230.
[49] William Hasbach, *A History of the English Agricultural Labourer*, 1st edn 1894 (London, 1966). There are several other books published around the turn of the century that attempt an overview of the history of the rural labourer. These include Russell M. Garnier, *Annals of the British Peasantry* (London, 1895); Revd. A. H. Beverstock, *The English Agricultural Labourer* (London, 1912); Montague Fordham and T. R. Fordham, *The English Agricultural Labourer, 1300–1925* (London, 1925) and F. E. Green, *A History of the English Agricultural Labourer, 1870–1920* (London, 1920), which concentrates on the growth of agricultural trade unionism in the late nineteenth and early twentieth centuries. Hasbach's remains the most comprehensive account, however.
[50] J. L. Hammond and Barbara Hammond, *The Village Labourer* (London, 1911).
[51] See Hammond and Hammond, *Village Labourer*, ch.11 and ch.12.

the agricultural revolution.⁵² From this work a very different picture of the agricultural history of the late eighteenth and nineteenth century emerged in which enclosure replaced an inefficient and outdated productive system with a highly successful one, providing the basis for the prosperity of the mid-Victorian period. According to Chambers and Mingay, the Hammonds exaggerated the costs of this change, and enclosure meant 'more food for the growing population, more land under cultivation and, on balance, more employment in the countryside'.⁵³ Yet this revisionist perspective itself has not gone unchallenged. J. M. Neeson has questioned the nature and effects of enclosure on small landowners and commoners in the Midlands region. 'In most villages studied', she argues,

> parliamentary enclosure destroyed the old peasant economy . . . by more than decimating small occupiers and landlords . . . and by expropriating landless commoners on whom much of the old economy had depended.⁵⁴

Leigh Shaw-Taylor's more recent work has added extra impetus to the enclosure debate, which rumbles on.⁵⁵

The impetus which has bolstered renewed thinking about the effects of enclosure – especially the changes wrought on the labouring poor – has been provided by the revival of social agrarian history since the 1960s. Other areas of rural research have been invigorated by this trend towards history 'from below', and new, innovative ways of viewing and understanding the nineteenth-century countryside have resulted. In books by A. J. Peacock, George Rudé and Eric Hobsbawm, the social history of the rural labourer is viewed through a particular episode: the 'Bread and Blood' riots in East Anglia in 1816 and the Swing riots in south-eastern England in the 1830s.⁵⁶

---

⁵² On the enclosure debate see also J. D. Chambers, 'Enclosure and labour supply in the industrial revolution', *Economic History Review*, V (1953), pp. 319–43; C. S. Orwin and E. H. Whetham, *A History of British Agriculture, 1846–1914* (London, 1964); Kerridge, *The Agricultural Revolution*; G. E. Mingay, *Enclosure and the Small Farmers in the Age of the Industrial Revolution* (London, 1968); Y. A. Yelling, *Common Field and Enclosure in England, 1450–1850* (London, 1977); M. E. Turner, *English Parliamentary Enclosure: Its Historical Geography and Economic History* (Folkestone, 1980); J. V. Beckett, *The Agricultural Revolution* (Oxford, 1990).
⁵³ Chambers and Mingay, *Agricultural Revolution*, p. 104.
⁵⁴ J. M. Neeson, *Commoners: Common Right, Enclosure and Social Change in England, 1700–1820* (Cambridge, 1993), p. 223.
⁵⁵ Leigh Shaw-Taylor, 'Parliamentary enclosure and the emergence of an English agricultural proletariat', *Journal of Economic History*, LXI (2001), pp. 640–62; 'Labourers, cows, common rights and parliamentary enclosure: The evidence of contemporary comment, c. 1760–1810', *Past and Present*, 171 (2001), pp. 95–126.
⁵⁶ E. J. Hobsbawn and G. E. Rudé, *Captain Swing* (London, 1969); A. J. Peacock, *Bread or Blood: A Study of the Agrarian Riots in East Anglia in 1816* (London, 1965).

An impressive body of research on rural crime and social protest has followed. Barry Reay's *The Last Rising of the Agricultural Labourers* concentrates on the uprising of Kent labourers in 1838, while John Archer's *'By a Flash and a Scare'* focuses on the wider incidence of incendiarism, animal maiming and poaching in nineteenth-century East Anglia.[57] The history of union activity among agricultural labourers has also emerged as an area of interest, and key texts by Alun Howkins and Howard Newby analyse the links between farmworkers, trade unionism and political radicalism in late nineteenth-century East Anglia.[58]

Amidst this reformation of rural history there has been little place for women. It has taken many years for rural women – and their roles as workers, rioters, family members and agents of social change – to materialise as topics worthy of academic interest. This exclusion is puzzling given that the founders of *History Workshop* had identified the invisibility of women in working-class history back in the 1970s.[59] Sally Alexander, Anna Davin and Eve Hostettler, writing in 1979, pointed to the outmoded generalisations which were used to describe rural labouring women, and by doing so offered a way forward for future research. 'Both married and single women worked in agriculture for the greater part of the nineteenth century', they claimed, 'and most textbooks on agricultural history say they disappeared from the rural labour force after 1870. This bland assertion conceals great diversity of

---

[57] Barry Reay, *The Last Rising of the Agricultural Labourers: Rural Life and Protest in Nineteenth-Century England* (Oxford, 1990); John Archer, *'By a Flash and a Scare': Incendiarism, Animal Maiming and Poaching in East Anglia, 1815–1870* (Oxford, 1990). The historiography of rural discontent is a growing field and includes J. P. D. Dunbabin, 'The "revolt of the field": The agricultural labourers movement in the 1870s', *Past and Present*, 26 (1963), pp. 68–97; J. P. D. Dunbabin, 'The incidence and organisation of agricultural trade unionism in the 1870s', *Agricultural History Review*, 16 (1968), pp. 114–41; J. P. D. Dunbabin, *Rural Discontent in Nineteenth-Century Britain* (London, 1974); Roger Wells, 'The development of the English rural proletariat and social protest, 1700–1850', *Journal of Peasant Studies*, 6 (1979), pp. 115–39; Andrew Charlesworth, 'The development of the English rural proletariat and social protest, 1700–1850: A comment', *Journal of Peasant Studies*, 8 (1980), pp. 101–11; Roger Wells, 'Social conflict and protest in the English countryside in the early nineteenth century: A rejoinder', *Journal of Peasant Studies*, 8 (1981), pp. 514–30; Andrew Charlesworth, *An Atlas of Rural Protest in Britain, 1548–1900* (London, 1983); Paul Muskett, 'The East Anglian agrarian riots of 1822', *Agricultural History Review*, 32 (1984), pp. 1–13; Mick Reed and Roger Wells, eds, *Class Conflict and Protest in the English Countryside, 1700–1880* (London, 1990); John Rule and Roger Wells, *Crime, Protest and Popular Politics in Southern England, 1740–1850* (London, 1997).
[58] Alun Howkins, *Poor Labouring Men: Rural Radicalism in Norfolk, 1870–1923* (London, 1985); Howard Newby, *The Deferential Worker* (Harmondsworth, 1977).
[59] See Raphael Samuel, ed., *Village Life and Labour* (London, 1975), p. xvii. This volume is sensitive to the role of women in rural areas and includes the essay by Jennie Ketteringham, 'Country work girls in nineteenth-century England', pp. 73–138, which has sections on farmwork, gangs, rural industries and morals.

patterns of employment over place and time.'⁶⁰ Only now are the implications of this statement being unravelled.

Some attempts to write women into the rural historiography have been more successful than others. Most efforts have centred on women's economic role. General texts aimed at popularising academic rural history – including numerous volumes by Pamela Horn and G. E. Mingay – have acknowledged women's contribution to the family income through paid work in agriculture and cottage industries, although it is a rather cursory treatment.⁶¹ More sensitivity to the position of women may be found in a number of scholarly overviews of agrarian England and the rural labour force in the eighteenth and nineteenth centuries. At the forefront has to be placed Keith Snell's *Annals of the Labouring Poor* which seeks to analyse the impact of long-term social and economic change within agrarian capitalism on the labouring poor of south-eastern England.⁶² Other texts by academics such as Alan

---

⁶⁰ Sally Alexander, Anna Davin and Eve Hosettler, 'Labouring women: A reply to Eric Hobsbawm', *History Workshop Journal*, 8 (1979), pp. 174–82 (p. 176).
⁶¹ See e.g. Pamela Horn, *Labouring Life in the Victorian Countryside* (London, 1976); Pamela Horn, *The Rural World, 1780–1850: Social Change in the English Countryside* (London, 1980); Pamela Horn, *The Changing Countryside in Victorian and Edwardian England and Wales* (London, 1984); Pamela Horn, *Life and Labour in Rural England, 1760–1850* (London, 1987); G. E. Mingay, *Rural Life in Victorian England* (London, 1976); G. E. Mingay, *A Social History of the English Countryside* (London, 1990). The two volumes of *The Victorian Countryside*, edited by Mingay, include only one essay specifically devoted to female labour. G. E. Mingay, ed., *The Victorian Countryside*, 2 vols (London, 1981). See Pamela Horn, 'Women's cottage industries', vol. 1, pp. 341–52. Howkins' contribution to this project, '"In the sweat of thy face": The labourer and work', vol. 2, pp. 506–20, does briefly mention the position of female workers. In the more recent *Agrarian History of England and Wales*, the massive vol. 6, covering the years 1750 to 1850, includes a section on the 'Employment of women and children' that runs to just five pages. W. A. Armstrong, 'Labour 1: Rural population growth, systems of employment, and incomes', in G. E. Mingay, ed., *The Agrarian History of England and Wales*, vol. VI, 1750–1850 (Cambridge, 1989), pp. 641–728 (pp. 683–8). Volume 7, published in 2000, incorporates scholarly work on rural women (see especially ch. 12 and ch. 23). However, the editor concludes that 'The role of women in the social, cultural and economic life of the countryside – not just women farm and industrial workers, but also women farmers, farmers' wives, farmers' female relatives living in the farmhouse, and "women of the gentry" – remains seriously under-researched.' E. J. T. Collins, ed., *The Agrarian History of England and Wales*, vol. VII, 1850–1914 (Cambridge, 2000), p. 2154. One of the few studies which has attempted an overview of the working lives of rural women from all social groups is Horn's *Victorian Countrywomen*. She looks at the working lives of professional women, farming women, domestic servants, agricultural labourers and women involved in rural industries. Although it provides much interesting material, the study is largely unsuccessful because it offers little interpretive perspective.
⁶² K. D. M. Snell, *Annals of the Labouring Poor: Social Change and Agrarian England, 1660–1900* (Cambridge, 1985).

Armstrong and Alun Howkins have also placed consideration of the regional diversity of female employment patterns within their analyses of the changing nature of the English countryside in the nineteenth century.[63]

Despite the growing appreciation of the meaningful presence women had in the nineteenth-century rural workforce, in many respects Pinchbeck's research on rural women still remains the major piece of analysis. Her book *Women Workers and the Industrial Revolution, 1750–1850* was first published in 1930 and provides a starting point for all historians interested in the question of women's labour in the countryside, particularly agricultural labour.[64] Indeed, as Hill has pointed out,

> The fact that today any investigation of women's work . . . must start with a study that is now over half a century old . . . is a tribute to the continuing importance of that study and a comment on the paucity of work that has followed it.[65]

Pinchbeck's method rested on a painstaking trawl through the range of printed sources available for the period she investigated. The scope of her inquiry and the minutiae of detail she extracted remain unsurpassed. A brief synopsis of her main argument is as follows. Before the agricultural revolution, although women worked in agriculture at hay and harvest time, and on other seasonal tasks such as weeding and stone-gathering, Pinchbeck argues that for many labourers' wives, agriculture was only a 'by-employment': women also exploited common rights and earned wages in the diverse range of industries located in rural districts, including spinning. Agrarian change destroyed many of these productive wage-earning opportunities, reducing women to increased dependency on their husbands. At the same time, new cultures and methods of cultivation 'combined to create a new class of women wage earners in agriculture': the day labourer.[66] According to Pinchbeck, the number of women employed as day labourers increased in the late eighteenth century and continued to do so throughout the course of the Napoleonic Wars. The post-war depression in agriculture led to unemployment and pauperisation across rural England, affecting male and female workers alike. However, after 1834, a combination of factors – the abolition of outdoor relief, the inadequacy of the male wage and the economising of farmers – led once more to a rise in women's agricultural labour. The increase of women

---

[63] W. A. Armstrong, *Farmworkers: A Social and Economic History, 1770–1980* (London, 1988); Alun Howkins, *Reshaping Rural England: A Social History, 1850–1925* (London, 1991). See also Howard Newby, *Country Life: A Social History of Rural England* (London, 1987).
[64] Pinchbeck, *Women Workers*.
[65] Bridget Hill, *Women, Work and Sexual Politics in Eighteenth-Century England*, 1st edn 1989 (London, 1994), p. 1.
[66] Pinchbeck, *Women Workers*, p. 28.

workers was most noticeable in eastern counties with the evolution of the gang system.[67] After the mid-nineteenth century women's labour force participation declined again, and with the progress in male wages and the formation of agricultural trade unions, the material life of rural families improved. 'By the end of the nineteenth century', Pinchbeck concludes, 'women had almost ceased to be employed as wage-earners in agriculture.' As a consequence, 'women day labourers as a class disappeared'.[68]

The chronology of women's work in agricultural day labour outlined by Pinchbeck has been highly influential and remains so today.[69] However, Snell's account of female participation and wage-earning in agriculture over the course of the eighteenth and nineteenth centuries has emerged more recently as the foremost account. Snell looks at long-term changes in the roles performed by women and men in the agricultural workforce between 1690 and 1860, basing his arguments on an analysis of settlement examinations taken from ten counties in southern and eastern England.[70] Snell also argues for a decline in women's agricultural labour, but he places the reduction in the demand for women workers in the late eighteenth century. This is at odds with Pinchbeck's view of increasing female employment as day labourers in the period up to the end of the French Wars.

Snell's argument cites changes in the use of agricultural technology as the crucial factor in transforming the seasonal basis of women's work. The expansion of grain production was accompanied by a greater demand for male harvest labour and heavier technology. Thus women's harvest employment was progressively marginalised as the sickle was replaced by the heavier scythe for the harvesting of wheat and rye. Consequently, female employment was increasingly confined to participation in spring weeding and early summer haymaking. The key period for this movement in women's employment was between 1751 and 1792. During the Napoleonic Wars this general trend continued but was temporarily disrupted due to shortages of male labour. By 1860 the shift towards greater employment security in the springtime was complete. According to Snell the sexual specialisation of agricultural labour did not stem from Victorian attitudes concerning the proper place of women: the decline in female work opportunities in the nineteenth century was the continuation of a prolonged process that began a century earlier.[71] Changes in female wage-earning potential occurred alongside the transformation in agricultural day labour, confirming the sexual

---

[67] Ibid., pp. 86–90.
[68] Ibid., p. 110.
[69] See e.g. Honeyman, *Women, Gender and Industrialisation*, pp. 77–80.
[70] Snell, *Annals of the Labouring Poor*, ch. 1. The counties are Cambridge, Bedford, Huntingdon, Norfolk, Suffolk, Essex, Hertford, Berkshire, Buckingham and Northampton.
[71] Snell, *Annals of the Labouring Poor*, pp. 21–2, p. 51.

division of labour. Thus, from 1760 women in eastern England found their real wages declining relative to men's. This pattern contrasted to the situation in the west, where livestock and dairy farming supported the continued employment – and stability of real wages – of female labourers.[72]

Snell's account draws on the earlier research of Michael Roberts. Roberts argues that with surplus grain production in early eighteenth-century agriculture, the scythe was extended from its traditional use for barley, oats, peas and beans to the harvesting of wheat and rye. This had the effect of relegating women harvest workers to the subsidiary task of raking, and 'as the male-dominated corn-scythe became more popular the value of men's wages was enhanced and women had to start looking elsewhere for well paid employment'.[73] A study of harvest technology in Lincolnshire and East Yorkshire also confirms that the relationship between various harvest workers – especially men and women – was altered by the use of the scythe over the sickle.[74] Eve Hostettler's illuminating study of the illustrations from Henry Stephen's *The Book of the Farm* also makes this point. This account of northern farming techniques was published in 1844, with several reprints appearing over the remainder of the century. Earlier editions include illustrations of female productivity in the harvest fields; by 1901 these women had been erased completely. With the advent of the scythe, Hostettler concludes, 'the woman's role in the harvest field began to change from cutting and gathering to gathering and making straw bands'.[75] The later introduction of the reaping machine was more devastating and 'removed at a stroke . . . the farmer's need to find extra labour every year at harvest time'.[76]

Snell's hypothesis on the impact of changing agricultural technology on the sexual division of agricultural labour has been embraced and extensively repeated by a variety of authors on women's history. Hill, in her investigation of eighteenth-century women, writes:

> Thus, with the specialisation on corn production and the consequent decline of traditional areas of agriculture in which women's labour had predominated, the potential in the south and east for a wide participation of women in agricultural labour was in decline long before the process of industrialisation got under way.[77]

---

[72] Ibid., p. 40.
[73] Michael Roberts, 'Sickles and scythes: Women's work and men's work at harvest time', *History Workshop Journal*, 7 (1979), pp. 3–28 (p. 19).
[74] J. A. Perkins, 'Harvest technology and labour supply in Lincolnshire and the East Riding of Yorkshire, 1750–1850', *Tools and Tillage*, 3 (1976), pp. 47–58 (p. 56).
[75] Eve Hostettler, 'Gourlay Steell and the sexual division of labour', *History Workshop Journal*, 4 (1977), pp. 95–100 (p. 97).
[76] Ibid., p. 98.
[77] Hill, *Women, Work and Sexual Politics*, pp. 53–4.

In her wide-ranging study of the 'industrial woman', Deborah Valenze argues that,

> for women, the chances of finding work in agriculture, at least in the major corn-growing regions of the south and east, grew slimmer toward the end of the eighteenth century and worsened later on.[78]

The consequences of this agricultural transformation on labouring women, she concludes, marginalised women who 'lost their claim to the traditional rural images of female productivity'.[79] Similarly, Sally McMurry contrasts the persistence of women's role in English cheese-making throughout the nineteenth century with their 'early disappearance' from arable agriculture which, she argues, has been 'convincingly' documented by Snell.[80]

But caution is needed. A number of concerns have been raised regarding Snell's thesis. First, the main source of data he used – settlement examinations – is not necessarily the best evidence for illustrating trends in agricultural day labour. Settlement examinations provide the date at which an examinant came to require parochial aid, and record details on sex, marital status and occupation. They refer mainly to farm and domestic servants rather than agricultural day labourers. Data on domestic servants are unlikely to depict patterns of unemployment in agricultural work.[81] Moreover, Sharpe has shown that changes in seasonal employment in counties like Essex could be accounted for by increasing work opportunities in 'seasonally-specific alternative employments' such as in the fashion and service trades.[82] Snell himself is aware of the tentative nature of his evidence. This can be seen in his defence of applying wage data taken from yearly hired servants to agricultural labour in general:

> But because the series presented here are for yearly hirings of unmarried people, inclusive of board and lodging, they have some disadvantages compared to labourers' wage rates. It seems likely that short-term trends in the latter, however, were closely paralleled by trends in wages paid for yearly hirings, and for the purpose of generalising about agricultural wages for married people this assumption has been made.[83]

---

[78] Valenze, *Industrial Woman*, p. 45.
[79] Ibid., p. 47.
[80] Sally McMurry, 'Women's work in agriculture: Divergent trends in England and America, 1800–1930', *Comparative Studies in Society and History*, 34 (1997), pp. 248–70 (p. 269).
[81] Pamela Sharpe, 'The female labour market in English agriculture during the Industrial Revolution: Expansion or contraction?', *Agricultural History Review*, 47 (1999), pp. 161–81 (p. 175).
[82] Pamela Sharpe, *Adapting to Capitalism: Working Women in the English Economy, 1700–1850* (Basingstoke, 1996), p. 76.
[83] Snell, *Annals of the Labouring Poor*, p. 24.

The ramifications of such remarks seem to have been overlooked by those duplicating his arguments.

The second major concern centres on Snell's assessment of harvest technology and the sexual division of labour. Snell argues that a more equal division of labour in agricultural work was found prior to the mid-eighteenth century. 'There is abundant supporting evidence' he contends, 'for a very wide range of female participation in agricultural tasks before 1750 in the south-east, when their work extended to reaping, loading and spreading dung, ploughing, threshing, thatching, following the harrow, sheep shearing, and even working as shepherdesses.'[84] Yet this view has been undermined by studies which reveal gender-specific employment patterns on farms in the sixteenth, seventeenth and eighteenth centuries in some of the same counties as Snell's.[85] In addition the implementation of new harvest technology was slow and uneven, with the sickle and scythe existing in tandem where this made economic sense. The replacement of the sickle by the scythe was not universal by the mid-nineteenth century, let alone the end of the eighteenth. E. J. T. Collins claims that before the 1830s a change in the adoption of new technology was regionalised, slow and generally exceptional. Instead, it was between 1835 and 1870 that the 'most active' phase of the hand-tool revolution occurred.[86] Sharpe, weighing up the contradictions in the evidence, outlines the current position as follows:

> In summary, close analysis of the sexual division of labour does not give as straightforward view as Snell and those who have repeated and extended his arguments have maintained, and would lead us to eschew a view of technological change explaining female expulsion, in favour of a more nuanced approach which gives greater weight to local variations due to geography, regional culture and time-honoured patterns of customary work.[87]

---

[84] Ibid., p. 52.

[85] These studies include Mrs Elizabeth Gilboy, 'Labour at Thornborough: An eighteenth-century estate', *Economic History Review*, 1st ser., III (1932), pp. 388–98; A. Hassell Smith, 'Labourers in late sixteenth-century England: A case study from north Norfolk [Part 1]', *Continuity and Change*, 4 (1989), pp. 11–52; A. Hassell Smith, 'Labourers in late sixteenth-century England: A case study from north Norfolk [Part 2], *Continuity and Change*, 4 (1989), pp. 367–94; Carole Shammas, 'The world women knew: Women workers in the north of England during the seventeenth century', in Richard S. Dunn and Mary Maples Dunn, eds, *The World of William Penn* (Philadelphia, 1986), pp. 99–114; Pamela Sharpe, 'Time and wages of west country workfolks in the seventeenth and eighteenth centuries', *Local Population Studies*, 55 (1995), pp. 66–9; Sharpe, *Adapting to Capitalism*, ch.4; Donald Woodward, ed., *The Farming and Memorandum Books of Henry Best of Elmswell, 1642*, British Academy of Social and Economic History, no. 8 (1984).

[86] E. J. T. Collins, 'Harvest technology and the labour supply in Britain, 1790–1870', *Economic History Review*, XXII (1969), pp. 453–73. This is an argument that Snell rejects, pointing to the adoption of new techniques in the south-east from the 1750s onwards. Snell, *Annals of the Labouring Poor*, pp. 49–50.

[87] Sharpe, 'Female labour market', p. 171.

Detailed research on rural women, using innovative sources and databases, has recently been carried out. The obvious potential for regional and local accounts of the diversity of female employment patterns in the nineteenth-century countryside is beginning to be realised. Studies have tended to focus on women's work in the agricultural sector, with the issues of female participation rates and the operation of the sexual division of labour commanding most attention. What emerges is a complex model of both continuity and change in female employment patterns that were dependent on regional circumstances. Joyce Burnette's study of the Oakes farm, four miles from Sheffield, indicates that work opportunities for female labourers fell considerably between the 1770s and the 1830s. This was due to a decrease in demand for women labourers and was linked to changes in husbandry that followed enclosure.[88] Therefore the trend Burnette detects from farm labour books is at odds with Pinchbeck's classic account of female agricultural employment, but reinforces Snell's periodisation of the diminution in women's labour.

Other studies tend to support the Pinchbeck view and point to a rise in female participation across the late eighteenth and early nineteenth centuries. Judy Gielgud's research on women employed in Northumberland and Cumbria shows that the number of female day labourers increased in regularity and diversity during the first half of the nineteenth century as improved farming methods were implemented in that region. Gielgud argues that women remained a vital component of the workforce into the twentieth century, being engaged as both yearly or half-yearly farm servants, as well as day labourers.[89] Similar patterns of employment for the first half of the nineteenth century have been uncovered in the south-west. Mary Bouquet claims that between 1800 and 1850 women in Devon were employed as day labourers on a regular and constant basis throughout the year, and that male and female unemployment patterns followed the same annual pattern 'with minor variations'.[90] According to Bouquet this sequence altered only in the late nineteenth century when women workers became more specialised within the dairy and household, marking

> the beginning of a gender division of labour related ... to the decline of female productivity in cultivation activities and ... to the development of the milk industry in which women initially played a significant role.[91]

---

[88] Joyce Burnette, 'Labourers at the Oakes. Changes in the demand for female day-labourers at a farm near Sheffield during the Agricultural Revolution', *Journal of Economic History*, LIX (1999), pp. 41–67.

[89] Judy Gielgud, 'Nineteenth-century farm women in Northumberland and Cumbria: The neglected workforce' (D.Phil. thesis, University of Sussex, 1992). See esp. ch. 3 and ch. 5.

[90] Mary Bouquet, *Family, Servants and Visitors: The Farm Household in Nineteenth and Twentieth-Century Devon* (Norwich, 1985), p. 40.

[91] Ibid., p. 44.

Helen Speechley also finds a rise in the employment of women as day labourers on Somerset farms in the late eighteenth century. In this county, farm records show that women constituted on average 20 per cent of the annual day labour force, 'a far higher proportion ... than has been previously acknowledged'.[92] Female agricultural work in Somerset was seasonal, centring on springtime activities such as planting and weeding, and summer work in the harvests, but 'both the nature and patterns of seasonal agricultural day labour changed little over the course of the seventeenth to late nineteenth century'.[93] Finally Celia Miller's analysis of Gloucestershire farm records reveals a substantial number of female day labourers being employed on the mixed farms in the Cotswolds region of that county, even after the 1870s. She shows that women were employed on a wide range of agricultural tasks including reaping and threshing, their peak period of activity extending into late summer harvesting. Thus, she concludes, 'the sexual division of labour was still incomplete in the last decade of the nineteenth century'.[94]

Scholars are also starting to address the complex issue of female agricultural wage rates. Were women paid a customary rather than a market wage for their labour, and could this explain the persistence of a male–female wage gap in agriculture? Burnette has rejected this opinion: she argues that women in agriculture received market wages based on their 'marginal productivity' and not simply on a customary value for their work.[95] Speechley found evidence in Somerset to back up this assertion. Throughout the seventeenth and eighteenth centuries, women's daily wage remained static in that county at 6d, but increased in the nineteenth century to between 7d and 10d a day. Men were paid at least twice this amount across the whole period.[96] Speechley maintains that women's inferior physical strength and shorter working hours go some way to explain the wage gap, although she acknowledges that wage discrimination existed in that 'societal opinion which held

---

[92] Helen V. Speechley, 'Female and child agricultural day labourers in Somerset, c.1685–1870' (Ph.D. thesis, University of Exeter, 1999), p. 76.
[93] Ibid.
[94] Celia Miller, 'The hidden workforce: Female fieldworkers in Gloucestershire, 1870–1901', *Southern History*, 6 (1984), pp. 139–61 (p. 151). This article is part of her thesis which assesses the impact of agricultural change in nineteenth-century Gloucestershire on all members of the agricultural community. Celia Miller, 'Farm work and farm workers in Victorian Gloucestershire' (Ph.D. thesis, University of Bristol, 1980). Barry Reay in his work on nineteenth-century Kent has also pointed out that extensive hop and fruit growing ensured an important role for women in the cycle of employment in the county. Thus, he contends, away from the pure corn lands of southern England, Snell's argument does not stand up. See Reay, *Last Rising of Agricultural Labourers*, p. 45 and Barry Reay, *Microhistories: Demography, Society and Culture in Rural England, 1800–1930* (Cambridge, 1996), pp. 109–12.
[95] Joyce Burnette, 'An investigation of the female–male wage gap during the industrial revolution in Britain', *Economic History Review*, L (1997), pp. 257–81 (p. 261).
[96] Speechley, 'Female and child day labourers', p. 116.

that women were the weaker sex' also had an impact on pay rates.[97] Sharpe makes more out of the endurance of fixed wage rates for women day labourers, suggesting that evidence for this practice across temporal and geographical divides indicates that 'women's wages contain a large customary element and the rate paid may bear little resemblance to the task carried out'.[98]

The diversity of women's experiences in the formal agricultural labour market is clearly apparent from the scholarship outlined above. Yet we have to add another layer to this: women's labour did not always readily translate into wages and a broader definition of 'employment' is necessary when considering women's economic activities in the nineteenth-century countryside. The ways women made productive contributions to labouring households through more informal channels of work and exchange are being identified. Humphries, for example, highlights how women and children were the main exploiters of common rights in the late eighteenth and nineteenth centuries, allowing them to contribute substantially to family earnings. The loss of these rights, she argues, led to the increased dependence of families on wages and wage-earners.[99] Peter King's work shows how gleaning, a customary task performed by women and children, remained a significant source of income for many rural labouring families into the late nineteenth century.[100] Finally, Reed's exploratory work on the nature of non-market-orientated exchange channels between small rural producers in the nineteenth century may have important implications for research into women's neighbourhood networks in the countryside.[101]

For too long the study of rural working women has been relegated to the periphery of nineteenth-century agrarian history. The neglect of rural women was often justified by recourse to a familiar grievance: lack of sources. While it is certainly true that good archival sources directly relating to the daily working lives of countrywomen are rare, there are a number of ways to approach this topic, as the studies by Burnette, Gielgud, Bouquet, Speechley and Miller indicate. These will be explored in the next section.

---

[97] Ibid., p. 129.
[98] Sharpe, 'Female labour market', p. 173. Sharpe does acknowledge instances when women were paid higher rates (for example, at harvest time) in some regions or in areas where alternative employers vied with agriculture for female labourers. She also points to the differences in wages paid to women based on whether they were married or widowed on the sixteenth-century Petre farms in Essex: see p. 174.
[99] Jane Humphries, 'Enclosures, common rights and women: The proletarianisation of families in the late eighteenth and early nineteenth centuries', *Journal of Economic History*, L (1990), pp. 17–42.
[100] Peter King, 'Customary rights and women's earnings: The importance of gleaning to the rural labouring poor, 1750–1850', *Economic History Review*, XLIV (1991), pp. 461–76.
[101] Mick Reed, '"Gnawing it out": A new look at economic relations in nineteenth-century rural England', *Rural History*, 1 (1990), pp. 83–94.

Researching the employment of rural women: the uses and limitations of sources

Official publications such as nineteenth-century Parliamentary Papers and census records are among the most accessible sources for historians, although they need to be treated with caution when researching female occupations. We should not dismiss these sources outright. However, their use in conjunction with other evidence – contemporary writing, local newspapers, farm records and autobiographical material – means that we can begin to move away from the official framework and biases inherent in formal published sources and build a more rounded reconstruction of rural women's working lives.

Census records

Census records have been widely used by historians to promote theories on women's participation in the nineteenth-century workforce. Scholars such as Michael Anderson and Eric Richards championed the use of census material in their studies of female occupations and lifecycle changes.[102] However, in recent years a considerable body of literature has emerged concerned with highlighting problems associated with using the occupational census records. As Edward Higgs puts it, 'the process of accumulating, arranging and analysing census data was not a value-free exercise, especially with regard to the work of women'.[103] The process of compilation and inspection was predominately male.[104] Assumptions about women's role in society governed the way female occupations were recorded. Family members were defined in terms of their relationship to the head of household (who was usually, but not always, male). Those filling in the returns varied in the extent to which they regarded women's work – both outside and within the home – as an occupation. It was often assumed that women, whatever their productive capacity, were dependants, while men were classified according to the nature of their work. The meanings attached to designations such as 'work', 'occupation' and 'labour force' were significant. According to Hill, from 1841 the

---

[102] Michael Anderson, *Family Structure in Nineteenth-Century Lancashire* (Cambridge, 1971); Eric Richards, 'Women in the British economy since about 1700', *History*, 59 (1974), pp. 337–57.

[103] Edward Higgs, 'Women, occupations and work in the nineteenth-century censuses', *History Workshop Journal*, 23 (1987), pp. 59–82 (p. 60).

[104] Higgs reveals that senior figures at the General Register Office were all male, that enumerators were appointed by male registrars and women were not eligible for this work until 1891. He also argues that the census office regarded motherhood as the prime function of women in the nineteenth century. Higgs, 'Women, occupations and work', p. 62.

values underpinning census collection and analysis were informed by classical economics. Thus 'work' was defined by the fact that it had a market value and could be measured in monetary terms.[105] Women's labour, characterised by part-time, casual and seasonal multi-layered activities, tended not to be classified as an 'occupation'. As a result such work often went unrecorded.

These issues were compounded by the changing and convoluted instructions circulated to enumerators and householders. The types of labour designated as an 'occupation' altered from census to census. In 1841 compilers were instructed that the 'profession etc' of wives 'need not be inserted'.[106] As a result, the under-recording of married women's work in the nineteenth-century censuses is commonplace, an omission revealed by cross-referencing census records with contemporary wage accounts and oral testimony.[107] The censuses of 1851, 1861 and 1871 did recognise that female work in the home could contribute to the market economy in that occupations of women who were 'regularly employed from home, or at home in any other than domestic duties' were to be 'distinctly recorded'.[108] By 1881 this clause was withdrawn: women's household manufacturing was excluded from the definition of economic activity. These women were now placed in a residual 'unoccupied' category. Female relatives who had previously been regarded as helping in the family business were now abstracted as dependants.[109] This makes comparisons between pre- and post-1881 censuses fraught with difficulties.

There are particular complications in the classification of rural women's work in the nineteenth-century census records. From 1841 onwards households were asked to give details of persons under their roof on one night of the year – usually in March or April. Therefore the extent of women's seasonal agricultural work in the summer months would not have been detected when the census was taken. In addition, the fact that women often worked on the

---

[105] Bridget Hill, 'Women, work and the census: A problem for historians of women', *History Workshop Journal*, 35 (1993), pp. 78–94 (p. 81). The work of Horrell and Humphries also shows how female participation rates differ according to whether an 'occupational' or 'earnings' definition is applied to women's labour. In their research on married women's employment in a cross-section of industries, an occupational definition produced lower estimates of participation than an earning definition. This was especially the case for women married to agricultural workers, particularly in low-wage counties which were located mainly in the south and east of England. Horrell and Humphries, 'Women's labour force participation', p. 97.

[106] Higgs, 'Women, occupations and work', p. 63. Children living with and assisting parents in their occupation, but not apprenticed or receiving wages, were also omitted from the occupational record in 1841.

[107] See Lown, *Women and Industrialisation*, p. 156; Elizabeth Roberts, *A Woman's Place: An Oral History of Working Class Women, 1890–1940*, 1st edn 1984 (Oxford, 1995), p. 136.

[108] Higgs, 'Women, occupations and work', p. 63.

[109] Ibid., p. 70.

same farms as their husbands may have led to the assumption that they were not following an independent 'occupation'. As a result, many women are not given occupational designations in enumerators' books. This omission also applied to female relatives of farmers, whose labour on family-run farms often went unrecorded. Female farm servants – who sometimes worked in the dairy, assisted in the fields at peak times and performed general household duties – were notoriously difficult to classify. It was not unusual for female servants who should have been recorded as farm servants to be classified in other occupational categories, notably domestic service.[110] The extent of this neglect – particularly of the casual and seasonal labour of women – is unearthed in studies by Jessica Gerard on country house servants and Miller on agricultural day labourers.[111] Miller's findings are telling: most women day labourers employed on the Gloucestershire farms she studied, many of whom worked in the fields for one-third of the year or more, were returned as 'unoccupied' by local enumerators.[112] This has serious implications for the conventional picture of the extent of female agricultural labour in the second half of the nineteenth century.

The weight of evidence challenging the reliability of nineteenth-century census material seems incontrovertible. Yet we should not abandon this source: census enumerators' books disclose interesting demographic details about families and individuals who would otherwise remain anonymous. Tentative conclusions on the marital and age specificity of rural labouring women can be deduced, as can the familial relationships between nineteenth-century farmworkers. The correlation between the ages and number of children a woman had and her ability to contribute to the household economy can also be analysed. While evidence from census records should be treated with care – especially in relation to female participation rates – it is one of the few sources we can exploit to uncover the shadowy and buried life stories of female labourers in nineteenth-century rural England.

---

[110] The main areas of under-recording of the agricultural workforce are explored in Edward Higgs, 'Occupational censuses and the agricultural workforce in Victorian England and Wales', *Economic History Review*, XLVIII (1995), pp. 700–16.

[111] Jessica Gerard, 'Invisible servants: The country house and the local community', *Bulletin of the Institute of Historical Research*, 57 (1986), pp. 178–88. This theme is further explored in her book, *Country House Life: Family and Servants, 1815–1914* (Oxford, 1994), esp. ch. 7; Miller, 'Hidden workforce'.

[112] Miller, 'Hidden workforce', p. 147.

Printed sources: Parliamentary Papers, contemporary writing and local newspapers

A large body of contemporary published material relating to agrarian matters exists for the nineteenth century. Indeed, the time-scale of this study was initially conceived in relation to two key reports: the investigations by David Davies and Frederick Morton Eden in the 1790s as the beginning, and the 1893 to 1894 Royal Commission on Labour, as the concluding point.[113] Between these two publications are to be found a plethora of books, journals, pamphlets and Parliamentary Papers issuing forth on rural matters. The most important and familiar government publications include the 1834 Poor Law Report, the 1843 and 1867 to 1870 reports on the employment of women and children in agriculture and the reports to the Children's Employment Commission in the 1860s.[114] Other significant evidence is contained in the General Views of Agriculture, published for all the English counties over the period of the Napoleonic Wars.[115] The *Annals of Agriculture, Journal of the Royal Agricultural Society, Journal of the Statistical Society* and the *Farmer's Magazine*, among other journals, contain relevant articles, while the rural 'journeys' of William Cobbett (1830), James Caird (1851) and Henry Rider Haggard (1902) are also useful.[116]

For the historian of female labour contemporary books, journal and pamphlet literature can be frustrating. Only occasionally do commentators directly address the question of women's work, usually when the issue became a point of contention. Parliamentary reports engage in the debate more

---

[113] David Davies, *The Case of Labourers in Husbandry, Stated and Considered* (London, 1795); Sir Frederick Morton Eden, *The State of the Poor*, 3 vols (London, 1797); PP 1893–4, XXXV, Royal Commission on Labour. The Agricultural Labourer. Reports from the Assistant Agriculture Commissioners.

[114] PP 1834, XXX, Report from His Majesty's Commissioners for Inquiring into the Administration and Practical Operation of the Poor Laws. Appendix (B.1). Answers to Rural Queries in Five Parts. Part I; PP 1843, XII, Reports of Special Assistant Poor Law Commissioners on the Employment of Women and Children in Agriculture; PP 1863, XVII, First Report of the Children's Employment Commission; PP 1864, XXII, Second Report of the Children's Employment Commission; PP 1867, XVI, Sixth Report of the Children's Employment Commission; PP 1867–8, XVII, First Report from the Commissioners on the Employment of Children, Young Persons and Women in Agriculture; PP 1868–9, XIII, Second Report from the Commissioners on the Employment of Children, Young Persons and Women in Agriculture.

[115] A good bibliography of the General Views is included in W. E. Tate, *The English Village Community and the Enclosure Movement* (London, 1967), pp. 177–8.

[116] William Cobbett, *Rural Rides*, 1st edn 1830 (Harmondsworth, 1985); James Caird, *English Agriculture in 1850–51* (London, 1852); Henry Rider Haggard, *Rural England: Being an Account of Agricultural and Social Researches Carried out in the Years 1901 and 1902*, 2 vols (London, 1902). See also Mark Freeman, 'Rider Haggard and *Rural England*: Methods of social enquiry in the English countryside', *Social History*, 26 (2001), pp. 209–16.

directly and contain a mass of information on male, female and child labour, wages and employment conditions, as well as much incidental material covering housing conditions, education, allotments, diet and living standards. These official printed sources are voluminous and have been widely used by historians. Early scholars, such as Hasbach and Pinchbeck, relied almost exclusively on this evidence. But the information contained in Parliamentary Papers is problematic, with the likelihood of bias high. Questions on the organisation, gathering and presentation of these reports need to be asked: why were these reports instigated? Who were the leading Commissioners and how would their sex, class and background affect their investigations? Who did the Commissioners approach for their information? The answers to such queries cast doubt on the validity of some of the details provided in the reports. Karen Sayer, who conceptualises the reports as social constructs, has highlighted this point. Given this, she argues, historians should treat them

> as historically specific cultural products, which belong to the ongoing construction and re-construction of the bounds and definitions of femininity and masculinity in the Victorian period, and which can be situated within the discourse of a newly professionalising bureaucracy.[117]

Despite these drawbacks, nineteenth-century literature does offer useful insights into the ways attitudes towards rural working women changed over the course of the century, an issue which will be explored in more detail in Chapter 2.

The final printed source that warrants investigation is the local newspaper. W. B. Stephens argues that 'for the nineteenth century . . . newspapers must be regarded as an essential source for the local historian'.[118] Before the nineteenth century local newspapers were largely weekly versions of the London press with much reprinted material. By the 1840s this had changed, and provincial papers began to carry a great deal of local news to appeal to resident farmers and gentry.[119] The wealth of detail contained in local newspapers is immense. When searching for information on female employment in the countryside, the use of newspapers is a time-consuming and often fruitless affair. There are exceptions to this however, and reports on the state of crops in the locality, local markets and the price of labour can be of particular interest.

---

[117] Karen Sayer, *Women of the Fields: Representations of Rural Women in the Nineteenth Century* (Manchester, 1995), p. 3.
[118] W. B. Stephens, *Sources for English Local History*, 1st edn 1981 (Chichester, 1994), p. 24.
[119] Howkins, *Reshaping Rural England*, p. 240.

Archival sources: farm labour and account books

The questionable nature of nineteenth-century printed sources makes it essential to use archival evidence when researching the working patterns of rural women. Farm records may be located in numerous locations: county archive offices, university manuscript collections and private holdings. Collins, writing in 1966, claimed that such 'records remain, by and large, a much neglected historical source'.[120] This comment is still pertinent. While work on farming output and productivity – particularly on the larger estates – has been produced, the use of farm records for the study of agricultural labour, especially female labour, is still largely untapped.[121] Farm records are not easy to use and this may account for the underemployment of the evidence at our disposal.

The majority of farm records still existing originate from large estates and are not necessarily representative of the average English farm in the nineteenth century. The estate farms were likely to be 'in-hand' or home farms. The latter were used to produce foodstuffs for the manor house, and were often showcase farms used by entrepreneurial landowners to experiment with new agricultural techniques and technology.[122] Such farms would certainly have employed a labour force sufficiently large to require a written record of payments and tasks.[123] A farm of under 100 acres would generally not employ sufficient workers from outside the family to require labour books: the smaller the farm, the less likely records were kept. As a result, 'those keeping farm records are unlikely to be representative of the class of farmers as a whole' and the labour performed by women on smaller holdings is therefore under-represented.[124]

There are considerable advantages in using farm records. They are a (largely) scrupulous account of employment and wages of workers. Whilst wage books only record names and payments, the best farm labour records that have survived include the full name, number of days worked per week,

---

[120] E. J. T. Collins, 'Historical farm records', *Archives*, 35 (1966), pp. 143–9 (p. 143). From the pages of surviving account and cropping books, herd and flock books, diaries and memoranda, he contended, numerous subjects relevant to the social and economic history of the countryside could be investigated: 'the levels of farm output, receipts, expenditure, profits and investment; the influence of price movements on individual farming systems ... crop and milk yields' (p. 145).
[121] M. E. Turner, J. V. Beckett and B. Afton, 'Taking stock: Farmers, farm records and agricultural output in England, 1700–1850', *Agricultural History Review*, 44 (1996), pp. 21–34. The work by Burnette, Gielgud, Miller and Speechley is beginning to change this.
[122] R. J. Colyer, 'The uses of estate home farm accounts as sources for nineteenth-century agricultural history', *The Local Historian*, 11 (1975), pp. 406–13.
[123] Turner *et al.*, 'Taking stock', p. 29.
[124] Ibid., p. 27.

tasks performed and payments made to all individual day labourers.[125] In some collections the sequence of labour books spans several decades and can reveal much about the changes in a farm workforce over time. However, even though farm accounts are mostly free from the urban, middle-class perceptions of Victorian Commissioners and commentators, farmers still much more consistently record male labour than female workers. Women (and children) are often bunched together under one heading at the bottom of a full list of male workers with only a note made of the payment given to women as a group. This in itself reveals much about the way contemporaries viewed the work of rural women in the nineteenth century. Thus, using sources such as farm wage and labour books, historians of labouring women, as Sharpe comments, 'have to learn to be perceptive about silences in the documentary coverage'.[126]

From these records it is possible to calculate labour payments made annually to male, female and child workers on farms. The continuities and changes in the employment of these workers over time and space can be determined. The seasonality of labour patterns can be explored through an examination of the number of days worked by farmworkers over the course of a year. The sexual division of agricultural tasks can be ascertained where individual work patterns are recorded. The nature of piece-work and day rates for men, women and children and the male–female wage gap can be examined. Where individual workers are named the familial relationships between workers on the farm – and the nature of family labour – can also be investigated. So, despite their problems, farm labour and wage books enable us to move towards a more sophisticated grasp of female employment patterns at the regional and local level. As Burnette argues, 'unless the account-keeper was cheating, the data in the wage books is an accurate report . . . much more exact than any other source'.[127]

Studying the informal economy: rural autobiography

Farm records, Parliamentary Papers, newspaper articles and census data have been used as the main sources in this book. These sources tend to focus on paid female employment in the formal sectors of the rural economy.

---

[125] Although, as Burnette notes, they do not include the age of workers or include a record of the tasks performed by the yearly farm servants. Burnette, 'Labourers at the Oakes', pp. 44–5.
[126] Sharpe, *Adapting to Capitalism*, p. 153.
[127] Burnette, 'Labourers at the Oakes', p. 44. For further exploration of farm records see Nicola Verdon, '". . . a much neglected historical source: The uses and limitations of farm account books to historians of rural women's work', *Women's History Notebooks*, 8 (2001), pp. 5–12.

Principally, women's work in agricultural day labour is discussed, although this material also pertains to female labour in farm service and domestic industry. The many ways village women 'made shift' outside the cash economy remain largely concealed in such evidence (although they are referred to in the government reports).[128] However, recognition of these strategies is key to appreciating the contribution made by women to the rural family exchequer. One way to begin to reveal the complex, multi-occupational nature of the daily pattern of rural women's working lives is through autobiographical writing and personal reminiscences of village life in the nineteenth century. David Vincent eloquently outlines the advantages of this type of source:

> There is a limit to the insights that can be gleaned from the most subtle analysis of census material, and while it is necessary to place this qualitative evidence in the context of the statistical data now available, it should be possible to use the memories and observations of these writers to help tease out the skein of human relationships that is family life. Furthermore, it is here that the autobiographers are most likely to discuss the crucial connections between their material lives, their existence as workers, both as children and adults, and the other basic areas of experience to which they attach significance.[129]

The working-class autobiography developed in the nineteenth century 'into a remarkably diverse and fertile genre' and became increasingly common in the latter decades of the century as literacy levels improved.[130] A number of working-class autobiographies and reminiscences centring on village life in nineteenth-century England exist, with work, childhood, home and family life forming the core themes in most accounts. In addition, sundry works by authors who rose out of the ranks of the labouring poor, but who look back and describe their formative upbringing in the countryside, are also available. Unfortunately, autobiographies written by working women are rare (although they do exist).[131] As a result it is virtually impossible for historians

---

[128] Penelope Lane, 'Work on the margins: Poor women and the informal economy of eighteenth and early nineteenth-century Leicestershire', *Midland History*, 22 (1997), pp. 85–99. Lane adopts this phrase from Olwen Hufton's research on eighteenth-century France in which she reveals 'an economy of makeshifts'. See Olwyn Hufton, *The Poor of Eighteenth-Century France, 1750–1789* (Oxford, 1974).

[129] David Vincent, *Bread, Knowledge and Freedom: A Study of Nineteenth-Century Working Class Autobiography* (London, 1981), p. 12.

[130] John Burnett, David Vincent and David Mayall, eds, *The Autobiography of the Working Class: An Annotated, Critical Bibliography, vol 1, 1790–1900* (Brighton, 1984), p. xiii.

[131] See e.g. Mrs Burrows, 'A childhood in the fens about 1850–60', in Margaret Llewelyn Davies, ed., *Life As We Have Known It*, 1st edn 1931 (London, 1977), pp. 109–14. The autobiography of Lucy Luck, a straw-plait worker, is reprinted in John Burnett, ed., *Useful Toil: Autobiographies of Working People from the 1820s to the 1920s*, 1st edn 1974 (London, 1994), pp. 53–63.

to probe women's own attitudes and outlook toward their working and family life. The invisibility of the female voice obligates a reliance on the male perspective. This is not ideal but can still be illuminating. Autobiographical material furnishes us with an alternative account of rural life. It produces an important comparison to records of labour in the formal employment market. It also offers a different perspective from the official opinion postulated in Parliamentary Papers. But before exploring the insights offered by autobiographical writing, we must assess the main trends in rural women's labour that emanate from the official and archival sources. The next chapter will examine the evidence contained in nineteenth-century printed sources.

2

Differing views of rural women's work in documentary material

An overview of printed sources

The significance of printed primary sources such as Royal Commissions to the study of rural women's work and wages has long been recognised. The scarcity of archival and personal records directly relating to poor labouring women bestows further value to documentary evidence. Early historians of rural England such as William Hasbach relied heavily on published sources, and we saw in Chapter 1 the results of Ivy Pinchbeck's comprehensive scrutiny of material pertaining to women's employment printed between 1750 and 1850.[1] Historians continue to make use of such documents today. One prominent example is Karen Sayer's cultural critique of the representations of rural women in nineteenth-century Parliamentary Papers.[2]

This chapter, then, does not introduce any new or unworked sources. It does however offer a fresh approach to the way historians can use such material. I have chosen a number of key printed sources to analyse, beginning with an examination of the household budget accounts of the labouring poor collected by David Davies and Frederick Eden in the 1790s. The General Views of the Agriculture of each of the counties of England will then be assessed for the possible insights they offer into the subject of female employment at the beginning of the nineteenth century. A number of well-known parliamentary commissions form the basis of the remainder of the chapter: specifically the 1834 Poor Law Report, the 1843 and 1867 to 1870 Royal Commissions on the employment of women and children in agriculture will be considered in detail. The result is an overview of the published account of rural women's employment patterns in the nineteenth century. The approach taken is chronological although the examination of each of the sources is thematic. In particular this chapter will consider what the documents reveal about the regional specificity of female employment

---

[1] William Hasbach, *A History of the English Agricultural Labourer*, 1st edn 1894 (London, 1966); Ivy Pinchbeck, *Women Workers and the Industrial Revolution, 1750–1850*, 1st edn 1930 (London, 1981).
[2] Karen Sayer, *Women of the Fields: Representations of Rural Women in the Nineteenth Century* (Manchester, 1995).

opportunities and wages, and the changing perceptions of rural labouring women across the nineteenth century.

The budget accounts of David Davies and Frederick Eden

The household accounts of the labouring poor assembled by Davies and Eden in the 1790s are unique. They form one of the earliest and most comprehensive samples of the earnings and expenses of a social class usually obscured in historical records: agricultural labouring families. Davies, rector of the parish of Barkham in Berkshire, amassed and printed over 120 budgets of the English labouring poor in the Appendix to his book *The Case of Labourers in Husbandry*, which was published in 1795.[3] Eden collected fifty-three household accounts. They were published in 1797 as Appendix 12 in the third and final volume of his tract *The State of the Poor*.[4] Both sets of records are printed in tabular form listing expenses and earnings by the week and year, together with additional information on the composition of the families involved and other relevant observations. Despite the similarities in methodology, these two men represented very different ideological viewpoints. Eden was critical of the Poor Law and sought to demonstrate that the labouring poor could lead independent, self-reliant lives without being a burden on the poor rates. Davies defended the right to relief and linked the pauperisation of the labouring poor at the end of the eighteenth century to wider economic factors such as enclosure and underemployment.[5]

Both writers offer extensive commentaries on the position of women workers in rural society.[6] The decrease in women's ability to contribute to

---

[3] David Davies, *The Case of Labourers in Husbandry, Stated and Considered* (London, 1795), 'Appendix containing a collection of accounts shewing the earnings and expenses of labouring families in different parts of the Kingdom'. He also collected five budgets from Wales and eight from Scotland which have been excluded from the analysis here.

[4] Sir Frederick Morton Eden, *The State of the Poor*, 3 vols (London, 1797), vol. 3, 'Appendix No. XII. Expenses and Earnings of Agricultural Labourers in various parts of England, collected in January and February 1796'.

[5] See Thomas Sokoll, 'Early attempts at accounting the unaccountable: Davies' and Eden's budgets of agricultural labouring families in late eighteenth-century England', in Toni Pierenkemper, ed., *Zur Ökonomic des Privaten Havshalts* (Frankfurt, 1991), pp. 34–58 (pp. 37–8); John Styles, 'Clothing the north: The supply of non-elite clothing in the eighteenth-century north of England', *Textile History*, 25 (1994), pp. 139-66 (p. 139).

[6] Although the evidence accumulated by Davies and Eden has been widely quoted by several generations of historians, so far the only extensive quantitative analysis of these data has been attempted by Thomas Sokoll. See Sokoll, 'Early attempts at accounting the unaccountable'. See also Thomas Sokoll, *Household and Family Among the Poor: The Case of Two Essex Communities in the Late Eighteenth and Early Nineteenth Centuries* (Bochum, 1993). Other historians who have utilised the accounts of Davies and Eden include

the family budget is noted by the two authors, linking this development to changes in both the agrarian and manufacturing sectors of the English economy in the 1790s. First, the loss of common rights through enclosure is highlighted. Davies argued that labourers were being denied the capacity to 'raise for themselves a considerable part of their subsistence' as a result of this process.[7] Eden, an enthusiastic advocate of agrarian improvement, is rather more sceptical about the value of commons and wastes to labouring families.[8] Recent research tends to reinforce Davies' account, pointing to the erosion of non-waged sources of subsistence which were extensively exploited by women and children before enclosure.[9]

Women also increasingly found themselves disadvantaged in the formal waged labour market. The loss of income from spinning was especially calamitous. Hand-spinning in the home was a ubiquitous female employment in the eighteenth century.[10] It was complementary to the other social and economic roles performed by women: seasonal agricultural labour, managing animals, appropriating common rights, taking care of the home and family. Both Davies and Eden – along with other contemporary commentators such as Arthur Young – recognised the significance of spinning wages. Davies claimed money earned by spinning allowed the purchase of 'clothes, linen and other necessities', enabling families 'to keep out of debt, and to live so decently'.[11] The distress wrought by the decline of hand-spinning was devastating. Young maintained that low wages for spinning in the 1780s had the consequence of 'almost starving the poor in the two counties of Norfolk and Suffolk', a situation confirmed by Eden across the English counties by

---

A. L. Bowlby, 'The statistics of wages in the UK during the last hundred years (part I). Agricultural wages', *Journal of the Statistical Society*, 61 (1898), pp. 702–22; Pinchbeck, *Women Workers*, pp. 44–52; Peter H. Lindert and Jeffrey G. Williamson, 'English workers' living standards during the industrial revolution: A new look', *Economic History Review*, XXXVI (1983), pp. 1–25; K. D. M. Snell, *Annals of the Labouring Poor: Social Change and Agrarian England, 1660–1900* (Cambridge, 1985), p. 56; George R. Boyer, *An Economic History of the English Poor Law, 1750–1850* (Cambridge, 1990), pp. 41–2.

[7] Davies, *Labourers in Husbandry*, p. 56. Davies calculates that a family could cut enough fuel for a year in a week, and to replace this after enclosure would cost anything from £1 15s to £4 3s. In this estimate the value of common fuel equalled 10 per cent of a labourer's wages. See J. M. Neeson, *Commoners: Common Right, Enclosure and Social Change in England, 1700–1820* (Cambridge, 1993), p. 165.

[8] Eden, *State of the Poor*, vol. I, p. 14.

[9] Jane Humphries, 'Enclosures, common rights and women: The proletarianisation of families in the late eighteenth and early nineteenth centuries', *Journal of Economic History*, L (1990), pp. 17–42.

[10] Deborah Valenze, *The First Industrial Woman* (Oxford, 1995), ch.4.

[11] Davies, *Labourers in Husbandry*, p. 84 and p. 86. Young argued that spinning established 'earlier habits of industry and good behaviour' and had 'a more extensive influence on the poor, than almost any other kind of industry'. 'T.B.' and Arthur Young, 'On spinning among the poor', *Annals of Agriculture*, 5 (1786), pp. 417–22 (p. 417).

the 1790s.[12] In Cumberland he found wages to be 'very inconsiderable', in Northamptonshire wages were 'much lower than formerly' and in Lincolnshire earnings from spinning were 'extremely low'.[13] The cause of this hardship was the transition to machine-spinning, which eventually concentrated production in factories and workshops in specific areas of the country. For great numbers of rural labouring women – and their families – who had profited by the wages of spinning, this transformation was disastrous. The precarious nature of alternative employment opportunities exacerbated the situation. Although Davies and Eden note the buoyancy of female wages in other domestic industries – particularly lace-making and straw-plaiting – these activities were mainly sited in the south Midlands region. Finally, agricultural day labour rates for women were shown to be generally low across England. Eden perceptively identifies the disparity between male and female wages in agriculture. In Cumberland he remarked, 'women, who here do a large portion of the work of the farm, with great difficulty get half as much. It is not easy to account for so striking an inequality; and still less easy to justify it.'[14]

If we look more closely at the accounts themselves, a number of significant themes emerge. First, it becomes clear that the typical agricultural labouring family lived below subsistence in the 1790s: 82 per cent of Davies' budgets and 83 per cent of Eden's show a deficiency of earnings compared to expenditure. Second, it is possible to calculate how much men, women and children earned annually and the extent family members contributed to the household income. The results are shown in Table 2.1. In Davies' accounts women earned on average £2 3s a year, while Eden's budgets show annual female wages to be slightly higher at £2 15s. The data contained in both studies suggest that women's earnings constituted just under 10 per cent of the family exchequer. Children's contribution was 13 to 14 per cent, while women and children together provided 22 to 23 per cent of yearly family incomes. Thus, even with the deterioration of spinning wages the value of women's earnings to family survival is revealed. This evidence also exposes the relationship between lifecycle, wage-earning potential and income deficit. The earnings women obtained were conditional not only on the availability of employment, but also on the number and age of children living in the household. Accounts recording excess earnings tended to belong to families with older,

---

[12] Arthur Young, 'On the price of wool, and state of spinning at present in England', *Annals of Agriculture*, 9 (1788), pp. 266–345 (p. 266). The decline of spinning employment is detailed in other volumes of this journal. See esp. Various, 'Replies to the editors circular letter', *Annals of Agriculture*, 24 (1795), pp. 239–93 and pp. 297–348, continued in vol. 25 (1796), pp. 473–506 and pp. 599–642, and vol. 26 (1796), pp. 1–26 and pp. 115–58.
[13] Eden, *State of the Poor*, vol 2, p. 84, p. 528 and p. 404.
[14] Ibid., p. 47.

Table 2.1 Average annual earnings of men, women and children in the household accounts of Davies and Eden

	Davies	Eden
Women's earnings	£2 3s	£2 15s
Children's earnings	£3 3s	£4 4s
Women and children	£5 6s	£6 19s
Men's earnings	£18 8s	£22 14s
Family total	£23 14s	£29 13s
Women's contribution	9%	9%
Children's contribution	13%	14%
Women and children	22%	23%
Men's contribution	78%	77%

Sources: Davies, *Labourers in Husbandry*, Appendix; Eden, *State of the Poor*, vol. 3, Appendix 12. In Davies' budgets, twelve accounts were left blank apart from the family total and have been excluded, as have four accounts that lump together the earnings of women and children.

economically active children at home.[15] However, both investigations include a preponderance of families with a large number of dependants: the mean number of co-residing children in Davies is 4.05, in Eden it is 3.62.[16] This would have adverse consequences for women's productive capacity. In addition, the types of families from which Davies and Eden collected budgets were restricted. Both focus on mature family groups. Only Davies includes some examples of families headed by widows or deserted wives and there is an absence of young families without children (whose economic position may have been much stronger).

Clearly this evidence has to be handled with care. In addition to the unrepresentative nature of the family groups there are other problems. Both sets of budgets were collected at a time of very high prices due to wartime inflation. The accounts do not cover the whole country. In fact both Davies' and Eden's budgets are biased in favour of families residing in low-waged southern England. Few of the printed accounts include harvest earnings. The significance of this omission is recognised by Eden: 'They go a great way towards making up the deficiency', he remarks.[17] Other forms of productive labour are also excluded from the printed accounts, although they are

---

[15] Davies, *Labourers in Husbandry*, p. 155.
[16] W. A. Armstrong, *Farmworkers: A Social and Economic History, 1770–1980* (London, 1988), p. 257. This can be compared to the average household composition in Ardleigh, Essex in 1795 to 1796 as compiled by Sokoll. He found 2.10 co-residing children in the average 'non-pauper' household and 3.41 in the average 'pauper' household ('pauper' being those in receipt of poor relief). Sokoll, *Household and Family*, p. 157.
[17] Eden, *State of the Poor*, vol 3, p. cccxxxix.

acknowledged in the narrative. Many of the activities were central to women's wage-earning capacity. For example, Eden noted that families could glean 'as much wheat as will serve them for bread for the whole year, and as many beans as will keep a pig'.[18] The cultivation of cottage gardens and rearing of cows, pigs, geese and chickens was shown to be beneficial.[19] Taking in washing and providing accommodation for lodgers are also mentioned.[20] Earnings gained in these ways, rather than representing strict monetary value, propped up the financial structure of the family. They point to the value of women's enterprises beyond the formal labour market. Thus, although Davies and Eden highlight the increasing pressures on women's employment opportunities in rural England at the end of the eighteenth century, the wages they did earn, by whatever means, are shown to be important – if not central – to the family economy.

The General Views of Agriculture

The first set of country reports to the Board of Agriculture were published in the mid-1790s; the second editions between 1804 and 1817. They are collectively referred to as the General Views of Agriculture. Their publication extends over the period of the Napoleonic Wars and provides us with one of the most complete published records of English agriculture in that period.

---

[18] Eden, *State of the Poor*, vol. 2, p. 547. This would have been worth around 6 per cent or more of the family's annual income. See Peter King, 'Customary rights and women's earnings: The importance of gleaning to the rural labouring poor, 1750–1850', *Economic History Review*, XLIV (1991), pp. 461–76 (p. 462).

[19] See Davies, *Labourers in Husbandry*, p. 179; Eden, *State of the Poor*, vol. 1, p. 628; vol. 3, p. cccxli. The value of land and animals to labourers is the subject of debate in several other contemporary publications. See e.g., Bishop of Durham, 'Extract from an account of three cottagers keeping cows and renting land in Rutlandshire', *Report of the Society for Bettering the Condition and Increasing the Comforts of the Poor*, vol. 1 (1798), pp. 116–19; Earl of Winchelsea, 'Extract from an account of the advantages of cottagers renting land', *Report of the Society for Bettering the Condition and Increasing the Comforts of the Poor*, vol. 1 (1798), pp. 129–39; Revd Dr Glasse, 'Extract from an account of the advantage of a cottager keeping a pig', *Report of the Society for Bettering the Condition and Increasing the Comforts of the Poor*, vol. 1 (1798), pp. 193–6; E. Harries, 'Land for cottagers', *Annals of Agriculture*, 36 (1801), pp. 355–9; Sir John Sinclair, 'Observations on the means of enabling a cottager to keep a cow', *Annals of Agriculture*, 37 (1801), pp. 225–45; Thomas Estcourt, 'An account of the result of an effort to better the condition of the poor in a country village', *Annals of Agriculture*, 43 (1805), pp. 1–9 and pp. 289–99; F. C., 'Agricultural labour', *Farmers Magazine*, 2 (1835), p. 114. See also William Cobbett, *Cottage Economy*, 1st edn 1822 (Oxford, 1979), pp. 96–7 on the advantages of keeping a cow. For a recent review of contemporary comment on cow-keeping see Leigh Shaw-Taylor, 'Labourers, cows, common rights and parliamentary enclosure: The evidence of contemporary comment, c.1760–1810', *Past and Present*, 171 (2001), pp. 95–126.

[20] See e.g. Davies, *Labourers in Husbandry*, p. 137, p. 143, p. 167 and p. 181.

Pinchbeck claims, however, that 'it is impossible' to accurately report the main trends in rural female labour during this time, as 'the only indications of its extent are the vague generalisations sometimes made by the reporters to the Board of Agriculture'.[21] In many ways Pinchbeck's assessment of this source is valid. The General Views were written by a variety of 'roving reporters' – or 'transient tourists' as William Marshall called some of them – not always familiar with local trends and reliant on second-hand accounts.[22] The employment of women was not central to their agenda: although all volumes include sections on labour and the poor, these are generally sandwiched between long descriptions of agricultural innovations, crop patterns and livestock. The information they include on wages is not as complete as that recorded by Davies and Eden: authors of the General Views did not collect annual incomes and budgets of the rural poor, for example. Yet despite these drawbacks, the General Views have yet to be fully and systematically exploited by historians, and the information they contain on a range of female employment opportunities – domestic industries, agricultural day labour and farm service – augment our understanding of the early nineteenth-century rural labour market.

First, the General Views enable us to follow the chronology and impact of one of the themes central to the writings of Davies and Eden: the decline of hand-spinning. Many of the first editions note the depreciation in wages earned by women through spinning; the second editions go beyond this and pinpoint the near-total decimation of the industry throughout the English countryside. The repercussions were felt on a number of levels. First, the lack of employment for women was lamented in many regions. In Devon, for example, the failure of spinning employment had relegated women to 'rummaging about for a few loose sticks in order to procure a scanty supply of fuel'.[23] The fall-off in work opportunities in turn affected the living standards of labouring families. In Gloucestershire it was noted that 'The families of labourers who were used to earning a good deal towards their maintenance by spinning, have no employment in the winter', while the rural poor of Wiltshire were found to be in a 'wretched condition' as a result of 'the failure of spinning work'.[24] The ultimate result was an increase in those applying for parish relief, adding to rising poor rates.[25]

---

[21] Pinchbeck, *Women Workers*, p. 63.
[22] Quoted in Neeson, *Commoners*, p. 40.
[23] Charles Vancouver, *General View of the Agriculture of the County of Devon* (London, 1808), p. 464.
[24] T. Rudge, *General View of the Agriculture of the County of Gloucester* (London, 1813), p. 341; Thomas Davis, *General View of the Agriculture of the County of Wiltshire* (London, 1811), p. 215.
[25] See e.g. G. B. Worgan, *General View of the Agriculture of the County of Cornwall* (London, 1811), p. 33.

One response to these conditions was the introduction of alternative domestic industries in some regions of the English countryside. Straw-plaiting in particular was viewed as useful employment for redundant female labour and was championed by philanthropic agents in the early nineteenth century. The second editions of Bedford, Buckingham, Hertford and Essex record this industry. Authors in Bedford, Buckingham and Northampton noted the presence of lace-making, while button-making was located in Dorset. Commentators welcomed the benefits bestowed by such employment, particularly in light of the high wages being earned by women as a result of wartime embargoes on foreign materials. Young claimed that the importation of straw plait into Essex by the Marquis and Marchioness of Buckingham had been 'one of the greatest of temporal blessings to that place', while in Hertford, he found it 'highly beneficial to the poor . . . and this has considerable effect in keeping down rates which would have been far more burdensome without it'.[26] Farmers in regions with thriving domestic industries were less enthusiastic about the apparent advantages of such work as they found it difficult to procure female labour for farm work. In Dorset, farmers complained that local women would not weed corn for 9d a day when they could earn nearly twice as much in button-making.[27] Similarly in Buckinghamshire, women who could earn up to 30s a week in straw-plaiting would not 'undertake work in the fields at such a rate as the farmer could afford to pay'.[28]

The General Views reveal the rarity of female day labourers in agriculture in counties with competing (and vibrant) employment opportunities. But what was happening to female agricultural day labour away from these areas? Pinchbeck asserts that the period covered by the General Views – c.1795 to 1815 – witnessed a rapid increase in this group of rural women workers.[29] Evidence can be found to reinforce this viewpoint, and many authors equated the introduction of drilling, dibbling, weeding and hoeing to the expansion of the female workforce.[30] However, the General Views do not provide any real

---

[26] Arthur Young, *General View of the Agriculture of the County of Essex*, 2 vols (London, 1813), vol. 2, p. 395; Arthur Young, *General View of the Agriculture of the County of Hertfordshire* (London, 1804), p. 223. See Pamela Sharpe, 'The women's harvest: Straw-plaiting and the representation of labouring women's employment, c.1793–1885', *Rural History*, 5 (1994), pp. 129–42, for the history of the straw plait industry in Essex. See also Thomas Bernard, 'Extract of an account of the introduction of straw platt at Avebury', *Report of the Society for Bettering the Condition and Increasing the Comforts of the Poor*, vol. 4 (1805), pp. 90–111.
[27] W. Stevenson, *General View of the Agriculture of the County of Dorset* (London, 1812), p. 453.
[28] Revd St John Priest, *General View of the Agriculture of Buckinghamshire* (London, 1813), p. 346. See Chapter 5 for further discussion of this point.
[29] Pinchbeck. *Women Workers*, p. 57.
[30] The introduction of new innovations in agriculture such as drill husbandry, dibbling, hoeing and weeding was welcomed by many observers as they not only aided the production of crops but also provided employment for women and children who could

Table 2.2 Male and female agricultural day rates as recorded in the General Views

County	Edition	Female rate	Male rate	Female-to-male wage ratio (%)
Hereford	1st (1794)	6d	10d–1s	55
Huntingdon	1st (1793)	6d	1s–1s 2d	46
Suffolk	1st (1794)	6d	1s 4d–1s 8d	33
Lincoln	1st (1794)	6d	1s–1s 2d	46
Wiltshire	1st (1794)	6d	1s–1s 2d	46
Durham	1st (1794)	6d–8d	1s–1s 6d	47
East Yorkshire	1st (1794)	6d–8d	10d–1s 6d	50
Gloucester	1st (1794)	6d–8d	1s–1s 8d	44
North Yorkshire	1st (1794)	6d–8d	1s–2s 6d	33
Northumberland	1st (1794)	6d–8d	1s–1s 4d	50
Somerset	1st (1794)	6d–8d	1s–1s 4d	50
Warwick	1st (1794)	6d–8d	1s–1s 4d	50
Worcester	1st (1794)	6d–8d	1s–1s 2d	54
Kent	1st (1794)*	8d	1s 6d–1s 8d	42
Westmorland	1st (1794)	8d–1s	1s 4d–1s 8d	56
Berkshire	2nd (1809)	6d–8d	1s 6d–2s	33
Cornwall	2nd (1811)	6d–8d	1s 6d–2s	33
Leicester	2nd (1809)	8d	2s	33
Oxford	2nd (1813)†	8d	1s 6d	44
Hampshire	2nd (1810)	8d	1s 6d–2s	38
Dorset	2nd (1812)	8d	1s 6d	44
Wiltshire	2nd (1811)	8d	1s 6d–1s 8d	42
Durham	2nd (1810)	8d–1s	2s–3s	33
Buckingham	2nd (1813)‡	8d–1s	1s 6d	56
Lincoln	2nd (1813)	9d	1s 3d–2s	46
East Yorkshire	2nd (1812)	9d	2s 6d–4s	23
Rutland	2nd (1808)	9d–1s	1s 9d–2s 2d	45
Kent	2nd (1813)	10d–1s	2s–2s 6d	41
Gloucester	2nd (1813)	10d–1s	1s 6d–2s	52
Warwick	2nd (1813)	1s–1s 6d	2s–3s 6d	45

Notes: * Isle of Thanet † Tetsworth area ‡ Stone district. The ratio is calculated from the mean female and male rates.
Sources: General View of Agriculture. See bibliography for full references.

easily be taught such tasks. One commentator called for all farmers to drill their turnips 'as well as pease and beans, as the hoeing may be then done by the women and children'. See Thomas Estcourt, 'Provisions for the poor', *Annals of Agriculture*, 34 (1800), pp. 145–50 (p. 149). Revd Glasse, writing in 1802, similarly argued that dibbling gave 'helpful and satisfactory occupation, and means of subsistence, to thousands of women and children, *at the dead seasons* of the year, when there is a general want of employment'. Revd Dr Glasse, 'Extract from an account of the superior advantages of dibbling wheat, or setting it by hand', *Report of the Society for Bettering the Condition and Improving the Comforts of the Poor*, vol. 3 (1802), pp. 85–92 (p. 91). See also Arthur Young, *General View of the Agriculture of the County of Suffolk* (London, 1794), p. 25, on the importance of wheat dibbling; William Mavor, *General View of the Agriculture of Berkshire* (London, 1809), p. 365, on women weeding; Worgan, *General View . . . of Cornwall*, p. 70, on the usefulness of hoeing; Stevenson, *General View . . . of Surrey*, p. 587, for a description of turnip drilling, and Vancouver, *General View . . . of Devon*, p. 123, on drill husbandry.

indication of the numbers of women actually employed on farms, making it impossible to track changes in the size of the female agricultural labour force in the early nineteenth century. Of more use is the information they provide on agricultural wages. Table 2.2 shows day rates recorded for male and female labourers in the first and second editions.[31] These sums represent the usual day wage: higher earnings at harvest time or on piece-work are not included. At the end of the eighteenth century female day wages in agriculture are shown to be between one-third and a half of the equivalent male rate. Across England women were normally paid between 6d and 8d a day. The spread of the male wage was wider, ranging from 10d to 1s 8d a day. The second editions show some movement in wage rates for both groups: women earned between 6d and 18d a day, men between 18d and 4s. Although these data do not reveal any striking regional trends, the persistence of the wage gap over the period covered by the General Views is clear (in the northern counties of Durham and East Yorkshire it appears to have strengthened). Where women were employed by farmers during the Napoleonic Wars they remained a cheap and flexible labour force: wartime conditions did not strengthen the remunerative position of women in the agricultural day labour market.

The General Views allow us some insight into the institution of farm service. Again, the nature of the evidence means that it is not possible to accurately map the regional incidence and extent of service in husbandry, but the issue of servants' wages can be analysed. Tables 2.3 and 2.4 show the annual wages of general female and male servants in the first and second editions (where these were recorded), along with the wage gap between the sexes expressed as a mean.[32] As with day labourers, female farm servants in the 1790s earned one-third to a half of the wage of their male counterparts. This was still the case in the early 1800s with the exception of two counties: in Hertford and Buckingham the presence of domestic industries vying for female labour raised the wages of women servants significantly. In Buckinghamshire the grievance of local farmers was clear: 'The wages of dairy-maids have risen much within a few years, on account of the lace and straw manufactories, and it is with difficulty they are procured at all.'[33] Although the male–female wage gap was a constant feature of farm service, the institution was clearly changing. Shorter hirings were prevalent in Dorset, Cumberland and Westmorland (to prevent parish settlements from being gained by servants). The expense of feeding and boarding servants was being seen as onerous; board wages were given in Norfolk and Middlesex as a

---

[31] Not all authors record wages and therefore Table 2.2 does not include all the counties of England.
[32] Some authors divide servants into different classifications and give more detailed wage rates, but here I have concentrated on 'general' servants.
[33] Priest, *General View . . . of Buckinghamshire*, p. 335.

Table 2.3 Wages of general male and female servants in first edition General Views

County	Year	Female wage	Male wage	Female-to-male wage ratio (%)
Worcester	1794	£2 10s–£4	£5–£7	54
Northumberland	1794	£3–£4	£7–£10	41
Hereford	1794	£3 3s–£4 4s	£6 6s–£9 9s	47
Cheshire	1794	£3 10s–£4 10s	£6–£9	53
Cambridge	1794	£4 10s	£10	45
Northampton	1794	£4 10s	£8–£10	50
Derby	1794	£4–£5	£10–£12	41
Cumberland	1794	£4–£6	£12–£14	38
Durham	1794	£4–£6	£10–£14	42
West Riding	1794	£5 5s	£10 10s	50

Sources: General Views of Agriculture

Table 2.4 Wages of general male and female servants in second edition General Views

County	Year	Female wage	Male wage	Female-to-male wage ratio (%)
Cornwall	1811	£3–£4	£8 8s–£12 12s	33
Leicester	1809	£3–£5	£6–£12	44
Cheshire	1808	£4–£6	£8–£10	56
Cumberland	1813	£4–£6	£10–£14	42
Derby	1817	£4 4s–£5 5s	£10 10s–£12 12s	41
Worcester	1813	£5–£6	£10 10s	52
Bedford	1808	£5 5s	£10 10s	50
Hertford	1804	£5 5s	£6 6s–£9 9s	67
Lincoln	1813	£5 5s	£14 14s	36
Lancashire	1815	£8	£15–£20	46
Durham	1810	£9	£21	43
Buckingham*	1813	£10 10s	£10 10s–£12 12s	91

Note: * Aylesbury region
Sources: General Views of Agriculture

substitute for living-in. Thomas Batchelor's description of farm service in Bedfordshire encapsulates these changes:

> The greatest part of the business of husbandry is performed by day labourers in every part of the county. It is common, however, on most farms of considerable size, to retain annual servants in the capacity of horse-keeper, cow-man, shepherd and

kitchen-maid, though the great advance in the price of provisions has apparently contributed to diminish the number of domestic servants of every description.[34]

The attitudes and behaviour of servants were also depicted as unsettled: the willingness of women to move into other occupations was just one sign of this.[35] Although the General Views reveal something of the underlying modifications taking place in farm service, the hiring of servants by the year was still economically viable in the early nineteenth-century countryside. The real decline in service – in the south-east at least – happened after the end of the Napoleonic Wars.

The position of rural workers – both male and female – appears to have deteriorated significantly after 1815. Agricultural depression followed the restoration of peace with demobilised soldiers flooding the rural labour market. Farmers responded by cutting day rates for agricultural work and, in the south and east, dismissing servants in favour of casual labour. William Cobbett notes the correlation between this trend and the pauperisation of rural workers:

> Why do not farmers now *feed* and *lodge* their work-people, as they did formerly? Because they cannot keep them *upon so little* as they give them in wages. This is the real cause of the change. There needs no more to prove that the lot of the working classes has become worse than it formerly was.[36]

Statements of agricultural distress throughout England after the Napoleonic Wars were recorded by various government enquiries: they reveal the want of employment in the countryside and the increased reliance on parish assistance.[37] The burden which underemployed rural labourers presented to the poor rates constituted one of the pivotal concerns of the early nineteenth century. The lack of employment for women was central to this matter and

---

[34] Thomas Batchelor, *General View of the Agriculture of the County of Bedfordshire* (London, 1808), p. 580.

[35] The servants in Middlesex were 'mostly a bad set'. John Middleton, *General View of the Agriculture of the County of Middlesex* (London, 1813), p. 500. In Surrey they were 'unsettled and continually wandering from one set of masters to another'. W. Stevenson, *General View of the Agriculture of the County of Surrey* (London, 1809), p. 540.

[36] William Cobbett, *Rural Rides*, 1st edn 1830 (Harmondsworth, 1985), p. 227. This view is reiterated by a correspondent to the *Farmers Magazine* who argued: 'the great cause, if not the sole cause, of this deplorable state of the agricultural districts, is to be attributed to the system of the Farmers discontinuing to board and lodge their men in their houses.' Anon, 'Suggestions for improving the moral character of the agricultural labourers, etc', *Farmers Magazine*, 1 (1835), pp. 8–9 (p. 8).

[37] See e.g. G. E. Mingay, ed., *The Agricultural State of the Kingdom in 1816* (Bath, 1970); PP 1821, IX, Select Committee on Petitions complaining of Depressed State of Agriculture of UK; PP 1824, VI, Select Committee on Agricultural Wages, and the Condition and Morals of Labourers in that Employment; PP 1833, V, Select Committee on State of Agriculture in UK.

was therefore one of the subjects investigated by the major parliamentary inquiry into the operation of the Poor Laws in the 1830s. This forms the basis of the next section.

The 1834 Poor Law Report*

The Poor Law Report has long been seen as a useful source for historians interested in the state of the rural employment market in the early 1830s. Mark Blaug has elucidated the background to the Report. Twenty-six commissioners were appointed by the central Poor Law Board to cover the whole of England and Wales. They were advised to visit as much of their region as possible in addition to distributing a questionnaire to all the rural parishes in the summer of 1832. By early 1833 most of the replies had been received and were printed as Appendix B of the 1834 Report.[38] The rural queries consisted of fifty-eight questions relating to, among other things, the administration of poor relief, laws and allowances regarding illegitimate children, the state of cottage accommodation, wage rates and employment opportunities for men, women and children. Of particular relevance to this analysis are questions 11, 12 and 13. Question 11 asked, 'Have you any and what employment for Women and Children?' Question 12 requested, 'What can Women and Children under 16, earn per week, in Summer, in Winter, and Harvest, and how employed?', and question 13 read, 'What might the Labourers Wife and four Children aged 14, 11, 8 and 5 years respectively, expect to earn in the year?'

Caution is needed when using this source. Only approximately 1100 responses were returned; that is, 10 per cent of the 15,000 parishes in England and Wales.[39] Clearly this raises doubts over the typicality of those parishes that replied. The wording of the questionnaire also creates problems. Three different editions of the rural queries were circulated, and although the substance of the queries remained the same, in all versions the questions are poorly phrased. This has led to problems of interpretation for both contemporary respondents and later historians. The way respondents understood terms such as 'earnings' and 'employment' was especially significant in relation to how women's labour was recorded. Employment was taken to mean paid employment, and earnings to denote payments made by an employer. Many aspects of rural women's productive activities were therefore ignored as they did not fit into the conventional view of work and wages used

---

[38] Mark Blaug, 'The poor law report re-examined', *Journal of Economic History*, XXIV (1964), pp. 229–45 (p. 234). See also Boyer, *English Poor Law*, pp. 127–8.
[39] Blaug, 'Poor law report re-examined', p. 231.
* A more substantial version of this section appears as Nicola Verdon, 'The rural labour market in the early nineteenth century: Women's and children's employment, family income, and the 1834 Poor Law Report', *Economic History Review*, LV (2002), pp. 298–322.

in the early nineteenth century.⁴⁰ The questions also unite the experience of women and children, rendering analysis of either group in isolation very difficult. Not surprisingly, many replies to the Report are incomplete, ambiguous or simply left blank. Nevertheless this is still an important source, and although many studies have taken advantage of its data, it remains the case that the information the Report contains on female (and child) employment across England, on wage rates and on annual family incomes, has not been systematically exploited.⁴¹

Replies to the Poor Law Report have been analysed to reveal the regional patterns evident in rural female occupations in the early 1830s. Figure 2.1 highlights the regional incidence of work in domestic industry as indicated in Question 11. This largely confirms the pattern disclosed by the General Views of Agriculture. Three regions of England had a concentration of domestic industries that employed women and children. The south Midlands counties of Northampton, Bedford and Buckingham recorded a high incidence of straw-plaiting and lace-making. Button-making, gloving and silk-throwing engaged women and children living in the south-west counties of Dorset and Somerset, while lace work for urban manufacturers was also recorded by several of the rural Midlands parishes in Derby, Nottingham and Leicester. Beyond these counties, the availability of domestic employment was scarce and in some areas non-existent. The totality of the destruction of the hand-spinning industry partly accounts for this. Thus in Norfolk we are told that 'the loss of wool-spinning has been a mortal blow to the comforts of our Poor'; in Essex, 'the long wheel is entirely discarded' and in Lincolnshire, spinning was 'almost profitless'.⁴²

Particularly in the region with the highest concentration of rural industries – the south Midlands – the employment of women in agriculture was virtually unknown. At Caddington in Bedfordshire, for example, the returnee claimed that 'women and Children are rarely, if ever, employed in field labour. All plats straw.'⁴³ But, in contrast to the prosperity reported by

---

⁴⁰ See King, 'Customary rights and women's earnings', p. 467; Hugh Cunningham, 'The employment and unemployment of children in England, c.1680–1851', *Past and Present*, 126 (1990), pp. 115–50 (p. 139). The interpretation of the wording of the report is significant, as an 'occupational' definition of work produced lower estimates of women's labour force participation than an 'earnings' definition. See Sara Horrell and Jane Humphries, 'Women's labour force participation and the transition to the male bread-winner family', *Economic History Review*, XLVIII (1995), pp. 89–117 (p. 97).
⁴¹ For studies which have incorporated analysis of the Poor Law Report see Pinchbeck, *Women Workers*, pp. 77–9; Snell, *Annals of the Labouring Poor*, ch.1; Cunningham, 'Employment and unemployment of children'; King, 'Customary rights and women's earnings'; Boyer, *Poor Law*.
⁴² PP 1834, XXX, Report from His Majesty's Commissioners for Inquiring into the Administration and Practical Operation of the Poor Laws. Appendix (B.1). Answers to Rural Queries in Five Parts. Part 1, p. 460a, p. 188a and p. 298a.
⁴³ PP 1834, XXX, p. 3a.

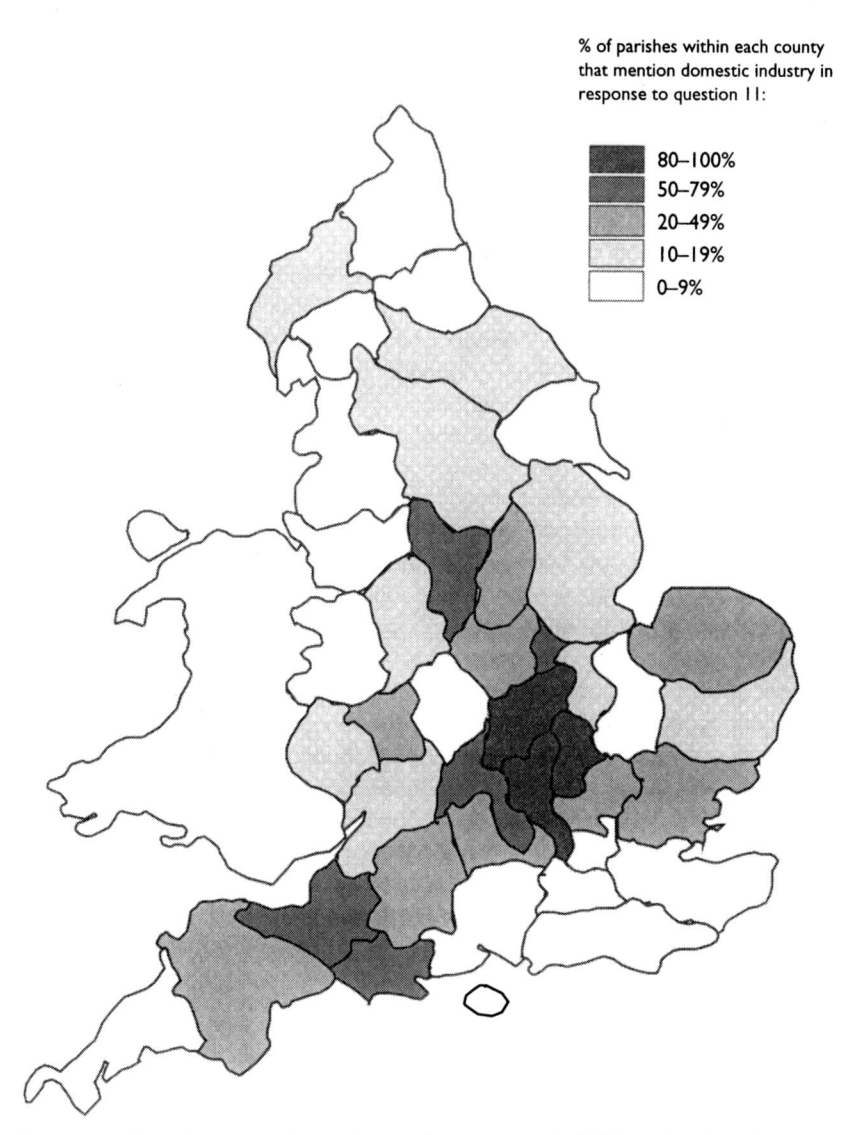

Figure 2.1 Distribution and prevalence of women's and children's work in domestic industry in England in 1834

Source: PP, 1834, XXX. Data compiled from responses to Question 11.

the General Views twenty years earlier, responses to the Poor Law Report reveal a collapse in wages for women engaged in these industries by the 1830s. Increased mechanisation and renewed foreign competition contributed towards this downturn. Thus in Bedford the lace trade was 'very bad', in

Northampton it was 'not a thriving trade', and in Buckingham lace work was 'badly paid for'.[44] Similarly, female button-makers in Dorset were paid little 'beyond the value of the materials' and Somerset glove-makers found their wages 'so much lowered'.[45]

Turning to agricultural employment, a high proportion of parishes reported some form of farmwork for women and children in their responses to Question 11. This is presented in Table 2.5. No distinct regional pattern emerges from these data. Counties that report farmwork in over 80 per cent of parishes emanate from across England: the north (Northumberland, Westmorland, Chester and Durham), East Anglia (Norfolk and Suffolk), the East Midlands (Nottingham and Lincoln) and the south-east (Kent and Sussex) are all represented. The correlation between low levels of agricultural work and high frequency of domestic employment is clearer (Somerset, Northampton, Buckingham and Bedford). The same is true where manufacturing opportunities drew women and children from the land into either outwork (Derby and Nottingham) or into local factories (Lancaster and West Yorkshire). These figures do not tell us anything about the number of women and children employed in agriculture in individual parishes: as with the earlier sources already considered, the Poor Law Report cannot be used to measure the size of the female agrarian workforce in England. However, it is possible to look more closely at the variety of jobs women and children were engaged to perform and determine whether there were any regional trends in such employment.

The established account of female agricultural employment by Keith Snell maintains that by the early decades of the nineteenth century women in southern and eastern England were becoming increasingly unlikely to retain their position in the harvest. Instead they found more security of employment in springtime activities such as weeding and in early summer work like haymaking.[46] We can assess this theory by looking at the frequency of women's and children's involvement in these three agricultural tasks as indicated by responses to Question 11 of the Report. The results are shown in Table 2.6. The mentions of haymaking in the English counties range from 60 per cent of returns in North Yorkshire to no mentions in Bedford, Derby and Stafford. Weeding was less frequently cited, with the highest prevalence being in the eastern counties of Norfolk, Lincoln and Cambridge. The range of harvest mentions is the largest: from 75 per cent of returns in East Yorkshire to no citations in Derby, Huntingdon and Middlesex. We can make more sense of these data by looking at the median value of parish mentions. For haymaking the median figure is 24 per cent, for weeding it is 20 per cent and for harvesting 17 per cent. Therefore these figures tells us that overall

---

[44] Ibid., p. 7a, p. 334a and p. 45a.
[45] Ibid., p. 140a and p. 409a.
[46] Snell, *Annals of the Labouring Poor*, ch.1.

Table 2.5 The incidence of women's and children's involvement in agricultural work in 1834

County	Number of parishes which returned questionnaire	Number of parishes which replied to question	Number of positive responses	Rate of incidence (%)
Middlesex	3	2	2	100
Norfolk	41	29	29	100
Northumberland	20	18	18	100
Kent	57	47	42	89
Berkshire	32	30	26	87
Southampton	58	48	41	85
Westmorland	21	20	17	85
Sussex	84	76	64	84
Hereford	19	17	14	82
Suffolk	51	32	26	81
Chester	16	10	8	80
Durham	38	35	28	80
Lincoln	20	15	12	80
Nottingham	28	20	16	80
Cambridge	44	41	32	78
Devon	24	22	17	77
Cumberland	47	42	32	76
Dorset	16	16	12	75
Rutland	4	4	3	75
Salop	22	20	15	75
Warwick	38	32	24	75
York – East	5	4	3	75
Wiltshire	29	25	18	72
Oxford	29	24	17	71
Surrey	29	24	17	71
Cornwall	30	27	19	70
York – North	12	10	7	70
Gloucester	28	22	15	68
Essex	50	43	29	67
Stafford	14	13	8	62
Hunts	13	10	6	60
Worcester	20	19	11	58
Somerset	25	23	13	56
Hertford	18	16	8	50
Northampton	18	14	7	50
Bucks	35	32	15	47
York – West	58	54	19	35
Bedford	16	15	5	33
Leicester	18	15	5	33
Derby	7	7	2	29
Lancaster	19	15	4	27

Note: Percentages in Tables 2.5 and 2.6 are based on parishes which replied to the question, not the number which returned the questionnaire.
Source: PP XXX, 1834. Data compiled from responses to Question 11.

haymaking was one-third more frequent in responses to Question 11 than harvesting, with the frequency of weeding falling between the two. Moreover, if we identify the upper and lower quartiles of this table, regional trends in the occurrence of the three tasks becomes evident. For haymaking, weeding and harvesting, there was a strong bias towards high prevalence in eastern counties of England. Conversely, western counties were least likely to mention these tasks, a trend that was particularly emphatic for haymaking. In harvesting, there is a high frequency of northern counties (East Yorkshire, Westmorland, North Yorkshire and Northumberland) in the upper quartile.

This data analysis of Question 11 seems to confirm that women and children were more likely to find employment in the spring and early summer tasks of weeding and haymaking, rather than harvest work. This trend was especially strong in eastern England. Women in northern regions were more widely employed in harvest work than women in the south. However, the placement of Kent and Sussex within the upper quartile of harvest returns sounds a warning to Snell's theory being 'pushed too far'.[47] The Poor Law Report indicates that women and children were involved in harvest work even in some southern counties where, as Alan Armstrong points out, 'the "surplus population" problem was held to be particularly acute'.[48] On the other hand, we do not know what respondents actually meant by 'the harvest': most do not specify in their returns the exact roles available to female and child workers at harvest time. Snell suggests that in some cases 'the harvest' could mean gleaning, and that 'by this date' women's role in the harvest 'was usually limited to the very short-term work of gleaning' in southern and eastern England.[49] King's analysis of the Poor Law Report indicates a broad north–south divide in the incidence of gleaning, with highest frequency of mentions of this task in central and eastern England.[50] Therefore the confusion over what harvest work consisted of may account for the high returns recorded in the southern counties such as Kent and Sussex.

This analysis of Question 11 may be repeated for questions 12 and 13 of the Report, although the wording of the queries means that the regional specificity of tasks as shown by responses to Question 11 is the most reliable.[51] Additional examination of the Report is possible: we can assess the broad seasonality of employment – the incidence of involvement in summer and

---

[47] Armstrong, Farmworkers, p. 40.
[48] W. A. Armstrong, 'Labour 1: Rural population growth, systems of employment, and incomes', in G. E. Mingay, ed., The Agrarian History of England and Wales, vol VI, 1750–1850 (Cambridge, 1989), pp. 641–728 (p. 685). This point is also made by Pinchbeck. See Pinchbeck, Women Workers, p. 72.
[49] Snell, Annals of the Labouring Poor, p. 54.
[50] King, 'Customary rights and women's work', pp. 467–8.
[51] For example, Question 12 – 'What can Women and Children under 16 earn per week, in Summer, in Winter, and in Harvest, and how employed?' – is suggestive, possibly prompting respondents to mention harvest work above all other tasks.

Table 2.6 The incidence of women's and children's involvement in haymaking, weeding and harvest work as indicated in Question 11 of the 1834 Poor Law Report

County	Parishes mentioning haymaking (%)	County	Parishes mentioning weeding (%)	County	Parishes mentioning harvest (%)
York – North	60	Norfolk	48	York – East	75
Middlesex	50	Lincoln	40	Westmorland	70
Rutland	50	Cambridge	39	York – North	60
Westmorland	50	Northumberland	39	Northumberland	56
York – East	50	Salop	35	Rutland	50
Sussex	49	Sussex	34	Kent	49
Surrey	42	Southampton	33	Lincoln	47
Northumberland	39	Devon	32	Sussex	43
Hertford	38	Hertford	31	Chester	40
Salop	35	Kent	30	Cumberland	33
Cambridge	34	Nottingham	30	Southampton	31
Lincoln	33	York – North	30	Nottingham	31
Kent	32	Warwick	28	Northampton	30
Chester	30	Suffolk	25	Surrey	29
Essex	30	York – East	25	Warwick	25
Hunts	30	Rutland	25	Hereford	24
Hereford	29	Cornwall	22	Cornwall	22
Warwick	28	Northampton	21	Oxford	21
Southampton	27	Surrey	21	Bedford	20
Cumberland	26	Westmorland	20	Berkshire	17
Norfolk	24	Hunts	20	Durham	17
Suffolk	22	Essex	19	Somerset	17

Northampton	21	Dorset	13
Nottingham	20	Somerset	13
Berkshire	17	Hereford	12
Oxford	17	Berkshire	10
Dorset	13	Chester	10
Lancaster	13	Durham	9
Durham	11	Stafford	8
Devon	9	Wiltshire	8
Somerset	9	Lancaster	7
Leicester	7	Leicester	7
Buckingham	6	Buckingham	6
York – West	6	Cumberland	5
Gloucester	5	Oxford	4
Worcester	5	York – West	2
Cornwall	4	Bedford	0
Wiltshire	4	Derby	0
Bedford	0	Gloucester	0
Derby	0	Middlesex	0
Stafford	0	Worcester	0
		Essex	16
		Suffolk	16
		Stafford	15
		Norfolk	14
		Hertford	13
		Lancaster	13
		Leicester	13
		Cambridge	10
		Salop	10
		Devon	9
		Gloucester	9
		Buckingham	6
		Dorset	6
		Worcester	5
		Wiltshire	4
		York – West	4
		Derby	0
		Hunts	0
		Middlesex	0

Source: PP 1834, XXX. Data complied from response to Question 11.

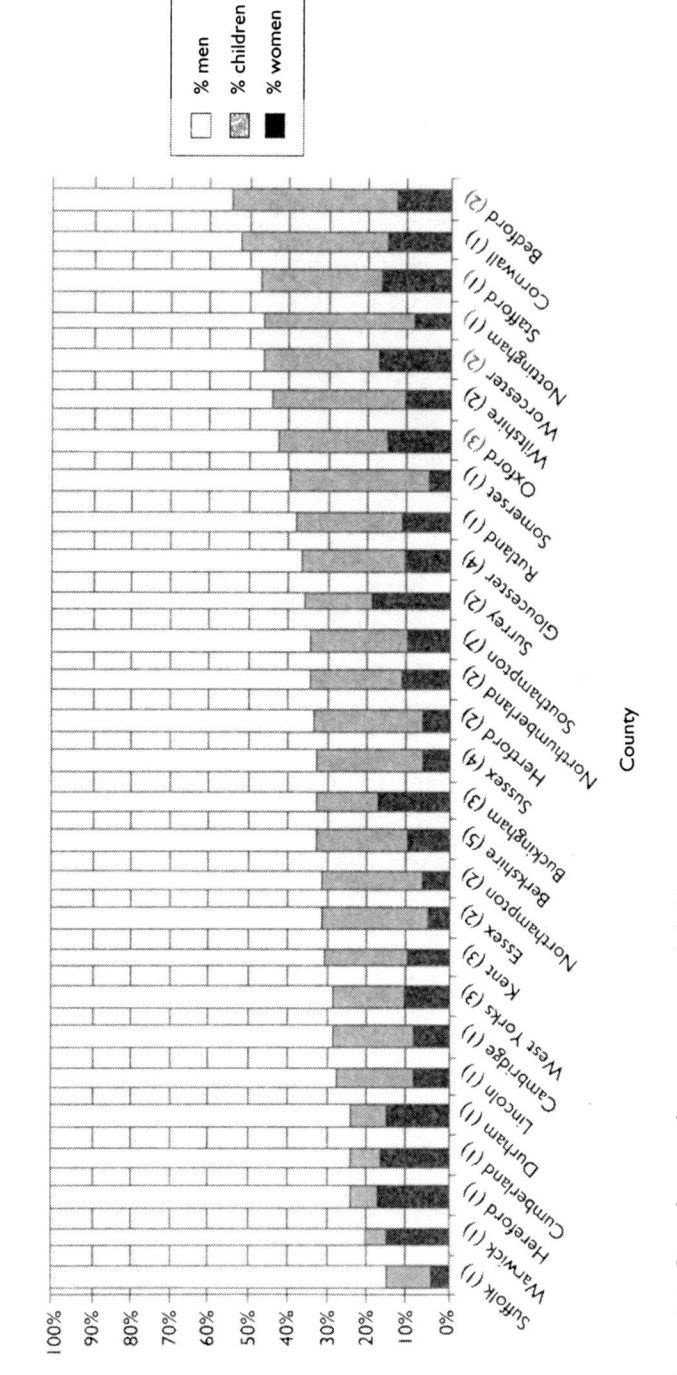

Figure 2.2 Contribution of men, women and children to annual family income in 1834

Source: PP 1834, XXX. Data compiled from responses to Question 13.

winter work – from responses to Question 12 for example. The results of this exercise are fairly predictable: most parish replies across England reveal wider opportunities for rural women and children to work in the summer. In nearly all counties 50 per cent and over of replies suggest summer work was available. Only half of the English counties record a similar percentage for winter employment. Moreover, even those counties that mention winter employment are clear on the short-term viability of such work, lasting only for the duration of specific tasks such as bean or wheat setting. More interesting is an investigation of the wage data provided in the Report. Question 12 covers day rates for female and child labour, but it is the issue of annual family income – dealt with by Question 13 – which throws up the most insightful information.

The Poor Law Report provides material on the average annual earnings of men, women and children in the 1830s. These data may be used to give an indication of the contribution which different household members made to the yearly income of rural labouring families. This is shown in Figure 2.2.[52] Women's yearly earnings range from £9 10s to £1 5s. The combined earnings of all the children in the family peak at £25 8s and fall to just £1 10s. Men's wages range from £35 to £18. Women contributed between 4 and 19 per cent of annual household income, children between 5 and 42 per cent and men between 45 and 84 per cent. The mean annual wage for women in rural England according to these figures was £5 11s 2d – or 12 per cent of the family total.

This mean percentage compares favourably to those recorded by Davies and Eden in the 1790s, and suggests a continuity – even a slight rise – in women's contribution to the family income across the turbulent decades of the late eighteenth and early nineteenth centuries.[53] However, this average figure obscures some region variance: women living in Suffolk and Essex, for instance, made the lowest contribution to household income, confirming the precarious nature of female employment in East Anglia in the wake of the disappearance of spinning. Children's mean earnings totalled £10 11s 11d, a quarter of the family income. This evidence therefore suggests child earnings were much greater than those of women in the 1830s. This is consistent with the findings of Horrell and Humphries, which showed that across

---

[52] The county coverage is not complete as many replies include inappropriate or inadequate information. Some respondents, for example, noted a daily or weekly wage but not an annual sum. Others record the earnings only of women, or only of children. A number of counties did not return any full replies and have been excluded from this analysis.

[53] The figures from the Poor Law Report for women's contribution to the annual family income are higher than those calculated by Horrell and Humphries, suggesting their data may underestimate female earnings in some regions, particularly northern counties. However, their comparative dataset covers the period 1821 to 1840. See Horrell and Humphries, 'Women's labour force participation', pp. 102–3.

occupations – including agriculture – the earnings of children outstripped those of adult women.[54] Not surprisingly children's average annual wages increase according to age; by the age of 14 children were earning considerably more than women although, as many respondents noted, the sex of the child would affect the amount they could earn.[55] The most valuable source of income for rural children in 1834 was not necessarily agricultural: it was in areas where children found non-agricultural employment in localised domestic industry (Bedford) or manufacturing and mining outlets (Cornwall, Stafford, Wiltshire and Worcester) that their earning capacity was greatest. The mean wage of men was £27 2s 3d, a contribution of 63 per cent to the whole. There is a correlation between the low earnings of women and the high contribution of male income to the family total (Suffolk). Conversely, men contributed the least where children earned the most (Bedford). It was child wages that had the major impact in offsetting the low earnings of men.

Rural labouring families in the early 1830s were reliant on the capacity of the (male) head of the household and the eldest children to earn a living. However, in many instances, while (married) women's earnings were not central to the family income, they were important and represented a significant contribution to the material well-being of the family. This casts doubt on previous studies of nineteenth-century standards of living that rely solely on male wage data.[56] Moreover, there are two key ways in which the Poor Law Report may underestimate the income generated by rural labouring women. First, we must remember that the Report represents only one subgroup of women: those married with four children under the age of 15. Yet for a whole range of women – single women, widows, married women without children – potential earnings may have been higher. Equally important is the fact that there were other avenues of income-generating labour that women (and children) participated in, but which were not represented in the estimates of annual incomes returned in Question 13. These included gleaning, picking fruit and other foodstuffs, taking care of domestic animals and gardens, taking in washing and lodgers, caring for the very young, the sick and the elderly, and tending allotments. The omission of such tasks is often recognised by those filling in the questionnaire. At Leamington Hastings in Warwick, it was noted that women and children would earn on average £3 7s 'besides her

---

[54] Sara Horrell and Jane Humphries, '"The exploitation of little children": Child labour and the family economy in the Industrial Revolution', *Explorations in Economic History*, 32 (1995), pp. 485–516.
[55] Only the child of 14 is revealed to be a boy; the identities of the younger children are not specified in Question 13.
[56] See e.g. Lindert and Williamson, 'English workers' living standards'; E. H. Hunt, 'Industrialization and regional inequality: Wages in Britain, 1760–1914', *Journal of Economic History*, XLVI (1986), pp. 935–66.

reaping, washing, and nursing, from which a willing and able woman would earn something considerable during the year'.[57] Similarly at Blechingley in Surrey, where women took in washing 'or can assist in household work occasionally, she can earn more', while at Sarston in Norfolk, women did not necessarily go out to work but did 'better by washing and taking in work'.[58] Earnings from such activities are difficult to translate into monetary terms, but are important to an understanding of women's economic participation in the early nineteenth-century countryside.

Interest in the productive capabilities of women residing in the countryside informs the content of material published between the 1790s and the 1830s. After the mid-1830s the context in which rural women are discussed begins to shift: from concern over employment opportunities (or lack thereof), to anxiety over the moral and physical effects of rural labour. This transformation is reflected in the types of information included in publications produced after the 1830s. Observers become less involved in tabulating annual budgets and income, or assessing the availability of different types of work. Instead, writing is focused on qualitative ideological debates: the age at which children should be allowed to work, the state of rural education, the impact on family life of married women working outside the household and the most suitable work for unmarried women are central themes. This change in the chronicling of rural women's work will become evident in the following section, which turns to a consideration of the mid-nineteenth-century Royal Commissions.

The Royal Commissions

Commentators observing the effects of the Poor Law after 1834 imply that more stringent conditions of relief led to an extension of female and child employment in rural areas. This was mostly viewed as a positive outcome, as Dr Kay's testimony to the Lords Committee on the Poor Law Amendment Act demonstrates. He claimed that 'The extent of employment for women and children has most wonderfully increased since the Poor Law came into operation.'[59] But the first major investigation of rural women's employment after the inception of the New Poor Law came in 1843. The report was written under the auspices of the Poor Law Commission and, as Sayer comments, 'provides our first example of an excursion by the state

---

[57] PP 1834, XXX, p. 547a.
[58] PP 1834, XXX, p. 475a and p. 325a.
[59] Quoted in Hasbach, *History of the English Agricultural Labourer*, p. 225. For similar views see *Second Annual Report of the Poor Law Commissioners for England and Wales* (London, 1836), p. 318 and p. 258.

into the countryside on a specifically gendered issue'.⁶⁰ The Home Secretary appointed it in December 1842 and the assistant commissioners were given thirty days to cover their designated region. Its coverage was selective: Alfred Austin inspected Wiltshire, Dorset, Devon and Somerset; Henry Vaughan covered Kent, Surrey and Sussex; Stephen Denison visited Suffolk, Norfolk and Lincolnshire, while Sir Francis Doyle looked at Yorkshire and Northumberland. This Commission was not a major parliamentary event – unlike the contemporaneous 1842 Report on women and children employed in mining – and its findings were not discussed in Parliament.⁶¹ In many ways the 1843 Report is a bridge between the broad socio-economic investigations of the labouring poor produced in the late eighteenth century and the reports published after the mid-nineteenth century which were informed by the stricter ideological and moral scriptures of the later Victorian period.

The commissioners in 1843 found women engaged in agricultural tasks across the areas they investigated, although they were sensitive to regional and local differences within and between counties. Austin commentated on the south-west:

> The practice of employing women in farm labour . . . prevails throughout the four counties mentioned . . . but the number of women so employed, and the kinds of work which they perform, are not always the same. A difference is sometimes found in their occupations on two adjoining farms.⁶²

An overview of the types of employment and the wages paid to women workers in 1843 is provided in Table 2.7. This shows that there were certain agricultural tasks universally performed by women. These fall into four categories: first, cleaning the land by weeding, hoeing, pulling thistles and stone-picking; second, haymaking; third, the planting, and finally, the harvesting of root crops such as potatoes and turnips. Women were engaged in the corn harvest in all areas, but with some regional diversity: in the north and south-east (Kent in particular), women cut the corn, while in East Anglia gleaning was the more usual task for women at harvest time. The regional specificity of English agriculture also accounted for some distinct differences in women's employment. The orchards, gardens and hop fields of the south-east furnished women with much seasonal work. The pastoral farms of the south-west provided dairy work. Women's agricultural employment in the

---

⁶⁰ Sayer, *Women of the Fields*, p. 34.
⁶¹ Ibid., p. 35. It was not until March 1844 that the Report was mentioned in the House of Commons, when William Cobden, a leader of the Anti-Corn Law League, referred to it. See Judy Gielgud, 'Nineteenth-century farm women in Northumberland and Cumbria: The neglected workforce' (D.Phil. thesis, University of Sussex, 1992), pp. 431–2.
⁶² PP 1843, XII, Reports of Special Assistant Poor Law Commissioners on the Employment of Women and Children in Agriculture. Report by Mr Alfred Austin on the counties of Wiltshire, Dorset, Devon and Somerset, p. 3.

Table 2.7 Women's agricultural work and wages in 1843

Region	Tasks	Wage rates
South-west: Wiltshire, Dorset, Devon and Somerset	Dairying, haymaking, harvest, weeding corn, stone-picking, hoeing, pulling and digging turnips, planting and digging potatoes, winnowing corn, beating manure, assisting on threshing machines (occasionally), leading horses at plough and filling dung carts (occasionally in latter two counties).	7d – 10d a day 10d – 1s a day harvest
South-east: Kent, Surrey and Sussex	Hoeing weeds, haymaking, reaping, turnip-pulling and topping, thistle-picking, orchard work, gathering and packing fruit, hop work – opening hills, poling, typing, picking and rag-chopping (for manure).	10d – 1s a day 1s 6d a day harvest Task work also available
The East: Suffolk, Norfolk and Lincoln	Hoeing wheat, haymaking, harvest and gleaning, topping and tailing turnips, pulling beets, weeding, stone-picking, dibbling and dropping wheat, spudding thistles, gathering potatoes, assisting on threshing machines, picking cockles on coast (Norfolk).	8d a day (Suffolk and Norfolk) 10d a day (Lincoln) 1s – 2s a day harvest (Lincoln)
The North: Yorkshire and Northumberland	Cleaning and manuring land, weeding, hoeing, topping and tailing turnips, haymaking, harvest (including shearing corn), barn work in winter, assisting on threshing machines, taking up potatoes, pulling flax (Yorkshire).	8d – 1s a day 10d – 1s a day haying 1s 6d – 2s 6d a day harvest

Source: PP 1843, XII.

north of England tended to be most extensive and year round, although Austin also found substantial employment of women in the winter months in Devon.[63] Alternatives to agricultural work were scarce: lace work was recorded around Honiton (Devon), button-making in the Blandford district of Dorset, gloving at Pocklington in Yorkshire and dressmaking near York. In

---

[63] PP 1843, XII, Report by Austin, p. 4.

Norfolk and Suffolk, Denison found 'no other domestic manufacture' had replaced spinning, the population being 'strictly agricultural'.[64] In terms of wages, English women working in agriculture were usually paid between 7d and 1s a day for their labour. Rates tended to increase in the harvest, with the highest wages paid in the north, Lincoln and Kent. Task work payments were also common in the south-east hop fields: working as a family group, with women tending and typing plants and men performing the groundwork, substantial earnings could be gained.[65] In addition to paid work, most labourers' wives were reported to assist in the maintenance of cottage gardens or allotments. Vaughan argued that this gave 'a more active character to the women's household employment', while Austin believed that such labour was 'by no means an unimportant addition to the means of subsistence to the family'.[66]

We have seen that the authors of the previous investigations analysed in this chapter viewed women's labour as an essential, necessary part of rural labouring life, their earnings facilitating family survival. The same perspective informs the 1843 Report. Generally, women's work was seen as being beneficial, both to women (in terms of physical health) and to the family (her earnings boosting household income). Austin found women labouring in agriculture to be 'active, energetic and well-disposed . . . working from the sole desire of increasing the means of subsistence of the family', and Vaughan considered women's work 'a mark of her activity and general providence', not 'a trespass upon her home duties'.[67] Denison found almost unanimous agreement in his region that outdoor labour was 'conducive to health', although gang labour was condemned by many witnesses as producing moral, physical and intellectual evil.[68] The economic contribution made by women was also recognised. As Austin commented, women's earnings were 'no inconsiderable part of the entire money-receipts of the family', being

> a benefit to their families which cannot be dispensed with without creating a great deal of suffering. And upon fullest consideration, I believe that the earnings of a woman employed in the fields are an advantage which, in the present state of the agricultural population, outweighs any of the mischiefs arising from such employment.[69]

[64] PP 1843, XII, Report by Stephen Denison on the counties of Suffolk, Norfolk and Lincolnshire, p. 220.
[65] PP 1843, XII, Report by Henry Vaughan on the counties of Kent, Surrey and Sussex, pp. 166–9.
[66] PP 1843, XII, Report by Vaughan, p. 143, Report by Austin, p. 15. George Nichols, writing in the Royal Agricultural Society journal, believed that garden work was much better suited to the 'sex and circumstances' of rural women than 'habitual field work at all seasons'. See George Nichols, 'On the condition of the agricultural labourer', *Journal of the Royal Agricultural Society*, 7 (1846), pp. 1–30 (p. 19).
[67] PP 1843, XII, Report by Austin, p. 23; Report by Vaughan, p. 139.
[68] PP 1843, XII, Report by Denison, p. 215.
[69] PP 1843, XII, Report by Austin, p. 17 and p. 28.

AN OVERVIEW OF PRINTED SOURCES

A quarter of a century later, the tone and content of the next parliamentary commission to enquire into rural female labour reveals a fundamental shift in the way women's work was viewed and documented.

By the 1860s mounting unease about women's employment – especially outdoor labour – induced the government to investigate the gang system as part of the Children's Employment Commission. The publication of the *Sixth Report of the Children's Employment Commission* in 1867 was a watershed in the perception of rural labour, inciting a public and parliamentary outcry. As a result of the 1867 Report, the government established a Royal Commission to fully explore the issue of child and female labour in British agriculture: two volumes relating to the English counties appeared in 1868 and 1869, the third and fourth reports on Wales and Scotland in 1870. Its brief was wide. The type and amount of work performed by women and children in agriculture were examined alongside a range of other issues: the state of children's education, cottage accommodation, gardens and allotments, modes of hiring and wage rates. While this has left us with a great deal of information on the state of the mid-Victorian countryside, it means that women are often marginalised within the reports.[70] Despite this we can pursue the key themes that have already emerged in this chapter.

First, regional differences in the availability of work for rural women still existed (see Table 2.8). The casualisation of the agrarian workforce in eastern England had led to the expansion of the gang system. This form of labour was reported in Lincolnshire, Cambridge, Norfolk, Suffolk and parts of Nottinghamshire, and it was viewed as being notoriously exploitative of cheap, casual female (and child) workers. How far the sensational reporting of the gang system exaggerated the extent and operation of gangs will be explored in greater detail in Chapter 4. Although domestic industries were said to be in distress in the 1860s, women living in areas where lace-making, straw-plaiting, gloving and button-making persisted were still rarely found to be engaged in agricultural labour. In the hop districts of Kent, and the sparsely populated districts of northern England, the need for women workers meant family hiring and the bondager system continued: it was a stipulation of male hiring that a female labourer would be available to work when required. Family hiring also remained in some regions of the south-west, although labour surpluses and the weak position of the agricultural labourer underpinned the system in this area.

The differences across England in the types and availability of work for women are also reflected in the wages women could expect to be paid for their labour. The best summary of agricultural wage rates are to be found in Frederick Purdy's estimates of the weekly earnings of rural labourers, published in 1860 (Table 2.9). The relative security of northern workers compared to their counterparts in the south (particularly the south-west)

---

[70] Gielgud, 'Nineteenth-century farm women', p. 416.

Table 2.8 Female agricultural work by county in 1867 to 1869

County	Tasks
Bedford	Lace and straw, market gardening and peeling onions
Berkshire	'Field work'
Buckingham	Hay and harvest, straw and lace, chair- and paper-making
Cambridge	Gang labour
Cheshire	Potato work, haymaking, milking (indoor service), beyond this 'very little'
Cornwall	Stone-picking, market gardening (Penzance)
Cumberland	Farm service, 'general' employment of women in some parts
Derby	Dairy work (north); general farm work elsewhere
Devon	Lace and gloving, stone-picking, apple-picking
Dorset	Gloving (Blandford), turnip work, threshing machines; family hiring
Essex	A little straw-plaiting, slop work,* hops and peas in some districts
Gloucester	Picking couch grass, haymaking, stone picking, spreading manure, gloving (Newent)
Hampshire	Weeding corn, picking stones and couch grass, dung-spreading, barn work, threshing machines
Hereford	Some gloving, orchards, hops and 'usual agricultural employment'
Hertford	Straw-plaiting, hay and harvest, but 'little farm work' done by women
Kent	Extensive hop work providing almost year-round labour; turnips, hay and harvest and weeding in non-hop districts although 'irregular and uncertain'
Leicester	Stocking-making and seaming
Lincoln	Gang labour, weeding, singling turnips, potato work, threshing machines
Norfolk	Gang labour, weeding; harvest labour rare
Northampton	Weeding, gathering stones, hoeing, spudding thistles, hay and harvest, cleaning turnips but women's field work exceptional
Northumberland and Durham	Bondager system; weeding, stone-picking, turnip hoeing, hay and harvest, rooting and cleaning turnips, barn work (thrashing and winnowing), filling dung carts, turning dung heaps, spreading dung and sowing artificial manure, turnip-cutting, driving carts or harrowing (occasionally); women employed throughout the year and their labour considered essential

Nottingham	Some gang labour, pea-picking
Oxford	'Field work', gloving and slop work
Rutland	Little employment
Shropshire	'Usual farm operations' (south-west); elsewhere 'little employed in outdoor work'
Somerset	Gloving (south), hay and harvest, turnip and mangolds (west); in west 'nearly every labourer's wife works'
Stafford	Threshing
Surrey	Hops, market gardening and 'usual agricultural employment'
Sussex	Hop work, harvest, trimming roots; women 'rarely employed' by the farmer
Warwick	Needle- and nail-making, gloving, orchards, hops, fruit and veg and 'usual agricultural employment'
Westmorland	Hay and harvest, dung-spreading, weeding, thinning turnips, taking up potatoes
Wiltshire	'Usual agricultural employment'; decline of cloth
Yorkshire	Farm service (East Yorks), potato work

Note: * Finishing machine-made clothing

Sources: PP 1867–8, XVII, First Report from the Commissioners on the Employment of Children, Young Persons and Women in Agriculture; PP 1868–9, XIII, Second Report from the Commissioners on the Employment of Children, Young Persons and Women in Agriculture

Table 2.9 Weekly earnings of agricultural labourers in England, Michaelmas 1860

Region	Men	Women	Children under 16	Female-to-male ratio (%)
South-east	11s 11¼d	4s 7d	3s 7d	38
South Midlands	10s 7½d	4s 7d	3s 5d	43
East	12s 1d	4s 4d	3s 7d	36
South-west	9s 6¾d	3s 9d	3s 4d	39
West Midlands	10s ½d	4s 2d	3s 3d	41
North Midlands	13s 1d	4s 8d	3s 2d	36
North-west	13s 3d	6s 11d	4s 9½d	52
York	14s 3½d	5s 9½d	3s 7d	41
North	14s 10d	10s 6d	5s 9½d	71

Source: Purdy, 'Earnings of agricultural labourers', p. 358.

Key
South-east: Surrey, Kent, Hampshire and Sussex
South Midlands: Hertford, Northampton and Bedford
East: Essex, Suffolk and Norfolk
South-west: Wiltshire, Dorset, Devon and Somerset
West Midlands: Gloucester, Hereford, Salop, Stafford, Worcester and Warwickshire
North Midlands: Lincoln, Nottingham and Derby
North-west: Cheshire
York: West, East and North Ridings of Yorkshire
North: Durham, Northumberland, Cumberland and Westmorland

is evident: women agricultural workers in Durham, Northumberland, Cumberland and Westmorland earned three times as much as female workers in Wiltshire, Dorset, Devon and Somerset. The wage gap between male and female workers persisted: the female weekly agricultural wage was between one-third and a half of that of men, with the exception of northern England. However, Purdy's wage estimates do exclude task work payments, perquisites from employers, produce from cottage gardens and gleanings. Women's involvement in such activities was recognised by the author.[71]

Although the types and amount of work available to women differed according to region, the commissioners' reports from the 1860s do point to the persistence of female labour in certain agricultural tasks across most of the English countryside. Women were still attractive as a cheap pool of labour for weeding and stone-picking, haymaking and harvest and for the planting and pulling of root crops. The Commissioner for Somerset, R. F. Boyle, summed up this situation:

---

[71] Frederick Purdy, 'On the earnings of agricultural labourers in England and Wales, 1860', *Journal of the Statistical Society*, 24 (1861), pp. 328–73.

from time immemorial there has been certain field work that is looked upon as women's work, and they are often to be seen working when men are out of work ... most of them only come for haymaking, harvest and to work among the turnips and mangolds, which seems to be always considered the principal women's work.[72]

Large-scale capitalist agriculture could not function without this seasonal input of women workers. One commentator in Lincolnshire stated,

> Each year more labour is required. Turnip cultivation has increased; corn crops are generally better. . . . These and other causes make more work, and consequently more hands are required to do it; and although machinery is to some extent employed, it tends more to increase production than to save labour.[73]

Yet the general impression promoted by the majority of the commissioners' reports is of a decline in women's participation in English agriculture. James Fraser, reporting on Norfolk, Essex, Sussex, Gloucester and Suffolk, claimed that: 'not a fifth part of the number of women is employed upon the farms in these counties now that was employed upon them 25 years ago.'[74] Edward Stanhope commented that the employment of women across the east Midlands was 'very general . . . although it is certainly decreasing'.[75] Stanhope echoes this observation in his Report on the counties of Dorset, Kent, Chester, Salop, Stafford and Rutland: 'the increasing disinclination of women to undertake any but light and occasional out-door labour was everywhere apparent.'[76] Similarly, in Devon and Cornwall 'women are not so much employed as formerly', and in Somerset 'with the spread of education and general improvement the labouring class are beginning to see that the woman's place is by her own fire-side'.[77] Although female labour was more widespread in the north, the withdrawal of women from field work was not unknown: in Westmorland Henry Tremenheere found women's labour to have 'considerably diminished'.[78] The reduction in the use of women for outdoor agricultural labour by the 1860s was not lamented by most of the commissioners; indeed, the prevalent attitude towards women fieldworkers was one of forthright disapproval. The following quotes from Edwin Portman and Fraser are illustrative of this viewpoint.

---

[72] PP 1868–9, XIII, Robert F. Boyle, Report on Somerset, p. 123.
[73] PP 1867–8, XVII, Hon E. Stanhope, Evidence to Report on Lincolnshire, Nottingham and Leicester, p. 294.
[74] PP 1867–8, XVII, Revd James Fraser, Report on Norfolk, Essex, Sussex and Gloucester, p. 18.
[75] PP 1867–8, XVII, Report by Stanhope, p. 76.
[76] PP 1868–9, XIII, Hon E. Stanhope, Report on the counties of Dorset, Kent, Chester, Salop, Stafford and Rutland, p. 14.
[77] PP 1868–9, XIII, Edwin Portman, Report on the counties of Hampshire, Devon and Cornwall, p. 35; PP 1867–8, XVII, Report by Boyle, p. 124.
[78] PP 1868–9, XIII, Henry Tremenheere, Report on Cumberland and Westmorland, p. 136.

> The effect of this constant field labour is that their cottages are in an untidy state, that the families are neglected, and where there are small children ... it is a common habit to give the infants an opiate for the purpose of keeping them quiet during the day.[79]

> It is universally admitted that such employment, not so much from causes inherent in it as from circumstances by which it is surrounded, is to a great extent demoralising. Not only does it unsex a woman in dress, gait, manners, character, making it rough, coarse, clumsy, masculine; but it generates a further pregnant social mischief by unfitting or disposing her for a woman's proper duties at home.[80]

Not all female field labourers were condemned in this way. Joseph Henley praised the physique of Northumbrian women labourers (they were 'physically a splendid race'), and was impressed by the homemaking skills of such women when they married and had children:

> There are those who hold the opinion that fieldwork is degrading, but I should be glad if they would visit these women in their own homes after they become wives and mothers. They would be received with a natural courtesy and good manners which would astonish them.... The visitor will leave that cottage with the conviction that field work had had no degrading effect, but that he has been in the presence of a thoughtful, contented, and unselfish woman.[81]

The 1867–70 Royal Commission is infused with biases. The commissioners occupied different social, economic and political viewpoints but they shared an urban, male, middle-class construction of gender that coloured their perceptions of rural labouring women.[82] But the Commission also contains evidence given by women themselves – as does the 1843 Report – providing rare examples of the testimony of labouring women in the nineteenth century. This evidence enables the historian to assess women's own attitudes towards their work. In doing so, a rather different standpoint emerges. Women labourers tended to highlight the physical – not moral – consequences of field work. Mrs Britton told Austin in 1843, 'Haymaking is hard work, very fatiguing, but it never hurts me. I am always better when I can get out to work in the fields.'[83] Women were critical of the conditions of their labour and were reluctant to send their children out to work under such circumstances. Mrs Sculfer of Castle Acre commented to Denison:

---

[79] PP 1867–8, XVII, Edwin Portman, Report on Cambridgeshire and Yorkshire, p. 96.
[80] PP 1867–8, XVII, Report by Fraser, p. 16.
[81] PP 1867–8, XVII, Joseph Henley, Report on Northumberland and Durham, p. 54. A deconstruction of the representation of Northumbrian women in the Royal Commissions (and other contemporary evidence) is provided in Sayer, *Women of the Fields*, pp. 79–81, and Jane Long, *Conversations in Cold Rooms: Women, Work and Poverty in Nineteenth-Century Northumberland* (Woodbridge, 1999), pp. 89–109.
[82] Sayer, *Women of the Fields*, ch.4.
[83] PP 1843, XII, Report by Austin, p. 66.

AN OVERVIEW OF PRINTED SOURCES

> I have six children; three girls and three boys; my two eldest girls go out – most to my grief that I am obliged to send them. . . . My eldest girl has a thorough dislike to it. She almost goes crying to her work. She would almost rather do anything than it . . . I wish I knew of any place I could get for her, but I don't. I am sure I don't know what to do.[84]

But time and again women point to the inevitability of field work out of sheer necessity, despite the laborious toil and low pay. Mrs Jenner told Stanhope on his visit to Kent in 1867,

> Women ought to go and do women's work and help their husbands, and not stay at home. I have taken my daughters out at 6 years old to hop tying . . . I go ladder tying too. I go and do more than a man would, and yet they give me 1s. instead of 2s. 6d. I work from 8 til 5. I had rather work by the piece, but they won't have it.[85]

Women's evidence is not totally reliable: we do not know the process by which the printed evidence was selected or how typical the views expressed are. But at a time when the value of rural female labour was being increasingly challenged in contemporary publications, the presence of the female perspective acts as a useful counterbalance to the official (male) viewpoint.

The disappearance of female labourers?

According to Arthur Wilson Fox a number of circumstances coalesced after 1870 to promote the decline of women's employment in the English countryside: higher male wages, the increased use of farm machinery and the demand for domestic servants in towns were the main factors. By the early 1880s, he claims, female labour 'had entirely ceased in many districts'.[86] There are a number of official publications from the last quarter of the century that substantiate this viewpoint. Census figures show a sharp decline in the number of women engaged as agricultural workers after the mid-nineteenth century (Table 2.10). Female participation peaked in 1851 with just under 71,000 women recorded as labourers in agriculture in England and Wales – 7 per cent of the total workforce. Over the next twenty years the numbers of women engaged declined by 47 per cent; by 1901 women constituted just 1 per cent of the total number of labourers. Various government reports from the 1880s and 1890s also confirm this trend. The most compelling evidence is to be found in the Royal Commission on Labour

---

[84] PP 1843, XII, Report by Denison, p. 275.
[85] PP 1868–9, XIII, Evidence to Stanhope's Report, p. 49.
[86] Arthur Wilson Fox, 'Agricultural wages in England and Wales during the last fifty years', *Journal of the Statistical Society*, 66 (1903), pp. 273–348 (p. 298).

Table 2.10 Number of agricultural labourers in England and Wales, 1841 to 1901

	Male	Female	Total
	Agricultural labourers		
1841	854,660	35,262	889,922
1851	1,006,728	70,899	1,077,627
1861	914,301	43,964	958,265
1871	764,574	33,513	798,087
	Agricultural labourers, farm servants and cottagers		
1881	807,608	40,346	847,954
	Agricultural labourers and farm servants		
1891	709,283	24,150	733,433
1901	573,751	4,254	578,005

Sources: Census Reports of Great Britain, 1841–1901

(1893–4). This was established in 1892 to inquire into working conditions and labour relations following many years of unrest.[87] The commissioners appointed to investigate agricultural labour were instructed to look at the supply of labour on the land, conditions of engagement and earnings, cottages and allotments, trade unions and general relations in the countryside. Women's labour was to be addressed where relevant, although it was not a specific area of concern. Throughout the reports in fact, women are largely invisible. In Nottinghamshire women took 'no appreciable part in the work in the land', in Lincolnshire 'men's wages are good enough now to relieve the women from the necessity of taking field work regularly', an opinion reiterated by the Commissioner for Dorset, Wiltshire, Kent and Somerset: 'the labourer is better off than previously, and can now afford to do without the extra earnings of his wife at hard field work.'[88]

But caution is required, since these reports from the late nineteenth century do not tell a straightforward story. As we saw in Chapter 1, there are many serious problems associated with the collection of occupational data for rural women workers. The census figures for the second half of the nineteenth

---

[87] Sayer, *Women of the Fields*, p. 137.
[88] PP 1893-4, XXXV, Royal Commission on Labour. The Agricultural Labourer. Report by Mr William Bear on the Poor Law Union of Southwell, p. 107; Report by Mr Edward Wilkinson on the Poor Law Union of Louth, p. 46 and Summary report from Mr Aubrey Spencer, pp. 10–11.

century are likely to under-record several categories of female labourers: seasonal workers, married women working alongside their spouses and farm servants. The changing way that occupations were classified also creates difficulties. After 1871 agricultural labourers were no longer tabulated separately from farm servants or cottagers. Moreover, in 1881 the census stopped counting the female relatives of farmers as economically active: this seriously misrepresents the position on many English farms.[89] Indeed, if we go back to the other official reports of this period, a second reading reveals that there were certain circumstances under which women's labour was still essential. In Northumberland women workers had 'stayed roughly the same ratio to all agricultural labourers' in the mid-1890s.[90] In the market-gardening regions of the Midlands and the hop districts of the south-east, women were still engaged in significant numbers. The 'opportunity which women and children have of earning money', the Commissioner for Kent wrote, 'is a special advantage of the labourer in this district, and materially conduces to their well-being.'[91] Even in some areas of East Anglia women were still crucial to the successful completion of certain agricultural tasks:

> Women are very generally employed in many of the parishes, and their employment usually consists in pulling and cleaning roots, stone-picking, weeding corn, singling turnips, and raking after the waggons in hay and harvest times. ... The labourers themselves generally dislike the employment of women, but look upon it as a necessity, in order to meet the expenditure of the family ... it often brings that additional money into a house, which just makes the difference in a large family, or where the man is wholly or partly incapacitated from work, between privation and what they would consider sufficiency.[92]

This quote is taken from the Swaffham area of Norfolk and tells a familiar story about the types of labour assigned to women and the economic significance their earnings to made to the family budget. In fact, it could have been written at any time during the nineteenth century.

The published sources analysed in this chapter have to be understood within the context of the era they were produced. The period from 1790 to the 1830s was one of increasing hardship for the rural labouring poor: changes in the institution of farm service, the undermining of customary rights and the

---

[89] Alun Howkins, *Reshaping Rural England: A Social History, 1850–1925* (London, 1991), p. 171.
[90] PP 1893–4, XXXV, Report by Arthur Wilson Fox on the Poor Law Union of Glendale, p. 54.
[91] PP 1893–4, XXXV, Report by Aubrey Spencer on the Poor Law Union of Hollingbourne, p. 53.
[92] PP 1893–4, XXXV, Report by Arthur Wilson Fox on the Poor Law Union of Swaffham, p. 68.

decline of real wages meant women's economic contribution to the rural household was a necessity. Writers acknowledged this and the notion of 'common interest' in the late eighteenth and early nineteenth centuries was prevalent. The Ladies' Committee for promoting the education and employment of women argued in 1805 that because female labour 'is for the benefit of all, looking to the increase of the general fund', women 'should not be precluded, from contributing their portion of productive industry'.[93] The sources we have looked at from this period show that rural women's labour was regionally specific and subject to a number of changes, but the capacity of women to contribute to the family income was crucial to the maintenance of the rural household. By the mid-nineteenth century the advantages gained by women's labour were being questioned so that the image of women as economically productive members of the rural labouring class was gradually eroded in most official accounts. In his 1870 book on agricultural labourers, Charles Whitehead believed that the 'gradual influence of public opinion' and higher male wages meant it was no longer expedient for women to go out to work, enabling them to remain at home 'in their proper sphere'.[94] The decline of women working in the formal rural workforce (particularly the agricultural sector) in the second half of the nineteenth century was drastic and continuous according to the printed sources, although it was still visible and viable in certain regions and industries. Whether this chronology of rural female employment stands up when we use other sources to look at three types of work in more detail – farm service, agricultural day labour and domestic industries – will be tested over the following three chapters.

---

[93] Thomas Bernard, 'Extract from an account of the ladies committee for promoting the education and employment of the female poor', *Report of the Society for Bettering the Condition and Increasing the Comforts of the Poor*, vol. 4 (1805), pp. 181–92 (pp. 184–5).
[94] Charles Whitehead, *Agricultural Labourers* (London, 1870), p. 53.

3

Women in the agricultural labour market

Female farm servants

> That so many women were, at some time in their lives, productive farm servants is of importance, because women were to lose much of this productive role in agriculture as a result of the decline of farm service.[1]

So wrote Ann Kussmaul in her classic account of farm service *Servants in Husbandry in Early Modern England*, which was published in 1981. The arguments she proffered have proved to be highly influential, although in recent years a number of scholars have begun to question her methodology, data and conclusions. While this has certainly widened our appreciation of the complexities of the regional incidence and structure of service, few studies have sought to explore in any detail the gendered experience of farm service. No single survey has explored to what extent women's economic role was undermined after the decline of service in southern England. In addition, the only detailed consideration of the productive functions performed by female servants in regions where the institution continued in the nineteenth century is Judy Gielgud's unpublished research on Northumberland and Cumbria.[2] This chapter seeks to add to our understanding of the second theme. I have chosen to concentrate on the experience of women farm servants in one county: the East Riding of Yorkshire. This county was unique in that it was the only arable county to continue hiring unmarried male and female farm servants as a fundamental component of its labour force into the twentieth

---

[1] Ann Kussmaul, *Servants in Husbandry in Early Modern England* (Cambridge, 1981), p. 15.
[2] Judy Gielgud, 'Nineteenth-century farm women in Northumberland and Cumbria: The neglected workforce' (D.Phil. thesis, University of Sussex, 1992). Jane Long's study of women and poverty in Northumberland also includes a chapter on female bondagers, although she concentrates on contemporary constructions of rural life, female bondagers and femininity, to reveal the complexities in 'the nature of women's work' and 'the operation of gender relations in daily life'. Jane Long, *Conversations in Cold Rooms: Women, Work and Poverty in Nineteenth-Century Northumberland* (Woodbridge, 1999), p. 88.

century. Therefore, this study allows us to investigate a number of questions: what productive roles did female servants perform and how essential was their labour? Was there a hierarchy among female servants and how was this reflected in their pay? How did their conditions of hiring and service compare to male servants? Can we detect any changes in the nature of female service in this region over the course of the nineteenth century, and how can we account for these? Before these questions can be investigated however, it is necessary to consider the ways historians have approached the study of servants to illustrate how, and discern why, women are marginalised in the historiography.

Farm service in the nineteenth century: persistence and decline

The centrality of service in husbandry to the lives of young rural workers in early modern England is without doubt. It was, according to Kussmaul, 'a major form of hired labour in early modern agriculture and the typical experience of rural youths'.[3] Kussmaul goes on to argue that the incidence of farm service did not remain static over the early modern and modern periods, with changes in the institution being linked to population fluctuations, the cost of living and relative prices.[4] Thus, the occurrence of service witnessed two peaks; the first in the fifteenth century and the second in the mid-eighteenth century, when declining population levels and relatively low-cost provisions made the institution of service attractive to farmers. A trough in the popularity of service in the late sixteenth and early seventeenth centuries was linked to population growth: a glut of adult labour seeking waged work enabled farmers to dismiss their annually hired servants. This pattern was repeated in the late eighteenth and early nineteenth centuries in the south and east at least, and led to the extinction of the institution in that region of England by the second half of the nineteenth century. Kussmaul writes,

> Service in husbandry did not evolve into a new form of labour. It collapsed.... Farm service is one of the larger reptiles of economic history, extraordinarily successful in its time, and driven rapidly to extinction when times changed.[5]

The deterioration of the environment in which service in husbandry flourished happened on a number of levels. The seeds of these changes were sown before 1750, intensified after the 1790s and strengthened inexorably

---

[3] Kussmaul, *Servants in Husbandry*, p. 11.
[4] Ibid., p. 98.
[5] Ibid., pp. 133–4.

after 1815. The large, newly enclosed arable farms prospering across the south and east – and a shift to wheat production, requiring large labour inputs at certain seasons – rendered the necessity of hiring servants on a yearly contact questionable. High grain prices and rising costs of living heightened the economic burden of boarding servants in the farmhouse. The authors of the General Views of Agriculture, as we saw in the last chapter, recorded the growing resentment farmers felt towards farm service at the beginning of the nineteenth century. Farmers were thwarted in their attempts to discontinue yearly hiring however by a series of temporary labour shortages during the French Wars. After 1815 demobilised soldiers flooded the countryside, creating a pool of labour that permitted farmers to discharge their servants and replace them with day labourers, hired and paid only for the work they performed. 'Farmers did not want to give annual contracts to servants,' Kussmaul claims; they 'did not want to live with them and ceased hiring them.'[6] Kussmaul cites Keith Snell's research on settlement examinations as evidence of 'the difference between the checked desire before 1815 and its fulfilment after 1815.'[7] A servant hired for a year gained settlement in that parish; as a reaction to rising poor rates farmers increasingly acted to deny this right. Snell shows that between 1780 and 1810 there was a noticeable upswing in shorter periods of hiring but after 1820 this trend escalated: the practice of yearly hirings in the south-east was persistently giving way to shorter hirings of periods from one week to fifty-one weeks.[8] Kussmaul concedes that this pattern was not uniform: by 1851 there were still pockets of south-east England where servants continued to be hired, including areas of Kent and Sussex. But on the whole it was only regions of small farms, rugged terrain and manufacturing (which drew labour off the land) that continued to rely on yearly farm servants. The implication is that service was not compatible with intensive, capitalist arable farming of the south-east and was only associated with backward, anachronistic ways of farming in the pastoral north and west. Thus, by the mid-nineteenth century, 'England had been divided between the low-service agricultural south and the high-service industrial north and west'.[9]

While Kussmaul's work should be regarded as 'a landmark for rural history', her conclusions have been recently challenged.[10] Early modern historian Donald Woodward casts doubt on Kussmaul's contention that long-term swings in the incidence of service were apparent before the mid-eighteenth

---

[6] Ibid., p. 129.
[7] Ibid., p. 125.
[8] K. D. M. Snell, *Annals of the Labouring Poor: Social Change and Agrarian England 1660–1900* (Cambridge, 1985), p. 75.
[9] Kussmaul, *Servants in Husbandry*, p. 130.
[10] Donald Woodward, 'Early modern servants in husbandry revisited', *Agricultural History Review*, 48 (2000), pp. 141–50 (p. 141).

century.¹¹ Historians of the modern period have disputed the distinction Kussmaul draws between the north and south of England, and between farm servants and day labourers. Alun Howkins has shown how Kussmaul's thesis is framed in a particularly English – as opposed to British – outlook, and in Scotland, Wales and Ireland the percentage of hired workers who were servants remained high into the late nineteenth century.¹² Moreover, it is clear that 'service' survived in many different forms and should not be used as a blanket term to describe a form of employment that was not uniform across the British Isles. Even in a specifically English context, Howkins identifies three kinds of farm service still extant in the nineteenth-century countryside. 'Classic' farm service, where a young person lived with a family, learned a trade and hoped one day to become an owner-occupier themselves, persisted in Lancashire, parts of Durham, Yorkshire, the Welsh borders and parts of Devon and Sussex.¹³ This assertion is validated by other studies. The continued centrality of service to the rural economy of north Lancashire is highlighted in Alistair Mutch's research (although the reality of the farming ladder is questioned).¹⁴ Brian Short and Mick Reed have both pointed to the survival of service – in much greater numbers than the census suggests – in nineteenth-century Sussex.¹⁵ The second form of service to survive in England was family hiring: the head of household (usually male) being hired for a year with his family to live and work on the farm. This persisted in the border counties, but also in Dorset and Kent. Finally, the hiring of young unmarried men and women into the farmhouse, with little hope of their ever becoming farmers, was still found in parts of Nottinghamshire, Lincolnshire

---

[11] Woodward, 'Early modern servants in husbandry'.

[12] Alun Howkins, 'Peasants, servants and labourers: The marginal workforce in British agriculture, 1870–1914', *Agricultural History Review*, 42 (1991), pp. 49–62 (p. 57). In Wales in 1871, for example, 52 per cent of all hired workers remained servants, in Ireland 60 per cent and in Scotland most permanent farmworkers, married and single, were hired servants. Even these figures are likely to be an under-representation as they refer only to actual living-in service.

[13] Howkins, 'Peasants, servants and labourers', p. 58.

[14] Alistair Mutch, 'The "farming ladder" in north Lancashire, 1840–1914: Myth or reality?', *Northern History*, 27 (1991), pp. 162–83. However, Andrew Gritt's detailed reassessment of the early nineteenth-century sources used by Kussmaul questions the extent of the distinction between the low service south and high service north. His investigation suggests the significance of the servant workforce in northern England – including Lancashire – has been exaggerated. Andrew Gritt, 'The census and the servant: A reassessment of the decline and distribution of farm service in early nineteenth-century England', *Economic History Review*, LIII (2000), pp. 84–106.

[15] Brian Short, 'The decline of living-in service in the transition to capitalist farming: A critique of the Sussex evidence', *Sussex Archaeological Collections*, 122 (1984), pp. 147–64; Mick Reed, 'Indoor farm service in nineteenth-century Sussex: Some criticisms of a critique', *Sussex Archaeological Collections*, 123 (1985), pp. 225–41.

and particularly the East Riding of Yorkshire.[16] Studies on the latter county by Stephen Caunce and Gary Moses have highlighted various aspects of servant life in the nineteenth and twentieth centuries.[17]

Kussmaul's contention that farm service, with its annual contracts and continuously available labour, distinguished servants 'from all other workers in agrarian society' – particularly day labourers – has also come under scrutiny.[18] This division, although accepted by Howkins, is questioned by other historians.[19] Both Caunce and Moses argue that farm servants, like day labourers, retained a reliance on waged labour, had little or no prospect of becoming farmers, developed 'an informal socio-political consciousness' through the hiring fair and experienced antagonistic relations between employer and employee on occasion.[20] In other words they were proletarians. Caunce writes, 'As Richard Anthony has argued for Scotland, there is no case for removing English servants from the landless labourer category *en masse*'.[21]

The issue of service in husbandry has been laid open by these debates and there is still much that remains inconclusive about this form of farm labour. This is most noticeable in the case of female servants. Confusion over exactly who female servants were may account for this neglect. The distinction between female farm servants and female domestic servants is blurred. Kussmaul adopts Adam Smith's terminology in describing farm servants as productive, 'hired not to maintain a style of life, but a style of work, the household economy'.[22] Bridget Hill casts doubt on the usefulness of this definition, especially after the mid-eighteenth century, when 'female servants in husbandry were also undertaking domestic work in the house and domestic servants were also performing "productive" work on the farm and in the dairy'.[23] Snell had also pointed to the indiscriminate use of terminology such as 'servant', 'servant in husbandry', 'house servant', 'house servant in

---

[16] Howkins, 'Peasants, servants and labourers', pp. 58–9.
[17] Stephen Caunce, *Amongst Farm Horses: The Horselads of East Yorkshire* (Stroud, 1991); Stephen Caunce, 'Twentieth-century farm servants: The horselads of the East Riding of Yorkshire', *Agricultural History Review*, 39 (1991), pp. 143–66; Gary Moses, '"Rustic and rude": Hiring fairs and their critics in East Yorkshire, c.1850–75', *Rural History*, 7 (1996), pp. 151–75.
[18] Kusmaul, *Servants in Husbandry*, p. 4.
[19] Howkins, 'Peasants, servants and labourers', p. 59.
[20] Stephen Caunce, 'Farm servants and the development of capitalism in English agriculture', *Agricultural History Review*, 45 (1997), pp. 46–60; Gary Moses, 'Proletarian labourers? East Riding farm servants, c.1850–1875', *Agricultural History Review*, 47 (1999), pp. 78–94 (p. 91).
[21] Caunce, 'Farm servants', p. 59. See also Richard Anthony, 'Farm servant vs agricultural labourer, 1870–1914: A commentary on Howkins', *Agricultural History Review*, 43 (1995), pp. 61–4.
[22] Kussmaul, *Servants in Husbandry*, p. 4.
[23] Bridget Hill, *Women, Work and Sexual Politics in Eighteenth-Century England*, 1st edn 1989 (London, 1994), p. 70.

husbandry' and 'housewifery' in indentures from the eighteenth and early nineteenth centuries.[24]

The nineteenth-century censuses did not resolve the problem. The census records a steady decline in the number of women employed as farm servants over the nineteenth century: between 1851 and 1871, for example, the number of female farm servants in England and Wales declined by nearly 80 per cent. By the mid-nineteenth century, according to Kussmaul, most female servants were domestics, 'hired to establish and maintain the status of the family and to attend to its personal needs'.[25] Edward Higgs, in his analysis of census records, has questioned the distinction between 'farm' and 'domestic' service, and the former's decline in favour of the latter. General female servants on farms, he contends, are likely to have been underenumerated in the census returns, being placed in the category of domestic service.[26] Guidance issued to enumerators in 1861 suggested that 'female servants of a farmers family' should be recorded as indoor farm servants, whereas 'if the duties of the servant are described as simply those of a household servant' she was to be classified as a domestic servant.[27] It seems highly unlikely that enumerators would have been able to determine whether a servant was hired purely for household duties, and an indiscriminate mixing of tasks in the house and on the farm was the norm for servants on many farms into the twentieth century. Mary Bouquet, for example, shows that female servants working on farms in Devon in the early twentieth century divided their time between the home and dairy.[28] In Lincolnshire a similar pattern has been uncovered: servants working in rural areas were expected to milk cows, make butter and cheese, and tend to livestock, in addition to performing their usual household duties.[29] Such workers, in all probability, were classified as domestic servants.

Thus, where farm service survived in the nineteenth century, historians have tended to submerge female farm service into domestic service. This not only distorts the situation, it also undervalues the labour women performed, both indoors and outdoors. Gielgud makes this point. The farm, she argues, could not function without the domestic and outdoor work women carried out: 'their contribution in both spheres was essential to the success of the

---

[24] Snell, *Annals of the Labouring Poor*, p. 283.
[25] Kussmaul, *Servants in Husbandry*, p. 4.
[26] Edward Higgs, 'Occupational censuses and the agricultural workforce in Victorian England and Wales', *Economic History Review*, XLVIII (1995), pp. 700–16 (p. 707).
[27] Edward Higgs, 'Women, occupations and work in the nineteenth-century censuses', *History Workshop Journal*, 23 (1987), pp. 59–82 (p. 71).
[28] Mary Bouquet, *Family, Servants and Visitors: The Farm Household in Nineteenth and Twentieth-Century Devon* (Norwich, 1985).
[29] J. A. S. Green, 'A survey of domestic service', *Lincolnshire History and Archaeology*, 17 (1982), pp. 65–9.

farm enterprise.'[30] Yet previous studies have tended to see women's labour as incidental to the real business of the farm performed by male servants. Caunce's illuminating research on East Yorkshire horselads literally consigns female servants to the footnotes. 'Girls were also hired to live in', he remarks, 'but with significant differences. There is no room to discuss their experiences here.'[31] The remainder of this chapter seeks to redress this oversight.

Hiring

The East Riding of Yorkshire was unique in the nineteenth century. It was a high-wage, arable county that continued with the system of hiring young unmarried male and female servants into the farmhouse on a yearly contract. The county was dominated by the pursuit of agriculture. Rapid enclosure in the late eighteenth and early nineteenth centuries resulted in the conversion of much unproductive grassland to arable, alongside the construction of new large farms and the adoption of new methods of cultivation.[32] Farms of 300 to 800 acres were normal in the Holderness region in the east of the county, while farms of up to 1000 acres were not unusual on the central Wolds.[33] The East Riding, then, faced the same pressures that had led to the abandonment of the institution of service across much of the arable south and east. However, a number of factors ensured that yearly hiring remained a central element of the East Yorkshire farm workforce. The county exploited its proximity to the industrial north, which provided an expanding market for agricultural produce throughout the nineteenth century. Isolated farmsteads and sparsely populated settlements meant that the hiring of servants continued to remain the most reliable and practical means of procuring and retaining labour for the whole of the year. During the prosperous years of the mid-Victorian period, farmers became more dependent on servants to fulfil their increased labour requirements: their share of the total agricultural workforce of the Wolds region, for example, increased in the middle decades of the century.[34] The attachment to yearly service in East Yorkshire did not

---

[30] Gielgud, 'Nineteenth-century farm women', p. 193.
[31] Caunce, 'Twentieth-century farm servants', p. 144.
[32] George Legard, 'Farming of the East Riding of Yorkshire', *Journal of the Royal Agricultural Society*, 9 (1848), pp. 85–136.
[33] Caunce, *Amongst Farm Horses*, p. 11. See also Barbara English, *The Great Landowners of East Yorkshire, 1530–1910* (Hemel Hempstead), 1990; K. J. Allison, *The East Riding of Yorkshire Landscape* (London, 1976).
[34] June A. Sheppard, 'East Yorkshire's agricultural labour force in the mid nineteenth century', *Agricultural History Review*, 9 (1961), pp. 43–54 (pp. 48–50). Holderness possessed fewer new farms and smaller scale enterprises than the Wolds and therefore required fewer living-in servants. Farmers on the Vale of York (in the south-west of the county) required more day labour and fewer servants as small-scale farming dominated the area. Family-run farms also remained common in the Vale of York.

indicate economic and technological backwardness: service adapted itself successfully to cope with the demands of the intensive, dynamic capitalist agrarian system of the county.[35]

Farm service occupied a distinct phase in the lifecycle of rural women. Girls left home to go into farm service between the ages of 12 and 14. They were hired by the year and boarded in the farmhouse, or in the house of the hind or foreman.[36] The system therefore continued to offer young single women the opportunity to leave home and enter the paid workforce in a relatively secure environment. In the process they also relieved 'their parents houses from overcrowding'.[37] The number of female servants hired varied from farm to farm and between regions. The larger, isolated farmsteads of the Wolds hired the most female servants, who worked under the supervision of the farmer's or hind's wife. In these circumstances a hierarchy existed within the female servant workforce: age and experience determined status, as they did among the male servants. Young girls embarking on their working lives began as 'nurse' girls, ostensibly to mind the babies and young children of the farmhouse. Higher up the ladder were the 'general' female servants, and by their early twenties women were described as 'upper' servants. All female farm servants in East Yorkshire were hired on a legally enforceable one-year contract, which ran from Martinmas to Martinmas (23 November). Any girls or women hired after this date were hired only until the following Martinmas. The yearly hiring included board and lodging for the whole year, with wages being paid at the end of the year's service. Female servants were hired on the same terms as men with one crucial exception: a system of one month's notice to terminate a contract by either party underpinned the hiring of women and reflected the arrangement for employing domestic servants in towns.[38]

Female servants – like their male counterparts – were a mobile workforce. It was exceptional for male or female servants to remain at the same farm for more than three years. The annual hiring fairs brought together farmers searching for new servants and workers seeking new positions. Each fair served a distinct district; few servants moved outside the district of their birth, and movement between the Wolds and the lowlands was especially

---

[35] Moses, 'Rude and rustic', p. 155.
[36] There was a shift from boarding servants with the farms to using the hind (foreman). He then took over from the farmer as the head of the servant household. Farmers themselves gradually withdrew from direct involvement, building new houses and housing the hinds and servants in the old farmhouse. See Caunce, *Amongst Farm Horses*, p. 197.
[37] PP 1867–8, XVII, First Report from the Commissioners on the Employment of Children, Young Persons and Women in Agriculture. The Hon. E. B. Portman, Report on the counties of Yorkshire and Cambridgeshire. Evidence to Portman's Report, p. 366.
[38] Mary Simpson, 'The life and training of a farm boy', in Revd F. D. Legard, ed., *More About Farm Lads* (London, 1865), pp. 75–100 (p. 90). An exploration of the legal basis of the servant contract is provided in Caunce, 'Farm servants and the development of capitalism'.

restricted.[39] A system of multiple hirings operated across the county. The first hirings were usually held around a fortnight ahead of Martinmas, and were used by servants to gauge wage levels and judge bargains being made. The serious business took place at the second hirings.[40] Some servants indicated their particular skill by pinning a symbol or badge on their clothing. Shepherds, for example, used bunches of wool, housemaids, a sprig of broom. But many servants – particularly female servants – would not have a clearly identifiable occupational symbol to display, being expected to perform a whole range of tasks over the year.[41] After a hiring was secured, servants pinned brightly coloured ribbons on to their coats to denote their hired status.[42] Terms of the agreement were verbally settled and sealed with a hiring or 'fest' penny. If the servant retained this, she was considered engaged until the following Martinmas. If it was returned at any time before the contract began, no agreement was upheld.[43] Acceptance of the hiring penny was considered binding for both parties and, as Gielgud argues, the breaking of a pledge was seen as dishonourable behaviour.[44]

Caunce compares the atmosphere of the hiring fair to an informal and temporary union: the bargaining was collective, with servants facing potential employers together, knowing the level of wages being demanded and received by friends and colleagues. It was 'one of the few places where a workman could genuinely negotiate his own contact directly with an employer without being at a gross disadvantage'.[45] Contemporary observers viewed the hiring fairs from a different perspective. To prominent local writers such as Mary Simpson and the Reverend Eddowes, fairs were degrading and demoralising.[46] Analogies were frequently drawn between the public

---

[39] Caunce, *Amongst Farm Horses*, p. 40.
[40] Ibid., pp. 67–9.
[41] Michael Roberts, '"Waiting upon chance": English hiring fairs and their meanings from the fourteenth to the twentieth century', *Journal of Historical Sociology*, 1 (1988), pp. 119–60 (p. 141). Caunce points out that this system of identification had ceased by the early twentieth century. Caunce, *Amongst Farm Horses*, p. 59.
[42] T. E. Keeble, *The Agricultural Labourer: A Summary of his Position*, 1st edn 1870 (London, 1907), p. 91.
[43] G. John Chester, *Statute Fairs: Their Evils and their Remedy* (York, 1856), p. 7.
[44] Gielgud, 'Nineteenth-century farm women', p. 192.
[45] Caunce, *Amongst Farm Horses*, p. 67. Fred Kitchen, *Brother to the Ox: The Autobiography of a Farm Labourer* (Horsham, 1981), pp. 97–101 provides a good description of the hiring fair for farm servants from south Yorkshire, north Nottinghamshire, north Lincolnshire and Derbyshire.
[46] See Revd J. Eddowes, *The Agricultural Labourer As He Really Is, or Village Morals in 1854* (Driffield, 1854); William Barugh, *Master and Man: A Reply to the Agricultural Labourers As He Really Is* (Driffield, 1854); Revd J. Eddowes, *Martinmas Musing: Or Thoughts About the Hiring Day* (Driffield, 1854); Revd F. O. Morris, *The Present System of Hiring Farm Servants in the East Riding of Yorkshire with Suggestion for its Improvement* (Driffield, 1854); Mary Simpson, *Gleanings: Being a Sequel to Ploughing and Sowing*

hiring of servants and slave markets, and farmers were criticised for looking only at the physical attributes of potential workers and ignoring their moral character. Eddowes believed that the hiring fair made

> servants of both sexes unduly and ignorantly independent, and to strengthen them in impertinence and disobedience. But – what is worse – it deadens, if not destroys, all their sense of self-respect; it gives a low, a depraved tone to their mind and their pursuits for the whole year.[47]

A public meeting at Howden in 1854 strongly urged the use of written characters for both male and female servants, stating the length of service, abilities and general conduct of servants as a prerequisite for hiring.[48] From the mid-nineteenth century, reformers increasingly targeted their activities towards female servants. The segregation of male and female hiring via the introduction of indoor accommodation and registration facilities for women was their main objective. Local newspapers first report the occupation of such facilities in 1860. In that year the Corn Exchange in Driffield was opened 'in order that females might not be exposed to the weather and the degradation of standing in the open street to be publicly hired'.[49] However, the same move in Bridlington indicates that there was initial reluctance on the part of women to make use of the amenities offered: 'owing to the favourable weather', it was reported, women 'did not avail themselves fully of this kind offer.'[50] Simpson records the tactics employed by reformers in Bridlington in 1862 to persuade female servants to use the indoor facilities. Circulars were sent to local clergymen and farmers, and placards were placed in blacksmith's shops advertising the amenities beforehand. On the morning of the hiring, clergymen stood directing the women to the Corn Exchange as they entered town, 'a work requiring a good deal of tact and diplomacy'.[51] The result was the

> room was soon filled, and the hiring went on briskly. The mistresses were greatly pleased, remarking with surprised satisfaction how much better behaved the girls were than when hired in the streets, where all was confusion and rude joking and jostling among the lads.[52]

(London, 1876); Revd Nash Stephenson, *On the Rise and Progress of the Movement for the Abolition of Statutes, Mops or Feeing Markets* (London, 1861).
[47] Eddowes, *Agricultural Labourer*, p. 22.
[48] *Eastern Counties Herald*, 2 November 1854.
[49] *Hull Advertiser*, 16 November 1860.
[50] Ibid.
[51] Simpson, *Gleanings*, p. 105.
[52] Ibid., pp. 105–6.

Over the next few years the success of the reformers was gradually achieved, and by the 1870s female servants were hired indoors, separated from the outdoor hiring of men. Along with the partial establishment of a system of register offices, this represents, according to Moses, one of 'the main long term achievements of the campaign against hiring fairs and constitute a major reform'.[53] Yet even indoor hiring did not prevent women from returning to the heady atmosphere of the fair after the contracts were agreed. Here, the morality of female servants was harder to control, if we are to believe the view of one local superintendent:

> Nor are the men-servants the only victims here, for the servant girls are as plentiful as the servant men at the Mop, and they throng the public houses, drinking, dancing and singing with drunken men and prostitutes, lying with the men in adjoining buildings, and taking part in scenes of which no-one can form a correct opinion unless they have witnessed them.[54]

Work

The Martinmas holiday extended to a week after which all servants were expected to report to their situations. Female servants were responsible for a number of tasks, both indoors and outdoors: preparing food for the household, cleaning the farmhouse, washing and ironing clothing, running the dairy, taking care of poultry and other small animals, and labouring in the fields when required. Although some female servants on the largest farms were hired to perform a particular role – dairymaid being the most obvious – it is clear that most servants undertook the whole range of jobs. This juxtaposition of outdoor and indoor tasks is confirmed by contemporary descriptions of the work female servants performed. Reverend Morris, for example, describes the position of a young teenage girl in her first hiring, who made 'herself generally useful in the house and out of it from morning till evening', while a dairy girl was expected to 'milk five or six cows every day and assist in the harvest-field and other out-door work'.[55] All types of work demanded of the female farm servant involved very long hours and hard physical labour. Caunce concedes that 'In terms of non-stop effort the inside servant worked even harder than the horselads, though the lads had the heavier jobs to do'.[56] While this may have been the case, the indoor work performed by women should not be dismissed or underestimated:

---

[53] Moses, 'Rude and rustic', p. 165.
[54] Quoted in Revd J. Skinner, *Facts and Opinions Concerning Statute Hirings, Respectfully Addressed to the Landowners, Clergy, Farmers and Tradesmen of the East Riding of Yorkshire* (London, 1861), Appendix II, p. 9.
[55] Revd M. C. F. Morris, *Yorkshire Reminiscences* (London, 1922), p. 311.
[56] Caunce, *Amongst Farm Horses*, pp. 148–9.

the reputation of a farm, and therefore the ability of farmers to attract the best servants, often depended on the quality of the food and the cleanliness of the house. As Gielgud comments, the indoor labour of hired female servants is generally overlooked as 'it is judged to require no skill . . . but such work was carried out to a high standard during the nineteenth century in most farmhouses'.[57] If we use contemporary accounts, it is possible to explore this point in more detail in the context of the East Riding.

Alice Markham, a hind's daughter from Paull, near Hull, describes the weekly routine of indoor labour at the turn of the twentieth century. This pattern is reminiscent of earlier decades:

> There was a regular routine of housework which was rarely changed. Monday, of course, was washday, followed by ironing on Tuesday. Wednesday was a baking day, and the bedrooms were 'done' on Thursdays. Friday was another day for a big baking session before the weekend, although no day went by without hours spent on baking.[58]

Washday was notoriously gruelling. Female servants would wash all the linen of the household but not the clothing of the male servants. The men usually took their washing home for their mothers to wash, or they paid a local village woman to perform the task. Before washing could commence, water had to be fetched and fires lit. The usual round of chores also had to be carried out alongside the washing. According to Morris, women would rise in the early hours and expected 'but little intermission for the rest of the day'.[59] Larger farmhouses had a separate washhouse attached to the kitchen, but on smaller farms the washing was carried out in the house itself.[60] In both, the copper and dolly tub were the main pieces of technology employed. The drying of the washing was no easy task either and poor weather could delay the process substantially. Given that the whole procedure of washing, drying and pressing was carried out by hand throughout the nineteenth century, the physical demands made on female servants were considerable. This was also true of the cleaning of the farmhouse and servants' quarters.

All the food that could be was hand-prepared by female servants on the farm. Pigs were usually the main source of meat. Pigs were killed on the farm, the meat was cured and by-products made into pies and puddings. Margaret Moate, who lived on a small farm at Cottingham near Hull in the late nineteenth century, describes this process:

---

[57] Gielgud, 'Nineteenth-century farm women', p. 196.
[58] Alice M. Markham, *Back of Beyond: Reminiscences of Little Humber Farm, 1903–1925* (North Ferriby, 1979), p. 27. Thanks to Gary Moses for this reference.
[59] Revd M. C. F. Morris, *The British Workman Past and Present* (London, 1928), p. 58.
[60] Colin Hayfield, 'Farm servants' accommodation on the Yorkshire Wolds', *Folk Life*, 33 (1994–5), pp. 7–28 (p. 24).

We always kept five pigs to be slaughtered for the house. They would weigh about twenty-five stone each and were always sows who had had one litter. The hams and fletcher would hang, after salted, from the kitchen rafters. Sausages, black puddings and pork pies were made after the pig killing, and the fat rendered down into lard for cooking.[61]

Fruits were preserved and bread was baked. Bakeries were not introduced until the early twentieth century, and then only in the large towns and seaside resorts of the county.[62] The daily round of baking and cooking was unremitting. Morris describes a large farm on the Wolds that employed fourteen male servants. Not surprisingly, the 'quantity of food consumed was enormous'. The two female servants would

> bake forty 'standing pies' together once or twice a week; these were made of meat in winter, fat mutton being commonly used, and fruit in summer. Eight stone of flour and one stone of bacon would be used, and a sheep killed every week.[63]

In addition, milk, butter, cheese and curds were made in the dairy; these were for consumption in the farmhouse and also to sell commercially at market. On Moate's farm, the milk 'from a herd of eight cows, would be separated into cream and churned into butter, which was sold to the local Dairy'.[64] Morris' description of dairy work again points to the physical nature of the work:

> I have heard of a girl . . . who had to help in the milking of nearly twenty cows daily. The cows would assemble on the back 'causer' in a ring; they would not be tied, for without the least trouble each would go to its accustomed place. It was reckoned rather a feat to milk these cows in an hour, but Jane was 'a rare strapping lass'. . . . Then came the diary work, 'siling' the milk, churning and what-not.[65]

Field labour took female servants away from the farmhouse and dairy, and away from the supervision of the farmer's wife. Agricultural work does not feature as prominently in contemporary accounts of working life as do other forms of labour, although it was clearly expected at peak times of the year. Morris argues that female servants 'would frequently lend a hand in the harvest field, and at odd times they would have other odd jobs to do such as "pulling" turnips'.[66] In 1848 the *Hull Advertiser* reported an accident

---

[61] Unpublished memoirs of Margaret Moate, born Cottingham, 1879. East Yorkshire Local Studies Library, Beverley. No page numbers. The farm employed three male and one female servant. When she was 13 the family moved to a farm in Holderness and Margaret began work alongside the female servant Lizzie.
[62] Caunce, *Amongst Farm Horses*, p. 150.
[63] Morris, *Yorkshire Reminiscences*, p. 311.
[64] Unpublished memoirs of Margaret Moate.
[65] Morris, *British Workman*, pp. 57–8.
[66] Ibid., p. 58.

involving Esther Scarborough, a female servant who had been assisting at the threshing machine when 'her clothes unfortunately became entangled in the wheel, and she was not rescued before one of her legs had been lacerated in the most dreadful manner'.[67]

Female servants interacted with male workers on a day-to-day basis, particularly at mealtimes, but in terms of their lodgings the two sexes were kept quite separate. Farm lads were usually housed in large dormitories, normally in the upper storey of the house, or in a separate wing. Female servants were boarded away from the men, often reaching their rooms via a separate staircase that was accessed from the kitchen.[68] Even where male servants were accommodated in a separate hind house, the female servants could still find themselves living with the farmer and his family. Whatever the circumstances, provisions for servants were sparse. Men usually slept two to a bed and the only furniture in their rooms was their 'clothing box', placed at the foot of the bed. The female servants often slept in small attic rooms, with little light, heating or furnishings. Colin Hayfield describes the room servant Ann Eccles slept in at Vessey Pasture in the early 1850s:

> the farmhouse included a small steep staircase off the main landing leading up to a 'garret' in the roof space lit only by a small roof light set in a heavy cast iron frame and with no fireplace or any other means of warmth other than any heat radiated from the chimney breast that passed up the gable wall.[69]

Moreover, their situations could be lonely and isolated. Women could be at risk of abuse from their employers, or more usually from the male servants on the farm. We know this because occasionally women resorted to the law. In 1861, for example, a Mrs Fuller (she had married on leaving service) took her ex-employer, Mary Edmond of North Cave, to court to recover £2 4s 9d in wages. She had run away from her service, arguing that the situation 'was anything but agreeable to her in consequence of being continually pestered by the men'.[70] In 1871, Elizabeth Grasby of Hotham, who had been employed in service by Thomas Craven, a farmer at Driffield, was charged with attempting to take her own life by laudanum. She claimed that an intimacy had existed between herself and Mr Craven, and that he had promised her marriage all the year, but had deceived her and turned her out of her place.[71]

---

[67] *Hull Advertiser*, 15 December 1848.
[68] Hayfield, 'Farm servants' accommodation', pp. 13–14.
[69] Ibid., p. 24.
[70] *Beverley Guardian*, 21 September 1861.
[71] *Beverley Guardian*, 25 November 1871. See also Jill Barber, '"Stolen goods": The sexual harassment of female servants in west Wales during the nineteenth century', *Rural History*, 4 (1993), pp. 123–36.

Many contemporary observers considered farmhouse life to be demoralising and degrading. They highlight poor supervision by masters and mistresses, and the mixing of the sexes in the farmhouse as the main causes of moral decay. Edwin Portman, reporting for the Royal Commission on women and children in agriculture in the 1860s, argued that following the hiring 'little or no trouble is taken to keep them in the right way. . . . The masters, taken as a whole, seem unaware that they are in duty bound to take some interest in the moral education of the servants.'[72] Simpson was similarly shocked by the way farmhouses were run:

> Every farmhouse I go into, I hear the same story. The master and mistress (strange misnomers!) have no control whatever over their servants, except in their actual work. . . . Seeing is believing. I had heard all my life with the hearing of the ear, that farmhouse life was 'so demoralising'. I had also heard pretty much what were its evils and dangers, but till I saw it with my own eyes . . . I never really believed it.[73]

What did Simpson find in the farmhouse kitchen that so troubled her? A rather innocuous scene it seems: seven male servants who had just finished their supper and were sitting on benches by the fire in the kitchen, with three females washing up after them. What shocked Simpson was the lack of supervision in this situation. But given the length of the working day and the lack of leisure time, the likelihood of misbehaviour would be slight. Servants were expected to be on hand for work whenever required, although Sunday was recognised as a day off. Male and female servants were certainly not always innocent, but observers like Portman and Simpson are recording the opportunity for impropriety rather than any actual misconduct. Indeed, they often seem to misread and misconstrue situations. Portman contended in his report that 'the separation of the sleeping rooms of the two sexes is very often most incomplete', which is not borne out by Hayfield's analysis of nineteenth-century farm architecture.[74] In reality, the opportunities for promiscuity on farms were rare. Simpson's and Portman's views are important because they were widely disseminated and had an impact on how farm service was viewed by some parties. But in many ways the scenes depicted by observers such as Simpson actually tell us more about the workings of her mind than about the reality of farm life for men and women servants in the nineteenth century. As Caunce puts it, 'Even though there was bound to be some sexual element in the contact on a few farms, the innocence of such evenings provides an interesting contrast to the dark scenarios of Mary Simpson's mind.'[75]

---

[72] PP 1867–8, XVII, Report by Portman, p. 100.
[73] Mary Simpson, *Ploughing or Sowing; or Annals of an Evening School in a Yorkshire Village* (London, 1861), pp. 2–3.
[74] PP 1867–8, XVII, Report by Portman, p. 100.
[75] Caunce, *Amongst Farm Horses*, p. 168.

Wages

The annual wages paid to female servants in the nineteenth century depended on several factors. Wages rose with age and experience, but the buoyancy of the local labour market and the state of the agricultural sector as a whole had a significant influence on the annual wage. At the beginning of the century, wartime labour shortages gave servants the upper hand in the hiring market. H. E. Strickland, reporting to the Board of Agriculture in 1811, found that the wages of servants throughout the East Riding were 'exorbitantly high', having doubled since his predecessor compiled his survey of the county in 1794.[76] Strickland divided the servant hierarchy into two classes. Young female servants ('undergirls' and 'dairymaids') received between £9 and £12 for their year's labour, while older women ('housekeepers') earned from £12 to £16. Teenage lads ('ploughboys') were worth £14 to £17, whereas the foremen could expect to be paid between £28 and £35.[77] The author was disturbed by the consequences of such high rates of pay, which he saw as encouraging a frivolous and irresponsible outlook among the servant population of the region. Strickland wrote,

> a passion for finery prevails so extensively that notwithstanding their exorbitant wages, the whole is commonly anticipated before the end of the year, and not unfrequently a considerable debt remains undischarged, very few laying by anything for their future establishment in life, or the assistance of their aged parents.[78]

The level of servant wages was significantly curtailed after 1815. The depressed state of agriculture in the second quarter of the nineteenth century led farmers to economise both in the numbers of yearly servants they hired and the level of wages they were willing to pay. Local newspaper accounts note the reluctance of farmers to hire large workforces. In the 1840s it was reported that 'a general disposition among masters and mistresses to economise in doing with as few servants as possible' existed across the county.[79] The cutback in the labour bill affected male and female servants of all ages. Thus we find that young teenage girls were being hired for as little as £4 at the Bridlington hirings of 1847, while foremen could only expect an annual wage of between £22 and £25 in 1848.[80]

By the mid-1850s, as East Yorkshire shared in the prosperity and progress of the Golden Age of agriculture, the demand for reliable year-round labour

---

[76] H. E. Strickland, *General View of Agriculture of the East Riding of Yorkshire* (York, 1812), p. 258.
[77] Ibid., p. 258.
[78] Ibid., p. 284.
[79] *Hull Advertiser*, 16 November 1849.
[80] *Hull Advertiser*, 19 November 1847; Legard, 'Farming of the East Riding', p. 125.

once again shifted the balance of power back to the farm servants. At Driffield, situated in the heart of the Wolds, servants 'stood out for higher wages' at the 1856 hirings and obtained them. Similarly, at Bridlington in the same year, wages were 'rather high for all descriptions of servants'.[81] The rise in wage levels was reflected in the improvement in servants' attire and conduct, according to a report in the *Hull Advertiser*:

> The conditions of the farm servants generally, from their outward appearance in dress etc., the conclusion would be that they are in comfortable and thriving circumstances especially when compared with their costume and general demeanour a few years since.[82]

One tactic employed by farmers to lessen their outgoings was to replace the older – and therefore more expensive – servants with less experienced, cheaper workers where possible. This meant that the market for female servants and teenage lads remained elastic across the mid-nineteenth century. At Driffield in 1869 it was recorded that 'much business was said to have been done in the hiring of under servants, both male and female', but fewer engagements with upper servants were reached, 'in consequence of their standing out for an advance of wages'.[83] Similarly, at Howden in 1868 'female servants hired well', with the 'demand for foremen and older class of farm labour less brisk than usual'.[84] The onset of agricultural depression in the mid-1870s caused servants to concede to reduced wages. On the Wolds, wages had been cut by £2 to £5 by the late 1870s. Similar reductions were recorded at Malton, while at Howden, in the south-west of the county, servants found themselves up to £8 worse off.[85] The *Driffield Times* summed up the current trends in its report on the 1878 fairs:

> More than usual interest is taken in the hirings this year on account of the depression in trade and its re-action on the agricultural interest, which has led the farmers to make a determined stand against the high wages paid for the last five or six years.[86]

The movement against high wages continued through the 1880s as farmers exercised prudence. Only by the last decade of the nineteenth century did fluctuations in wages begin to stabilise.

---

[81] *Hull Advertiser*, 15 November 1856.
[82] *Hull Advertiser*, 18 November 1854.
[83] *Hull Advertiser*, 19 November 1859.
[84] *Eastern Counties Herald*, 18 November 1868.
[85] *Eastern Counties Herald*, 20 November 1878; *Eastern Counties Herald*, 20 November 1879.
[86] *Driffield Times*, 16 November 1878.

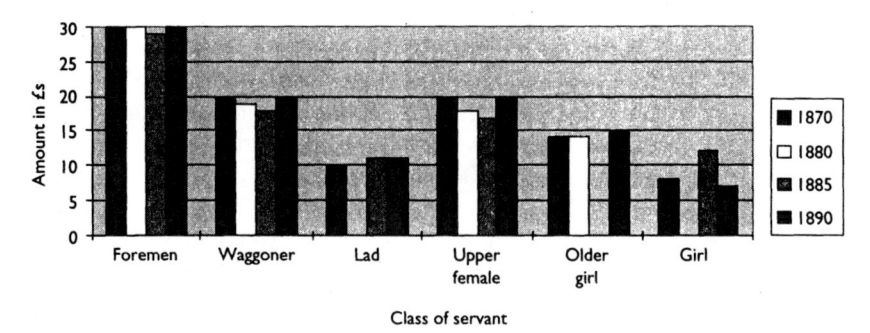

Figure 3.1 The movement in servants' wages at Driffield, 1870 to 1890

Sources: *Eastern Counties Herald*, 17 November 1870; *Driffield Times*, 13 November 1880; *Driffield Times*, 14 November 1885; *Driffield Times*, 15 November 1890. In some years not all information was available.

Local newspapers begin to record wages agreed at hiring fairs more systematically by the last quarter of the century, making it easier to plot the movement in servant wages over that period. Figure 3.1 represents annual wage levels of servants hired at Driffield between 1870 and 1890. The amounts shown are the highest servants were contracted for. Waggoners and upper female servants were most directly hit by the decrease in wages in the 1880s, although foremen also witnessed a slight reduction in income in 1885. By 1890 wages had risen to their pre-depression levels for these servants. The wage gap between female and male servants on the highest rung of the hierarchy remained stable across the late nineteenth century at 60 per cent. Middle-ranking female servants received from 60 to 75 per cent of their male equivalents' annual rate. Younger girls were paid yearly wages nearer to their male counterparts than any other class of female servants: the gap between men's and women's wages thus began to widen with age and experience. Lads and girls experienced an increase in annual wages in the 1880s. The appeal of cheap labour partly accounts for this trend, but by the 1880s another factor was coming into play: as the decade wore on farmers were finding it increasingly difficult to attract young women into farm service and offered higher wages as an inducement. A report in the *Beverley Guardian* in 1892 highlights this pattern:

> The scarcity during the past two or three years of good domestic servants is more than ever acutely emphasised this Martinmas, and at all the Yorkshire statutes mistresses are finding the greatest difficulty in procuring useful girls for general domestic work, although more liberal wages are being offered. The advertising columns of the county newspapers also bear out these facts, and certainly the state of the labour market in this direction seems undergoing a remarkable change.[87]

[87] *Beverley Guardian*, 26 November 1892.

By the late nineteenth century farmers in East Yorkshire were complaining that they could not find women servants to undertake certain kinds of farm labour traditionally associated with the female workforce. The most persistent lament was linked to the scarcity of women who would work in the dairy. This had been reported at Driffield in the late 1860s as a distinct new feature in the hirings. The result 'was the extensive requirement for girls who would undertake milking the cows, which the females are now beginning to think too slavish and dangerous a duty to be performed by them'.[88] This pattern was routinely noted by the 1870s: at Hedon in 1874, for example, milkmaids were 'in great demand, the supply being far short of previous years'.[89] The dearth of dairymaids induced farmers on the Wolds to turn the work of the milkmaid over to a young male servant. This, in turn, had led the women to 'make a stand against carrying the milking pail in the future'.[90]

These reports are interesting for a number of reasons, highlighting significant changes taking place in the nature of female farm service in East Yorkshire. First, it is suggested in some instances that farmers were increasingly willing to substitute the labour of women with that of young lads. It may have been that farmers acted to push troublesome female servants out of the dairy (and other outdoor work), thereby promoting a more segregated workforce on the farm, with women servants increasingly confined to indoor, domestic labour and men monopolising outdoor, agricultural work.[91] The extract from the *Beverley Guardian* quoted above attests to this transformation, clearly stating that young women were sought as 'good domestic servants' for 'general domestic work' in the farmhouse. Moses argues that this process helped facilitate the acceptance by women servants of segregated hirings at the Martinmas fairs, as indoor hirings mirrored the 'already established trend towards gender segregation within the farm service labour force'.[92] But the newspaper accounts also suggest that women were by no means passive bystanders in this process of change. Farmers were reacting to the refusal of female servants to perform certain tasks on the farm in the 1860s and 1870s. By the 1880s women were showing an unwillingness to be hired into yearly rural service at all. Most county newspapers are witness to this trend. In Bridlington in 1887, it was reported that 'there was a falling off in the attendance of females' at the hiring fair; at Malton in the same year, 'Female servants were very scarce. There were more employers than servants amongst the females', and at Market Weighton in 1889, 'the streets were

---

[88] *Eastern Counties Herald*, 18 November 1869.
[89] *Eastern Counties Herald*, 19 November 1874.
[90] *Eastern Counties Herald*, 18 November 1869.
[91] Higgs suggests that farm service for women as a whole was not declining but rather 'the use of space on the farm changed' with the farmhouse increasingly 'a space dominated by the work of women'. Higgs, 'Occupational censuses and the agricultural workforce', p. 708.
[92] Moses, 'Rude and rustic', p. 168.

crowded with male servants, but the attendance of female servants was very small... hiring among them was virtually at a standstill'.[93] The necessity of attending the hiring fairs had decreased by the 1880s: those women who were looking for a place of service on a farm increasingly used newspaper advertisements and registration offices to find positions prior to the Martinmas fairs. However, many women were turning their backs on farm service.

As farm servants were unmarried, it is highly unlikely that these women were dropping out of the labour market altogether in the late nineteenth century. Instead, they may have been increasingly attracted to domestic service in local towns. Richard Jefferies noted the restlessness of rural girls in service at this time:

> The girls are not nearly so tractable as formerly – they are fully aware of their own value and put it extremely high.... Most of them that are worth anything never rest till they reach the towns, and take service in the villas of the wealthy suburban residents.[94]

Census figures indicate that the movement from farm to domestic service was drastic. Between 1851 and 1871 the number of female farm servants in East Yorkshire declined by some 80 per cent, while those recorded as domestic servants shot up by 95 per cent between 1861 and 1891. As we have seen, problems over classification challenge the validity of this data, but population statistics reinforce the notion of widespread rural to urban migration among the East Riding's female population in the late nineteenth century. Between 1871 and 1891, the number of women (aged 15 years and over) residing in Bridlington and Beverley increased by 22 per cent and 19 per cent respectively. In both towns the expansion of young women in the age group 15 to 19 was particularly noticeable: 26 per cent in Bridlington and 24 per cent in Beverley. In the same period, the male population aged 15 and over increased by only 4 per cent in Bridlington and 11 per cent in Beverley. If we take two rural districts over the corresponding period, the movement of women from country to town becomes evident. Patrington and Howden witnessed a decline in their female populations of 5 per cent and 8 per cent (aged 15 and over).[95]

So, as farmers acted to replace women servants in some aspects of farmwork, women themselves were moving away from farm service altogether.

---

[93] *Driffield Times*, 15 November 1887; *Driffield Times*, 18 November 1876; *Beverley Guardian*, 16 November 1889.
[94] Richard Jefferies, *Hodge and His Masters*, 1st edn 1880 (Stroud, 1992), p. 185.
[95] Census Reports of Great Britain: Population Tables, PP 1871, LXXI, vol. 3 (1873); PP 1881, LXXX, Ages, Condition as to Marriage, Occupations and Birthplaces, vol. 3 (1883); PP 1891, CVI, Ages, Condition as to Marriage, Occupations and Birthplaces, vol. 3 (1893–4). See also Susan Neave and Stephen Ellis, eds, *An Historical Atlas of East Yorkshire* (Hull, 1996), pp. 46–9.

FEMALE FARM SERVANTS

Were women in East Yorkshire becoming conscious of the disreputable reputation middle-class commentators attached to farm service? Were they attracted to domestic service because it was seen as more respectable and becoming for young women? Lack of firsthand accounts from the county means that we can only speculate on such issues. However, this seems to have been the case in other parts of the country. At Lark Rise, in late nineteenth-century Oxfordshire, Flora Thompson claims that female farm servants were viewed by villagers as 'a class apart' and mothers were 'ambitious for their daughters' to enter domestic service in respectable country and town houses.[96] The decline of the bondager system in late nineteenth-century Northumberland is also partly attributable to women's increasing distaste for the work, according to Jane Long. She argues that the resistance of hinds to hire bondagers, and a general exodus of labourers from country to town were significant factors in weakening the institution of hiring bondagers. But women's acceptance of codes of femininity also 'played a role in the decline of bondage work', with 'some women who might previously have "naturally" worked the bondage were instead employed in country towns, meeting the increased demand for servants and shop assistants'.[97]

Farm service in East Yorkshire was not a static institution. It successfully adapted to fulfil the demands of the intensive arable farming of the region. Women formed an important component of the farm service labour force, although their productive role as servants is often overlooked. For most of the nineteenth century farm service served an important function in providing young, unmarried women with a relatively secure and sometimes well-paid employment opportunity. Evidence suggests that by the last quarter of the century girls and women were increasingly turning their backs on this option. But for women who lived in southern England, this choice probably did not exist after the end of the Napoleonic Wars. There, women were forced to search for work in the often saturated agricultural day labour market. Their success in procuring a living varied from region to region, and sometimes from farm to farm. Chapter 4 will consider the position of women in the agricultural day labour force.

---

[96] Flora Thompson, *Lark Rise to Candleford*, 1st edn 1939 (Harmondsworth, 1984), p. 157.
[97] Long, *Conversations in Cold Rooms*, p. 109.

4

Women in the agricultural labour market

Female day labourers

The position occupied by women workers in the nineteenth-century agricultural day labour force in England is the focus of this chapter. This is a remarkably complex issue. An appreciation of local and regional distinctions in farming systems and hiring patterns, and how these changed over the century, are essential to understanding the level of women's involvement in agriculture. But we also have to be mindful of a variety of more intangible ideological and lifecycle factors, and assess how these also affected women's access to work. Judging the relationship between all these components – and measuring their relative importance – is no easy matter. Attempting to do this for the whole of England over a significant length of time is perhaps over-ambitious. Yet it is well overdue. We saw in Chapter 1 that there is comparatively little published research on women's employment as agricultural day labourers in the nineteenth-century English countryside. For many historians, the publication of Keith Snell's highly influential study of agricultural seasonal change and women's work offered a neat solution to the issue. Recent research has suggested that this is far from correct and there is still much that remains inconclusive about the subject. This chapter aims to do a number of things. By bringing together previous analyses of women's agricultural employment and introducing new research, an overview of the continuities and changes in female participation as day labourers in the nineteenth-century English agricultural workforce will be attempted. The ways in which agricultural labour was gender divided with regard both to tasks performed and wages received will then be explored. An assessment of the impact of lifecycle changes on women's agricultural labour in the nineteenth century will conclude the chapter.

Women in the agricultural day labour force, 1800 to 1850

Two accounts of women's employment as agricultural day labourers in the early nineteenth century dominate the literature. The chronologies posited by Pinchbeck and Snell have been outlined in Chapter 1, but the main themes are worth reiterating here. Pinchbeck identified two peaks in the employment of female day labourers on English farms. The first, during the French Wars, was linked to agrarian change and male labour shortages. The second, in the 1830s and 1840s, was associated with economic necessity (for both rural labouring families and farmers). Snell argues for a decline in women's agricultural labour over the first half of the nineteenth century in south-eastern England. This was an extension of a process begun in the middle decades of the previous century, and meant that women's work in nineteenth-century agriculture was relegated to a number of seasonally specific tasks. Pinchbeck based her arguments on an analysis of printed sources, while Snell used settlement examinations for his main evidence. As we have seen, both sets of sources have significant problems and may not be ideal in identifying trends in women's agricultural day labour. By using farm labour and wage books it is possible to avoid the disadvantages associated with the other types of evidence, permitting a more accurate measurement of the extent of women's involvement in the agricultural workforce. Looking at the period 1800 to 1850 first, several questions can be addressed which will enable a thorough examination of the complexity of the issue. Do the patterns that emanate from farm records concur with those uncovered by Pinchbeck? Is Snell correct to claim a prolonged diminution in women's agricultural labour in the south-east region? What was happening in other regions of the country? Can we detect clear regional patterns of women's work in England?

The first investigation of labour trends is from Home Farm at Earsham in Norfolk.[1] In 1807, of the total number of days worked by male, female and child day labourers for the year, women performed a quarter of these. Eighteen per cent of work days may be attributed to children and 57 per cent to male labourers. The employment of women day labourers was therefore fairly substantial. Can we attribute this sizeable female presence to the lack of male workers during the war years as Pinchbeck's account claims? Unfortunately, records for the farm do not survive to enable us to compare the employment of female day labourers in the early 1800s to that in the period before the 1790s. However, analysis of records from other regions in East Anglia suggests that, contrary to Pinchbeck's view, there was not a noticeable expansion of the female day labour force at this time. In Essex, Pamela Sharpe argues that while some farm accounts reveal a rise in the employment of women in the early war years, farmers were keen to secure the supply of male workers through the use of contract labour. This ensured

---

[1] Norfolk Record Office (hereafter NRO), MEA 3/27–51, farm accounts of Meade of Earsham, 1807 to 1838. The years 1807, 1827 and 1837 were chosen as random samples from the accounts. During the 1810s the surviving accounts are very sketchy and could not be transcribed effectively. Earsham is situated on the Suffolk border, one mile from Bungay. Dominant crops in the parish were wheat, barley and beans.

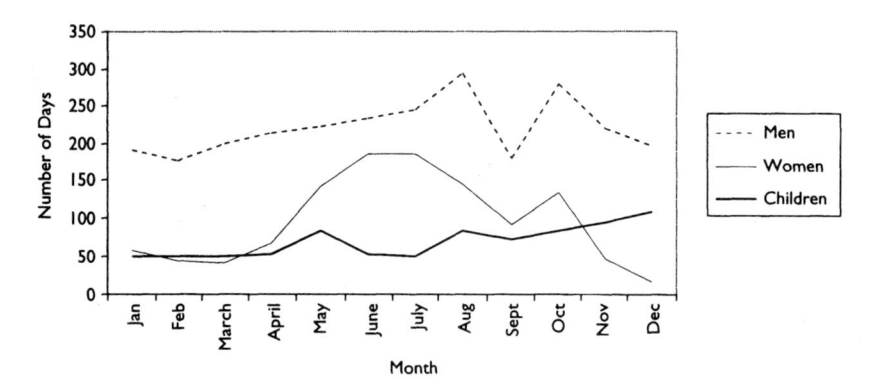

Figure 4.1 Days worked by male, female and child labourers on Earsham Home Farm, Norfolk in 1807
Source: NRO, MEA 3/27.

that the sexual division of agricultural labour remained steadfast: men were available to complete tasks such as ploughing and harvesting whereas women continued to be engaged for jobs conventionally characterised as 'women's work'.[2]

This gender-specific pattern of farm labour was replicated at Earsham and is shown in Figure 4.1. Women's labour was most in demand in the springtime for weeding and hoeing, in July for haymaking and to a slightly lesser extent in the corn harvest. Of the women employed, a number were engaged nearly all year round. Cress Read worked 238¾ days in 1807, earning over £8 for her labours. Letty Read worked 215½ days for £7, Sarah Kerry worked 212 days for £7 3s 4d and Mary Cooper's 166½ days earned her £5 13s. Other women were employed on a more casual basis between May and October. Children's employment remained fairly constant across the year; in fact two teenage lads worked all year round tending cattle and assisting with the horses. In addition, a number of younger boys worked on seasonal tasks such as crow scaring and cleaning the farmyard, particularly in the winter months. The employment of female children on this farm was rare. Male workers were also hired by the day and on piece-work (including the harvest).[3] None of these men found constant year-round employment, although a number of them – Ben Fickling, William Goldsmith, William Read, John Henry, John Read, John Flowerdew and John Norman – worked for over 250 days in 1807. It is impossible to know whether these men worked for other farmers in

---

[2] Pamela Sharpe, *Adapting to Capitalism: Working Women in the English Economy, 1700–1850* (Basingstoke, 1996), p. 86.

[3] Because harvest work was paid by the piece, this may account for the dips in recorded days worked for men and women in September.

FEMALE DAY LABOURERS

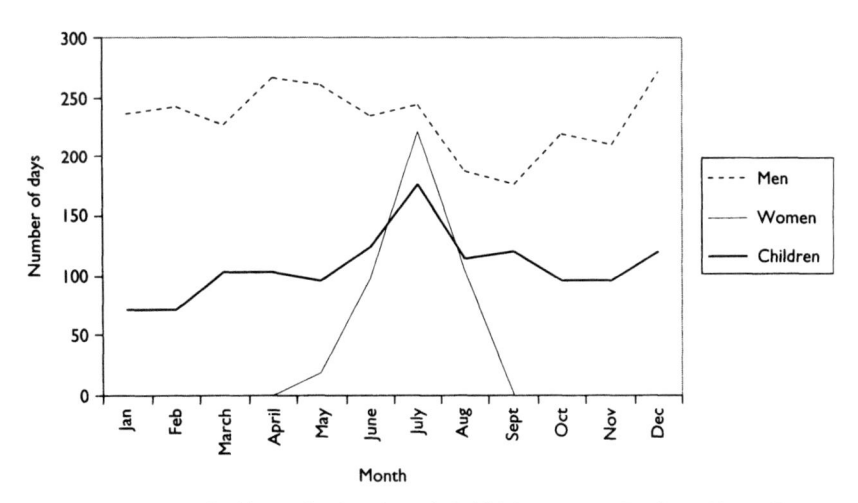

Figure 4.2 Days worked by male, female and child labourers on Earsham Home Farm in 1837
Source: NRO, MEA 3/51

the neighbourhood, or were unemployed, when they were absent from the Earsham accounts. But as Susanna Wade Martins and Tom Williamson argue, such gaps in the records suggest 'at the very least a degree of insecurity'.[4] Two men were also hired for fifty-one weeks and paid board wages, confirming the changes taking place in farm service in southern England in the early nineteenth century.

Although these accounts cannot offer firm evidence for changes in the female day labour market during the Napoleonic Wars, they do present interesting insights into the post-war agricultural workforce in south-east Norfolk. By the late 1820s significant changes in the employment of female and child workers are apparent at Earsham. In 1827 women account for 15 per cent of the total days worked in the year – a 10 per cent decrease over twenty years. Conversely, the employment of children has increased: they worked just under one-third of the total labour days in 1827. The use of male day labourers remained similar to that in 1807. If we look at the accounts for 1837, we find the employment of women had declined further. In that year, women labourers worked 10 per cent of total labour days, men worked 63 per cent and children 27 per cent. Women's total labour participation was not only diminishing, it was also becoming increasingly seasonally specific by the 1830s. This trend can be seen in Figure 4.2. In 1837 female labourers were present in the fields from May to August for weeding, stone-picking,

---

[4] Susanna Wade Martins and Tom Williamson, 'Labour and improvement: Agricultural change in East Anglia, c.1750–1870', *Labour History Review*, 62, 3 (1997), pp. 275–95 (p. 282).

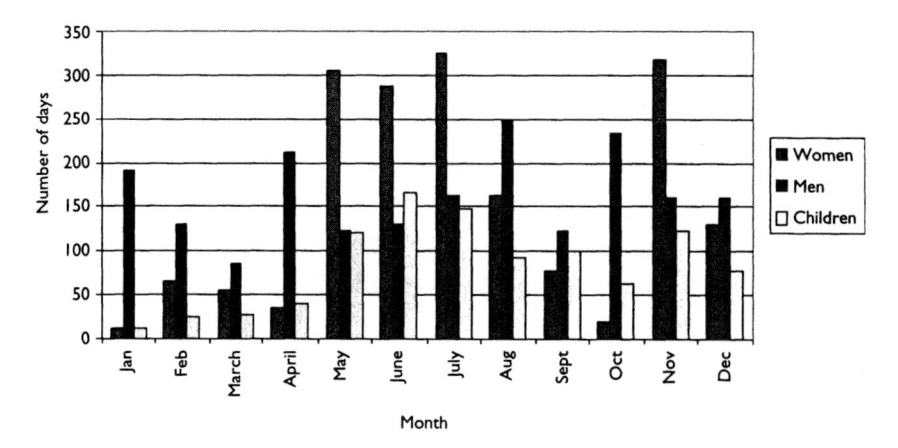

Figure 4.3 Days worked by male, female and child day labourers on Saltmarshe Home Farm, East Yorkshire in 1820

Source: ERRO, DDSA, 1219/1; DDSA 1203/3

haymaking and for just a few days in corn harvesting. The main concentration of their work lay in June and July, and from September to March women found no work at all on the farm. So, on Earsham Home Farm, women's employment shrank appreciably after the French Wars, while that of young lads rose proportionally. There is little evidence to indicate that women farmworkers became more common after the implementation of the New Poor Law, although we do not know the composition of the workforce after the late 1830s. This analysis largely corroborates the Snell thesis: at Earsham women's agricultural labour became progressively seasonal and marginal in the first three decades of the nineteenth century.

Moving away from south-eastern England, is a reduction in the female day labour force also apparent in other arable regions? Snell claims that although 'regional differences certainly existed, they should not be overstressed'. The census of 1841 revealed that women constituted less than 4 per cent of the agricultural workforce, 'suggesting that the argument for significant diminution of female labour having already taken place by the early nineteenth century has a wider applicability'.[5] Very detailed accounts of the workforce on Saltmarshe Home Farm in East Yorkshire enable us to explore this contention. In 1820 women performed 38 per cent of the total labour days recorded. Male labourers account for 41 per cent of days worked and children 21 per cent. Numerous women were engaged on a casual basis in certain seasons: May, June and July for weeding, hoeing and haymaking, and November and December for potato planting and harvesting represent

---

[5] K.D.M. Snell, *Annals of the Labouring Poor: Social Change and Agrarian England, 1660–1900* (Cambridge, 1985), p. 57.

peaks in the employment of casual female workers (Figure 4.3).[6] Women were also employed on the specialised task of flax-pulling which took place in late August and early September. Most female labourers in 1820 worked for less than 100 days a year, but there were exceptions: Hannah Tuke worked 158½ days for £6 14s, Sarah Jewitt 137 days for £5 10s 1d and Mary Baxter for 130 days, earning £5 14s 10½d. Among the child labourers, boys were engaged more consistently, although girls were employed for a considerable number of days between May and August: Ruth Longfield, Hannah Robenson and Hannah Thompson worked between sixty-eight and ninety days each. Figure 4.3 implies that at certain times of the year more women and children were employed at Saltmarshe Home Farm than male day labourers. This is somewhat misleading. Men were also widely engaged on piece-work operations (including the harvest). The days spent on such tasks are not recorded separately in the accounts and therefore the total days worked by men are seriously underestimated in the graph. This discrepancy may also disguise other labour that women (and children) performed over the year, particularly if they worked in the harvest fields with their families.[7]

The accounts at Saltmarshe for 1840 show little change in the scale of female employment. Women carried out 35 per cent of the total labour days for the year. Children's work increased, seemingly at the expense of men. Thirty-four per cent of days worked can be ascribed to men in 1840, 31 per cent to child workers, although the labour of men is again significantly under-represented. Figure 4.4 shows that women's labour was still in demand for weeding, hoeing and haymaking, but in 1840 they were also more consistently employed across the winter months. The increasing cultivation of potatoes may account for this.[8] Six women (twice the number in 1820) were recorded as working for 100 days or more. Nine women worked between fifty and 100 days, while the names of another forty-three women appear in the accounts on a more casual basis. Evidence from Saltmarshe does not signify an increase in female day labourers after 1834 but neither does it fall off. Women were an integral component of the workforce in 1820 and remained

---

[6] East Riding Record Office (hereafter ERRO), DDSA 1219/1–2, Women's labour journals, Saltmarshe, 1818 to 1822 and 1835 to 1841; DDSA 1203/1–6 Farming receipts and expenses, Saltmarshe, 1801 to 1846. The latter includes the labour of men only. Child labour is included in the women's accounts. The farm, covering 311 acres, was part of the estate of Philip Saltmarshe who owned land in Saltmarshe, Laxton and Kilpin totalling 2700 acres.

[7] Saltmarshe Home Farm also employed four to five male servants and one or two female servants in the nineteenth century, hired by the year. Their presence would have an impact on how many day labourers were needed across the year.

[8] This region of East Yorkshire became renowned for its potato cultivation in the early nineteenth century. Saltmarshe was situated on the banks of the River Ouse and vessel loads of the crop were transported by water from the village to markets in the south. ERRO, DDSA, 1198, Saltmarshe, MSS. History of the village and family written in 1894.

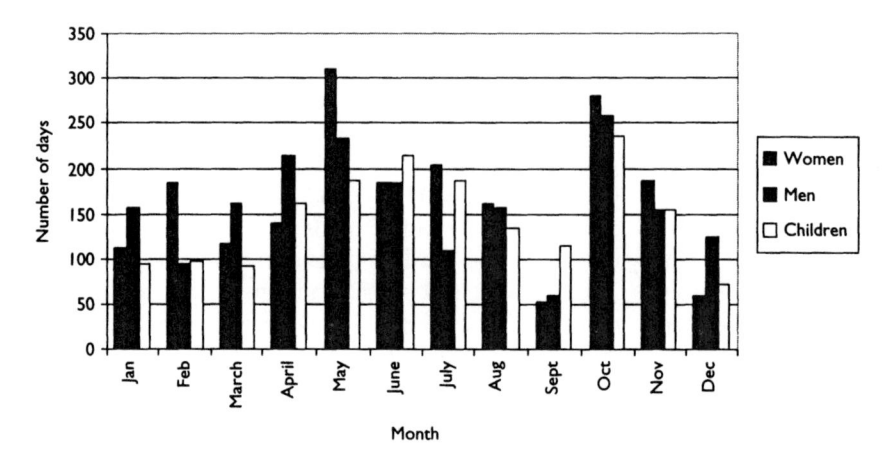

Figure 4.4 Days worked by male, female and child day labourers on Saltmarshe Home Farm in 1840

Source: ERRO, DDSA 1219/2; DDSA 1203/3

so in 1840. Away from the pure corn lands of south-east England, the marginalisation of women agricultural day labourers was far from complete by the mid-nineteenth century.

Still staying in the arable east, but shifting the focus to the far north of England, Judy Gielgud's research on Northumberland and Cumbria substantiates this model of women's employment. Labour books from Seaton Delavel in late eighteenth-century Northumberland show women working considerable, but seasonal, days on the farm. In the winter months (October to April) three or four women worked for two or three days a fortnight. Springtime saw the number of women employed increase, culminating in the August harvest, where the ratio of male to female labourers was 19:71.[9] By the early nineteenth century, changes in crop cultivation – particularly the move to increased potato growing – meant women labourers were more regularly employed. This corresponds to the pattern at Saltmarshe Home Farm in East Yorkshire. Using the accounts from Hutton John Farm (near Penrith), Gielgud traces the transition to year-round employment for women in the 1830s, highlighting the case of Mary Bell, who worked 130½ days from May 1837 to April 1838. By 1840 there were three women regularly employed on this farm for the whole year. They did not work continuously – January and February provided the least amount of labour – but Gielgud argues that as male labourers 'also worked episodically', the contribution of females 'should not really be categorised as "part-time" as is so often the

---

[9] Judy Gielgud, 'Nineteenth-century farm women in Northumberland and Cumbria: The neglected workforce' (D.Phil. thesis, University of Sussex, 1992), pp. 155–8.

case'.[10] Therefore, the decisive factor that enlarged women's day labour in the 1830s and 1840s in this region was agricultural (new crops); the impact of the New Poor Law was secondary.[11]

The Pinchbeck case for an advance in the employment of women in agricultural day labour over the late eighteenth century can also be made for certain areas of western England. Helen Speechley's analysis of farm records from Dunster Castle and Nettlecombe Barton in Somerset confirms this contention. The percentage of days worked by female labourers at Dunster Castle, for example, increased from 27 per cent in the 1770s, to 42 per cent in 1794 to 1795.[12] Male labour shortages during the early years of the French Wars probably do not explain this rise. The more likely reason, Speechley contends, is linked to 'increased arable output and the more extensive cultivation of new crops'.[13] The employment of female labourers in the county begins to change over the first decades of the nineteenth century. On the Poulett estate, the proportion of total labour days worked by women fell between 1810 and 1818 from 36 per cent to 27 per cent. Similarly, at Dunster the days worked by women dropped between 1801 and 1803 and 1836 and 1839 from 35 per cent to 26 per cent of total work days. This offers evidence for the shrinkage of the female labour force during the post-war agricultural depression. Figures from Dunster for the late 1840s reveal a slight rise in the employment of women: during the period 1846 to 1849 women were working on average 29 per cent of labour days on the farm. Although these findings indicate a decline in the female day labour force from the high point of the 1790s, it may be argued that women in Somerset still constituted a high proportion of the agricultural workforce until the mid-nineteenth century.

Individual farm accounts from northern and western England show women were a core component of the agricultural day labour force in the first half of the nineteenth century. This line of argument should not be pushed too far however. In a different region of Yorkshire, Joyce Burnette found clear evidence for a diminution in female day labour over the late eighteenth and early nineteenth centuries. Her analysis of Oakes Farm, near Sheffield, shows that women were mostly casual labourers (working less than sixty days a year), and their employment centred on the hay harvest. Accounts survive for two periods: 1772 to 1775 and 1831 to 1845. In the 1770s, women represent 18 per cent of days worked. By the later period they account for just 6 per cent of labour days.[14] Although it is not possible to date the beginning of the

---

[10] Ibid., p. 173.
[11] Ibid., p. 177.
[12] Helen V. Speechley, 'Female and child agricultural day labourers in Somerset, c.1685–1870' (Ph.D. thesis, University of Exeter, 1999), p. 63.
[13] Speechley, 'Female and child agricultural day labourers', p. 64.
[14] Joyce Burnette, 'Labourers at the Oakes. Changes in the demand for female daylabourers at a farm near Sheffield during the Agricultural Revolution', *Journal of Economic History*, LIX (1999), pp. 41–67 (pp. 55–6).

decline, Burnette links the fall-off in women's work to changes in the farm's labour demands. 'The changes in husbandry which followed enclosure', she maintains, 'both increased the demand for men in the spring and decreased the demand for women during hay-making.'[15]

What conclusions may we draw from the material outlined in this section? The picture presented of female participation in the agricultural labour force in the first fifty years or so of the nineteenth century is not straightforward. Although they offer a more reliable indication of the agrarian workforce than other sources, there are still a number of problems related to the evidence from farm books. First, where female (and male) labourers are missing from the accounts at some periods in the farming year, it is not possible to ascertain how far they moved between local farms looking for work. Only the survival of records from a number of adjacent farms would resolve this issue. Second, the data points from the various farms are not homogenous. Surviving accounts do not necessarily correspond in terms of the size and type of farm, or in the sequence of years for which labour is recorded. In addition, some of the records analysed come from home farms. Although the general pattern of farming on these enterprises would reflect farming conditions in the locality, the type and amount of labour engaged on home farms (with their access to capital and technical expertise) may have differed considerably from other tenant farms and smaller concerns.[16]

The third major problem concerns regional differences in farming operations. The crops grown on a farm, the extent of pastoral land and the degree of animal husbandry varied across the English farming regions. These factors determined the size and composition of the labour force. The majority of the farms examined here concentrated on arable production, including those in Somerset. Of these arable enterprises, only the farm in Norfolk reveals a significant and unbroken decline in the employment of female day workers in the first half of the nineteenth century, reinforcing the Snell thesis for south-eastern England. In East Yorkshire and Cumbria, the adoption of widescale cultivation of potatoes and other root crops fostered more regular work for women. The farm investigated by Burnette, on the other hand, was largely concerned with animal production. As a pasture farm, the hay harvest was the key operation in the annual calendar and the demand for female labour outside of this peak time was relatively small. Therefore the discrepancies found in the size of the female workforce in England between 1800 and 1850 have to be understood in relation to the circumstances of individual farms: their size, location and output. This helps us to make sense of the different patterns of labour suggested by Pinchbeck and Snell. Their models of change fit certain farms from certain areas and not others. Generalisations have to be tempered by recognition of the overriding importance of region.

[15] Ibid., p. 65.
[16] R. J. Colyer, 'The use of estate home farm accounts as sources for nineteenth-century agricultural history', *The Local Historian*, 11 (1975), pp. 406–13 (pp. 407–8).

Women's work in agricultural gangs

A crucial element in Pinchbeck's account of women's work in early nineteenth-century agriculture focuses on the extension of the gang system of labour in eastern England after the mid-1830s. In areas such as Norfolk, Lincolnshire and Cambridgeshire, where 'a great deal of weeding and light labour was required', Pinchbeck maintains that 'almost all the work was done by the gangs which grew up naturally in the open villages'.[17] This view has endured. The gang system has been represented by historians such as Alun Howkins as a widespread form of organised labour that drew heavily on a surplus of cheap child and female labour across the eastern counties.[18] Other historians have been more cautious, suggesting that the system was specific to certain areas of the east.[19] Either way, few studies of the nineteenth-century agrarian workforce fail to mention the existence of gang labour. Despite this awareness of the existence of gangs, no research has hitherto examined the scale, structure and functions of the system in any detail. It is therefore worth assessing the role of gangs, and women's involvement in them, in isolation from farmwork in general. In fact, farm records throw little light upon this question, as farmers who employed gangs tended to note only the final payment for the task given to the gangmaster. Thus the individual women and children engaged in the work remain obscure in the written records. However, despite the obvious problems associated with nineteenth-century government reports, some knowledge of the scale and composition of gangs may be gained from this evidence. Because we have already looked at women's agricultural work on Norfolk farms, I have chosen to concentrate on the operation of the gang system in that county. The applicability of the arguments may also be extended to other eastern counties where gangs were established.[20]

According to contemporary accounts agricultural gangs in nineteenth-century Norfolk fell into two categories: public and private. The public gang system originated in the Norfolk parish of Castle Acre in the mid 1820s.[21] It

---

[17] Ivy Pinchbeck, *Women Workers and the Industrial Revolution, 1750–1850*, 1st edn 1930 (London, 1981), p. 87.
[18] Alun Howkins, *Reshaping Rural England: A Social History, 1850–1925* (London, 1991), p. 106. See also Katrina Honeyman, *Women, Gender and Industrialisation in England, 1700–1870* (Basingstoke, 2000), p. 79, for a restatement of the Pinchbeck view.
[19] See Jennie Kitteringham, 'Country work girls in nineteenth-century England', in Raphael Samuel, ed., *Village Life and Labour* (London, 1975), pp. 73–138 (p. 98); G. E. Mingay, *A Social History of the English Countryside* (London, 1990), p. 102.
[20] A longer version of this section may be found in Nicola Verdon, 'The employment of women and children in agriculture: A reassessment of agricultural gangs in nineteenth-century Norfolk', *Agricultural History Review*, 49 (2001), pp. 41–55.
[21] John Todd, overseer of a gang, stated in the 1843 Royal Commission that the system had been running for seventeen years. PP 1843, XII, Reports of Special Assistant

was essentially a system of subcontracting between farmers and gangmasters. Farmers with a particular piece of work to be done which demanded a large number of labourers would contract a gangmaster to carry out the work for an agreed sum of money. The gangmaster would then employ sufficient numbers of women and children to perform the task, working in gangs and paid at a daily rate. Private gangs, which were defined in the 1860s as 'a group of children, young persons and women in a farmer's own employ, and superintended by one of his own labourers', existed alongside the public gang system in Norfolk.[22] It was the public gang system which aroused most contention in the mid-nineteenth century however. It was usually considered to be exploitative, with farmers and gangmasters benefiting at the expense of workers. Legislation was directed only against the public gang system. Numbers employed in public gangs typically totalled around twenty, while private companies tended to be smaller.[23] Standard jobs performed by both public and private gangs varied according to the season but consisted principally of three main tasks: the cleaning of land by weeding and stone-picking, the planting and then the harvesting of root crops such as turnips, potatoes and mangolds. Hours of work were generally 8 a.m. until 5 p.m., with an hour's break in the middle of the day, although working days were shorter in winter. Bands of workers travelled to their work on foot, often covering distances of up to eight miles each way. Occasionally the farmer would provide a cart for excessive distances or gangs would stay overnight in a barn, although both were exceptional practices. Remuneration for women gang members was typically 8d or 9d a day in the mid-nineteenth century. Children normally received 3d or 4d a day. Labourers employed in the Norfolk gang system thus obtained day wages on piece-work tasks, forgoing the increased profits usually associated with the latter.[24] Moreover, if bad weather curtailed the day's work, labourers were not paid for their time.

Why did this system develop in Norfolk? Contemporary accounts posit two reasons. The role played by village settlement patterns in encouraging gang labour is highlighted by many commentators. Stephen Denison, who reported on Norfolk, Suffolk and Lincolnshire for the Report on the Employment of Women and Children in Agriculture in 1843, drew attention to the 'open' and 'close' parish system in Norfolk. He uses the example of Castle Acre as a case study. Castle Acre, an 'open' parish, was surrounded by 'close' villages, where cottage building and parish settlements were closely

---

Commissioners on the Employment of Women and Children in Agriculture. Report by Stephen Denison on the counties of Norfolk, Suffolk and Lincoln, p. 276. That date – 1826 – is the one Pinchbeck uses in her analysis. Pinchbeck, *Women Workers*, p. 87.

[22] PP 1867–8, XVII, First Report from the Commissioners on the Employment of Children, Young Persons and Women in Agriculture. Report by Revd James Fraser on Norfolk, Essex, Sussex, Gloucester and parts of Suffolk, p. 11.

[23] The term 'company' was used interchangeably with 'gang' by contemporaries.

[24] PP 1843, XII, Report by Denison, p. 276.

controlled by landowners. Thus Castle Acre became 'overstocked with inhabitants that do not properly belong to it', while adjoining parishes did not accommodate enough residents to cultivate the soil.[25] According to Denison, Castle Acre was 'the most miserable rural parish I ever saw'.[26] Later nineteenth-century reporters drew on this argument, as have historians such as Pinchbeck.[27] But the relevance of this argument has been questioned recently. Sarah Banks' analysis of mid-nineteenth-century population patterns suggests that Castle Acre's burgeoning population was caused by low levels of out-migration from the parish, not an influx of people from neighbouring villages. Opportunities to work in local crafts and trades, as well as agriculture, sustained Castle Acre's population.[28] A more plausible alternative explanation for the growing importance of gangs centres on local farming patterns. Farmers, landowners and other experts interviewed by Denison in 1843 often mention improved agricultural techniques and widespread cultivation of root crops (especially turnips) as a causal link.[29] As these features were adopted more widely during the mid-Victorian agricultural boom, the seasonal demands for gang labour grew. Pinchbeck argues that although the gang system was condemned in 1843 for its moral and physical dangers, it continued unrestricted as both local farmers and labouring families found gangs economically attractive.[30]

It was not until the 1860s that agricultural gangs emerged as a national scandal. By this time the rural woman worker was being represented as a social problem. Women who participated in gang labour in eastern England were especially vilified as being a disgrace to the female sex. We saw in Chapter 2 that disquiet over the public gang system led Lord Shaftesbury to extend the remit of the existing Children's Employment Commission to investigate organised gangs in eastern England. The publication in 1867 of its Sixth Report fuelled sensational reporting. The parliamentary investigators in 1867 were clearly shocked that exploitative systems of labour were not

---

[25] Ibid., p. 221.
[26] Ibid., p. 226.
[27] See e.g. PP 1867, XVI, Sixth Report of the Children's Employment Commission. Summary Report by H. S. Tremenheere and E. C. Tufnell, p. xxi; PP 1867–8, XVII, Report by Fraser, p. 95. Pinchbeck, *Women Workers*, p. 87; Kitteringham, 'Country work girls', p. 98.
[28] Sarah Banks, 'Nineteenth-century scandal or twentieth-century model? A new look at "open" and "close" parishes', *Economic History Review*, XLI (1988), pp. 51–73 (pp. 68–70).
[29] See e.g. PP 1843, XII, Report by Denison, p. 277. Turnips were by far the most dominant root crop grown in the Freebridge Union where Castle Acre was situated. In 1854 they made up 87 per cent of all root crops grown in the region. Susanna Wade Martins, *A Great Estate at Work. The Holkham Estate and its Inhabitants in the Nineteenth Century* (Cambridge, 1980), p. 265.
[30] Pinchbeck, *Women Workers*, pp. 87–8.

unique to urban, industrial manufacture. They were particularly struck by the similarities between the operation of the gang system and other forms of subcontracting in urban trades. This view is most clearly expressed by an anonymous correspondent to the *Quarterly Review*:

> The report is one of the most painful which it has been our duty to pursue, for it proves to distraction that the social evils which were long supposed to be peculiar to manufactures exist in an even more aggravated form in connection with the cultivation of the soil. Great numbers of children, young persons and women are, it appears, employed in companies or 'gangs' in certain counties which have acquired an odious notoriety for one of the most flagrant abuses which has ever disgraced a civilised land.[31]

The recommendations set down to regulate gangs in the Sixth Report formed the core of the 1867 Gangs Act. The age of children working in gangs and the distance they were allowed to travel to work were targeted, and a system of licensing for male and female gangmasters was instigated. This was the only government legislation aimed specifically at curtailing the agricultural employment of women and children in the nineteenth century (although it was only public gangs that were addressed). In addition to the 1867 Act, the government appointed the Royal Commission on the Employment of Children, Young Persons and Women in Agriculture to investigate the issue on a nation-wide footing. It is from these two reports of the late 1860s that the most complete evidence on the nature and extent of ganging in nineteenth-century Norfolk is found.

Mr White and Mr Longe were instructed to investigate the incidence of ganging in the eastern counties by the Children's Employment Commission in 1867. Across the whole district they found the total number of labourers employed in public gangs to be between 6000 and 7000 persons.[32] In Mr White's district – covering Norfolk, Suffolk, Nottinghamshire and parts of Northamptonshire and Cambridgeshire – the total number was estimated at 3017.[33] In Norfolk itself twenty-six parishes returned circulars, indicting that 956 people worked in public gangs in that county.[34] The Commission acknowledged that this figure was only an approximate calculation and would be 'subject to considerable variations at different periods of the year'.[35] Moreover, as only twenty-six parishes in Norfolk returned data, the figure is not an approximation of the total number of gang labourers across the whole county. However, the returns do begin to indicate the regional distribution

---

[31] Anon, 'Agricultural gangs', *Quarterly Review*, 123 (1867), pp. 173–90 (p. 174).
[32] PP 1867, XVI, Summary Report, p. xxiii.
[33] Ibid., p. x.
[34] Ibid., p. ix.
[35] Ibid.

of gangs: those parishes with a concentration of gang labour were situated in the west of the county, with the addition of some gangs operating around Wymondham and Diss. Detailed responses from a good number of these twenty-six parishes also offer information on the age and sex of those employed. Three-fifths of the gang members were female workers. Of these, 32 per cent were aged between 7 and 13 years, 30 per cent were between the ages of 13 and 18, and just under 40 per cent were 18 years old and above. Of the women aged over 18, the majority (71 per cent) were married. The bulk of males employed (87 per cent) were boys and lads aged between 7 and 18, with only thirty-seven men over 18 working in gangs. Only two children under 7 years of age – one male and one female – were recorded.[36]

Some tentative conclusions may be drawn from these data, placing the composition of public gangs in an interesting perspective. First, White's Report indicates that very young children were rarely employed in Norfolk gangs in the mid-nineteenth century. The exploitation of children under 7 years old was extremely rare. Second, it appears that only around two-fifths of public gang members in Norfolk were adult women. Gang work was a viable option to only a small proportion of women in the county aged 18 and over. In fact the majority of those employed in gangs were children and teenagers between the ages of 7 and 18. These findings have important implications for the way gang labour has been represented in the past.

Turning to evidence contained in Fraser's report for the Royal Commission on the Employment of Children, Young Persons and Women in Agriculture it is possible to obtain some insight into the regional incidence of gangs in Norfolk. Fraser's report focuses on only four of the Poor Law Unions in the county: St Faith's, Depwade, Docking and Swaffham. Each represented a general area of the county (central, south, north and west Norfolk respectively), and his choice was based on unions which he believed could 'be considered typical' of their locality.[37] In the evidence attached to his report, which in total covered 127 parishes, only nine mention the existence of public gangs within their borders. Only in Swaffham, the most purely agricultural region, was the gang system found to prevail extensively, and was, according to Fraser, still the 'most deeply rooted'.[38] In the Swaffham Union five parishes refer to the existence of public gangs: Ashill, Saham Toney, Great Cressingham, Gooderstone and Swaffham. The return from Ashill stated, 'There are three or four public gangs in the parish constantly employed throughout the year'.[39] In the Docking Union, factors which underpinned the widespread employment of gangs in the Swaffham area

---

[36] Ibid., pp. x–xi. These percentages have been calculated using the highest estimates of the numbers employed.
[37] PP 1867–8, XVII, Report by Fraser, p. 4.
[38] Ibid., p. 7.
[39] PP 1867–8, XVII, Evidence to Fraser's Report, p. 59.

(large farms, sparse population settlements and light lands) also characterised the region. Yet public gangs, to Fraser's surprise, were not a central component of the farming system in Docking. 'The gang system exists,' he writes, 'but to a smaller extent than might have been expected under the circumstances.'[40] Moving to the Depwade Union, Fraser found that the gang system was diminishing in importance. At Stratton St Michael, one witness noted that the system was generally 'dying out in this neighbourhood'. Whereas several farmers in the village had found work for gangs in the 1830s and 1840s, the present situation was that 'only one farmer employs a gang'.[41] At another parish in this region (Pulham Magdalene) the one gang that was recorded was said to consist entirely of boys.[42] Other respondents from Depwade insisted that gangs had never been established in their parishes, and residents of most villages in the vicinity would not understand the meaning of the term 'gang'. At Drayton the return insisted that 'A gang has never been heard of in the parish'.[43] Similarly at Bunwell and Carleton Rose, it was reported that 'no gangs' were employed in either parish, where 'many people would not know what the system means'.[44] In the final union under investigation by Fraser in 1867, St Faith's, evidence for the presence of gangs was also slight. Only one gang, operating out of Haverland and Weston, was declared.

This evidence suggests that by the late 1860s the existence of ganging was very regionally based in the western portions of the county around Swaffham. A sense of decline pervades the parochial replies from across the rest of Norfolk. By this time, it seems likely that employment in agricultural gangs was an option open to only a limited number of female and child labourers where the successful cultivation of the land still required some system of organised labour. Indeed, gangs were part of the agricultural landscape in the Swaffham area until the turn of the twentieth century. In the 1890s it was reported that the system was still economically attractive to farmers and labourers. A gangmaster from Swaffham told the Royal Commission on Labour that without gangs, 'there would be some families here without anything to support them'.[45] The persistence of ganging in this region into the late nineteenth century was certainly exceptional however. Elsewhere, the system – where it existed at all – became redundant from the early 1870s as farmers began to abandon cleaning operations such as weeding and stone-picking in response to the agricultural depression. It was mainly economic

[40] PP 1867–8, XVII, Report by Fraser, p. 7.
[41] PP 1867–8, XVII, Evidence to Fraser's report, p. 43.
[42] Ibid., p. 41.
[43] Ibid., p. 31.
[44] Ibid., p. 47.
[45] PP 1893–4, XXXV, Royal Commission on Labour. The Agricultural Labourer. Report by Mr Arthur Wilson Fox on the Poor Law Union of Swaffham, p. 86.

pressures that dictated the final demise of the gang system in Norfolk. However, evidence given to the nineteenth-century commissioners reveals the reluctance of local women to work – and to send their children out to labour – in the Norfolk gangs. Even in times of economic necessity, rural labouring families viewed gangs as a last resort and any opportunity to cease working under gang conditions was readily seized.[46]

The data on gang labour in Norfolk are obviously not ideal. Two specific difficulties are apparent. First, we have to question the typicality of those parishes that gave evidence to White's and Fraser's reports. Fraser's investigation rests on information from only one-sixth of the total number of parishes in Norfolk; the percentage of returns White received was significantly smaller. However, both commentators were aware of this drawback and were confident their findings could serve as a useful indicator of gang labour trends. The second problem concerns the type of gang labour which the parliamentary investigators examined. Most of the evidence relates specifically to public gangs. But by concentrating on the public gang system are we in danger of underestimating the scale and importance of private gangs on mid-nineteenth-century Norfolk farms? The Summary Report of the 1867 Children's Employment Commission argued that the number of women and children employed in private gangs in Norfolk was 'greatly in excess' of those employed in public ones: 'Where the numbers of the latter "are", to use a common mode of designating them, "counted by hundreds, those in the former are counted by thousands".'[47] Moreover, the authors drew little distinction between the two types of gang. The report claimed that 'There is no practical difference between the ages and hours of work, the modes of work, the composition of the gang, the state of education and the moral condition, in the case of those employed in the private and the public gangs'.[48] After the 1867 Gangs Act it was reported that farmers were substantially increasing their use of private gangs, thereby avoiding the restrictive regulations set out in 1867. However, Fraser was very sceptical about the widespread existence of private gangs in Norfolk. In reference to the Sixth Report he comments dryly, 'I have not been able to discover the foundation of this impression in any part of the district that was assigned to me'.[49] During his investigation Fraser found only seven parishes from the county willing to acknowledge the existence of private gangs on farms in their locality. These were limited in scale, with only the largest farms finding continuous employment for them, and were 'without the accompaniment of any of those circumstances of physical or moral degeneration which

---

[46] See Verdon, 'The employment of women and children', pp. 51–2; Sayer, *Women of the Fields*, pp. 54–7.
[47] PP 1867, XVI, Summary Report, p. xxiii.
[48] Ibid.
[49] PP 1867–8, XVII, Report by Fraser, p. 11.

startled and shocked the public mind when it first read the revelations of the system of public gangs'.[50] The contention of the Children's Employment Commission that private gangs were very widely established in Norfolk was not borne out by Fraser's inquiry of the following year.

These reports do not provide us with a complete account of the scale and composition of gang labour across Norfolk in the nineteenth century, but they do yield enough information to cast doubt on some previous interpretations – including Pinchbeck's – of agricultural gangs. Gangs have hitherto been largely seen as a widespread system of organised labour that exploited female and child labour to feed the demands of an increasingly capitalist farming system. Yet the evidence suggests that the scale of agricultural gangs was relatively small in nineteenth-century Norfolk, that the distribution of gangs was regionally specific within the county and that the composition of the typical gang workforce was youthful. The position of women workers in nineteenth-century Norfolk agriculture as a whole appears to have been precarious. Farm accounts from the county show the encroaching marginalisation of women day labourers by the 1830s. Few of these labourers would have found alternative work in gangs; although it is impossible to measure the true extent of the numbers engaged by gangmasters, it seems that adult women constituted only a minority of gang workers. Moreover, even where gangs did exist, by the late 1860s the usefulness of the system to Norfolk farmers was declining, and when Fraser investigated the region, the overall impression conveyed in his report is of a dwindling and largely obsolete arrangement. Whether this pattern of decline is replicated on Norfolk farms outside the gang system over the latter decades of the century – and the applicability of this model of decline to other English counties – will now be examined.

Women in the agricultural day labour force, 1850 to 1900

It was shown in Chapter 2 that official sources such as the occupational censuses record a dramatic decline in the numbers of women employed as agricultural day labourers in the second half of the nineteenth century. Parliamentary commissioners also intimated that women were withdrawing from the agricultural workforce by the late 1860s, although their reports do point to the persistence of female labour in certain seasons and regions. Are these patterns confirmed in farm records?

Several farm labour accounts from the period after 1850 indicate a decline in the level of women engaged as agricultural day labourers. The most useful way to illustrate this is to revisit some of the counties we have already looked

[50] Ibid.

Table 4.1 Days worked by women, men and children, 1861 to 1891, at Hoverton St Peter, Norfolk

Year	Days worked by women (%)	Days worked by men (%)	Days worked by children (%)
1861	12	62	26
1871	7	70	23
1881	2	77	21
1891	1	79	20

Source: University of Reading Library (hereafter URL), NORF, 9.1/1–75, Farm account books, 1859–1938.[51]

at in this chapter. Table 4.1 shows the employment of day labour on Old Hall Farm, Hoverton St Peter in Norfolk in the second half of the nineteenth century. This was an arable farm of 420 acres, employing around fifteen men and four boys. Women and younger children were also engaged for certain seasonal tasks. Accounts survive for a long time span – from 1859 to the 1930s – and here the census years 1861 to 1891 have been taken as points of analysis. Between these years the employment of women falls considerably. As records from the early part of the century have not survived, it is impossible to date the beginning of this shrinkage. By 1891 however, it is clear that women played little part in the agricultural labour on this farm. The employment of male day labourers rose steadily over the same period. These changes in the employment of day labour occurred across the years of agricultural depression, suggesting that the casual labour of women was particularly affected by farmers' efforts to cut back labour bills. Tasks usually associated with female workers – weeding, hoeing and stone-picking – were dispensed with as the depression wore on. These transformations resulted in the employment of a core male workforce, assisted by a number of teenage boys.

Surviving evidence from Sewerby Home Farm in East Yorkshire covers the same years as those from Hoverton and allows a unique comparison of labour trends. The diminution in the days worked by women at Sewerby replicates the pattern uncovered in Norfolk (Table 4.2). In 1861 female labourers worked just under one-fifth of total labour days. They were engaged for a few days in the winter threshing, but their labour consisted mainly of weeding, hoeing, haymaking and harvesting in the spring and summer months. A decade later, 1871, the volume of women's day labour had nearly halved. By 1891 women worked just 5 per cent of labour days, employed only in April

---

[51] These accounts are recorded in the archives as belonging to a farm in the village of Neatishead, but cross-referencing with the census reveals the accounts emanate from Old Hall Farm, Hoverton St Peter.

Table 4.2 Days worked by women, men and children on Sewerby Home Farm, East Yorkshire, between 1861 and 1891

Year	Days worked by women (%)	Days worked by men (%)	Days worked by children (%)
1861	19	74	7
1871	10	88	2
1881	7	93	–
1891	5	95	–

Source: Brynmor Jones Library, University of Hull, DDLG 43/5–15. Farm and private accounts, Lloyd-Greame family of Sewerby, 1821 to 1893. These are not an unbroken set of accounts and those from the earlier years in particular are difficult to decipher.

and May for weeding and hoeing, and in July and August for the hay and corn harvests. The decline in women's work in the harvest over this time period is particularly apparent. In 1861 fourteen women worked a total of 210 days in the harvest; by 1891 only four women were recorded as working in the harvest fields, engaged for forty-eight days over the period. The growing importance of the male workforce in the second half of the nineteenth century is also highlighted in these accounts, while child workers were employed only in small numbers. After the 1870s the employment of child labour appears to cease altogether.

The decrease of women day labourers on these two farms after 1860 is incontrovertible. At Sewerby women's day labour participation contracted by 75 per cent between 1861 and 1891, while at Hoverton the disappearance of women workers was virtually complete by the end of the nineteenth century. The sustained decline in the appropriation of women on these farms mirrors the downward course suggested by the official census figures. Moreover, these accounts are not exceptional. Both Speechley and Gielgud uncovered evidence to confirm the fall-off in women's agricultural labour in the second half of the century. On Chilcot Manor Farm in Somerset, for example, women workers performed just 1 per cent of days worked in the late 1860s. Again their labour was very seasonal: women were engaged for weeding and stone-picking in the spring, and for haymaking and harvesting in the summer, but they were not employed for the remainder of the year. In 1868 there were no female labourers engaged on this farm.[52] At Hutton John Farm in Cumbria, Gielgud shows that female day labour peaked in the 1840s and 1850s. By the early 1860s the number of labour days carried out by women on the farm had halved from previous levels.[53]

[52] Speechley, 'Female and child agricultural day labourers', p. 68.
[53] Gielgud, 'Nineteenth-century farm women', p. 388.

These farms in Norfolk, East Yorkshire, Somerset and Cumbria denote an uninterrupted decrease in the use of women day labourers. But again we need to handle this material with care: proclaiming that these farms are representative of the whole of the English agricultural labour force in the second half of the nineteenth century would be imprudent. Other farms – some from the same counties examined here – offer a somewhat different account. Laxton Manor Farm in the East Riding is a good illustration of this point. Laxton parish was situated in the south-east of the county and adjoined the village of Saltmarshe. It has already been shown that the large-scale cultivation of potatoes in this region furnished women with plenty of work in the period between the 1820s and 1840s. The presence of women workers was still appreciable in the 1880s, although not as high as it had been in the earlier decades. Records from Laxton survive for only one complete year – May 1882 to April 1883.[54] In that year women performed 20 per cent of total labour days on the farm. Children account for 19 per cent of days and men 61 per cent. There had been other shifts in female labour patterns since the 1840s. Women's work was more seasonal than it had been at Saltmarshe forty years earlier. In 1882 to 1883 days worked across the winter months between November and April were minimal (in December only one-and-a-half days were worked by women), but from May to October, female workers at Laxton were a significant part of the day labour force. In July, for instance, fifteen women worked 191 days, while eleven men laboured for 228 days. An additional change was apparent in the number of days worked by individual women. Women at Laxton worked on a more casual basis than their counterparts at Saltmarshe had done earlier in the century. At Laxton in the 1880s no woman worked more than eighty days in the year. Significantly however, few of the women who worked on this farm seem to have been recorded as agricultural labourers in the occupational census.

Although the surviving farm records from Laxton do not exactly match the census year, most of the women who were employed on the farm in 1882 to 1883 have been located in the census of 1881. The results of this exercise are shown in Table 4.3. The lack of occupational designation for women is striking. In many instances the enumerator in Laxton simply added the word 'wife' to the occupation of the woman's spouse. Thus Harriet Marshall, who worked seventy-nine days in 1882 to 1883, earning £4 12s 3d, was returned as an 'agricultural labourer's wife', as were Hannah Morley and Dinah Poole. Ann Roberts, who worked forty-nine days was returned as a 'shoemaker's wife', Sarah Sims a 'ratcatcher's wife' and Elizabeth Waterland a 'butcher slaughterman's wife'. Ann Wainman, a widow aged 40, was recorded as a 'charwoman' although she worked for over seventy days on Laxton Manor Farm and earned £3 16s 6d in agricultural labour. Only one woman – Jane

---

[54] ERRO, DDSA 1067, Labour journals of Laxton Manor Farm, May 1882 to January 1884.

Table 4.3 Women workers on Laxton Manor Farm, May 1882 to April 1883 and their occupational designation in the 1881 census

Name	Days worked	Age	Marital status	Occupation of husband	No.+ age of children	Amount earned in 1883	Occupational description in 1881
Hannah Briggs	55	55	Married	Railway gateman	1 (16)	£3 7s 4d	No occupation
Alice Marshall	12½	27	Married	Agricultural labourer	2 (3+2)	12s 6d	No occupation
Harriet Marshall	79	57	Married	Agricultural labourer	None	£4 12s 3d	Agricultural labourer's wife
Jane Marshall	68	62	Married	Farm labourer	None	£3 13s 3d	Farm labourer occasionally
Hannah Morley	64	53	Married	Farm labourer	2 (24+12+grandson)	£3 14s 9d	Farm labourer's wife
Mary Morton	75½	28	Married	Railway signalman	1 (7)	£3 19s 4d	No occupation
Dinah Poole	28	49	Married	Agricultural labourer	1 (14)	£1 7s	Agricultural labourer's wife
Ann Roberts	49	41	Married	Shoemaker	None	£2 8s 4d	Shoemaker's wife
Sarah Sims	34½	27	Married	Ratcatcher	4 (10,4,4+2)	£1 14s 6d	Ratcatcher's wife
Jessy Steels	78	29	Married	Railway signalman	4 (9,6,4+1)	£4 2s 6d	No occupation
Ann Wainman	72	40	Widow	–	6 (19,15,10,9,8+4)	£3 16s 6d	Charwoman
Emma Wainman	59½	35	Married	Labourer	2 (14+1)	£3 3s	No occupation
Elizabeth Waterland	58	34	Married	Butcher slaughter Man	6 (12,10,8,6,4+2)	£3 2s 6d	Butcher slaughterman's wife
Mary Wilson	23½	34	Married	Agricultural labourer	3 (13,12+9)	£1 5s 3d	No occupation

Sources: ERRO, DDSA 1067; East Yorkshire Local Studies Library, Beverley, Census Enumerators' Book, Laxton parish, 1881.

Marshall – was noted as a 'farm labour occasionally', although the number of days she worked was on a par with the other women in the village. Six women were entered as having 'no occupation' in 1881. The enumerator in Laxton parish clearly did not recognise the seasonal agricultural labour of women in the village as an occupation. The recording of women in different occupational categories – in this case charring – is also evident. The casual, but significant, agricultural work performed by women on Laxton Manor Farm in the early 1880s was essentially omitted from the official occupational tables in the census. This blinkered approach to documenting women's agricultural work is not idiosyncratic: similar cross-referencing of farm accounts with census records from Norfolk and Somerset endorses these findings from East Yorkshire.[55] Although the census underestimates the real size of the female agricultural labour force, it does provide useful information on the familial and lifecycle circumstances of working women. This will be explored later in the chapter.

Celia Miller's research on the mixed farming region of Gloucestershire also shows the persistence in female day labour in the last quarter of the nineteenth century. On a farm in Dymock (north-west Gloucestershire), the female workforce actually increased over the course of the 1870s. In 1872 women worked 12 per cent of labour days. Seven years later the volume of their labour had nearly doubled, to just over 22 per cent of days worked.[56] On farms in the Cotswolds region of the county, female workers were also present in considerable numbers. At Fairford, one farm records women performing just under one-third of all labour days in the early 1870s. Nineteen women on the farm worked for 100 days or more over the year, while a further five females were engaged for more than 200 days. This trend was replicated on a farm at Snowshill in the early 1890s, where female day labourers accounted for 33 per cent of days worked, with many women again labouring for one-third or more of the year.[57] As with Laxton, the census enumerators seemed to have ignored most of these female agricultural workers, particularly those women who worked on the Cotswolds farms. Miller argues that this evidence shows

> The census of 1871, and by implication, the censuses of 1881 and 1891, greatly underestimated the size of the female agricultural labour force in the arable and mixed farming areas of Gloucestershire. There can be little doubt that the type of field work performed by women continued to be economically viable from both labourers' and farmers' viewpoints after 1871.[58]

---

[55] See Verdon, 'Changing patterns of female employment', pp. 214–17; Speechley, 'Female and child day labourers', pp. 29–31
[56] Celia Miller, 'The hidden workforce: Female field workers in Gloucestershire, 1870–1901', *Southern History*, 6 (1984), pp. 139–61 (p. 145).
[57] Ibid., p. 145.
[58] Ibid., p. 147.

Even in a county like Norfolk, where the evidence for the marginalisation of female workers seems most compelling, women were still important to the cultivation of some farms after the mid-nineteenth century. On one farm at Wereham, payments to women labourers constituted 15 per cent of the total labour expenditure for the year 1856.[59] The farm was a small occupation employing only two or three male workers, with labourers' wives being called upon to assist at certain seasons. On another farm at Winfarthing, women were employed to work 17 per cent of the 3013¾ total labour days for 1881.[60] Moreover, as both male and female labourers were paid piece rates for work in the hay and corn harvests, this figure is likely to be an underestimate of the total labour performed by women on the farm in that year. These cases are interesting, as they highlight two ways in which women's labour on nineteenth-century farms is consistently overlooked or under-represented. The Wereham farm reminds us that the bias in the survival of farm records towards the larger, more commercially orientated farms may obscure the wider and crucial role afforded to women on smaller farms.[61] The Winfarthing example reveals that a great deal of labour undertaken by women with their families in the harvest fields (and at other task work) is disguised, as wages were mostly paid to the male head of the group. In Norfolk in 1867 it was noted that in the wheat harvest 'when it is put out by the acre, women would take part with their husbands in the work'.[62] Local reminiscences from the same area also show the continued presence of women in the harvest fields in the late nineteenth and early twentieth centuries. Arthur Randall recalls that his mother 'was especially busy' at harvest time, tying and shocking sheaves all day 'as fast as any man'.[63] That the whole family was called upon to participate in this activity is reflected in the following passage:

> As soon as I could toddle I used to run about alone in the harvest field while my parents and older brothers and sisters were at work there. My parents

---

[59] URL, NORF 11/4/1, labour book, Wereham, 1855 to 1868.

[60] NRO, MC 229/28. Farm account book of Betts of Forncett, Tibenham and elsewhere, including farm labour book, 1880 to 1902.

[61] Robert Allen argues that the employment of women and children declined as farm size increased during the conversion to large-scale capitalist farming in south-eastern England in the eighteenth century. 'The shift to large farms', he contends, 'meant that only the husbands in labourers' families were employed in agriculture' and that 'eighteenth-century farm amalgamation rendered most rural women and children redundant in agriculture'. This claim is clearly overstated, as women and children were still engaged as day labourers on large farms in many areas of southern England after 1800. R. C. Allen, *Enclosure and the Yeoman: The Agricultural Development of the South Midlands, 1450–1850* (Oxford, 1992), pp. 18 and pp. 215–17.

[62] PP 1867–8, XVII, Evidence to Fraser's report, p. 39.

[63] Arthur Randall, *Sixty Years a Fenman* (London, 1966), p. 17.

had harvested on the same farm for many years, and as soon as we children were able to do so we had to tie the corn, and then, as we got older, to tie and shock alongside our elders.[64]

However, it was his father who fixed a price per acre for tying, shocking and carting in the harvest field, and who was given the final payment. Thus the labour of the rest of the family would have gone unrecorded. Such evidence intimates that Pinchbeck was overstating the case to suggest that female day labourers in agriculture had vanished by the late nineteenth century. While many farm records confirm the general impression of a decline in the numbers of women employed in the second half of the century others also demonstrate that in certain circumstances the input of female labour was still essential and could not be dispensed with, even in the 1880s and 1890s. Thus farm records from the period after 1850 largely endorse the pattern of female agricultural labour promoted in the published documentary material.

Gendered labour: the sexual division of work and wages

So far, data from farm records have been used to ascertain the extent of women's work in agriculture and how this changed over the nineteenth century. This evidence also reveals a great deal of information about the operation of the sexual division of labour in agriculture and differentials in wage rates paid to male and female workers. Analysis of nineteenth-century Parliamentary Papers in Chapter 2 has already disclosed regional distinctions in the types of tasks women performed and the rate of remuneration they received for agricultural work. Farm account books also testify to this paradigm. While there were certain jobs that were framed as 'women's work' across England, close examination of sources indicates subtle regional patterns of work and wages for men and women. These did not remain static over the course of the century and we have to be mindful of regional, socio-economic and customary factors when considering how trends in work and wages shifted.

If we look at the south-east region to begin with, Snell suggests that before the mid-eighteenth century, men's and women's work in agriculture was far more equitable than in subsequent periods. Differences in seasonal patterns of work and wage rates were 'less notable' before 1750, and 'abundant supportive evidence for a very wide range of female participation in agricultural tasks' exists. Thus women's work 'extended to reaping, loading and spreading dung, ploughing, threshing, thatching, following the harrow, sheep shearing, and

---

[64] Ibid., p. 22.

even working as shepherdesses'.[65] Yet A. Hassall Smith's analysis of the farm books of Nathaniel Bacon of Stiffkey unearthed clear distinctions in men's and women's farmwork in late sixteenth-century Norfolk. Women were engaged on a range of 'seasonal and occasional tasks' including weeding in the spring and autumn, haymaking in June and July, harvesting in August and sorting wool and picking over seed corn in winter.[66] In addition, women worked on the specialist crop of saffron, planting in the summer and harvesting in autumn. Male labourers were engaged as shepherds, hedgers and ditchers, furze-cutters, grain-threshers, ploughers and dung-carters. In the hayfields men mowed and carted; in the harvest men scythed, while women sheared and tied the wheat. According to Hassell Smith, women's labour 'was not interchangeable with that of men; rather it was complementary'.[67] So the sexual division of labour described earlier at Earsham Home Farm in the early nineteenth century was nothing new. Women were still employed on many of the same seasonal tasks in nineteenth-century Norfolk as they were in the sixteenth century.

Yet there are differences between the two sets of records that indicate a strengthening of gender-specific work in the early nineteenth century.[68] At Earsham we have already seen that women's work was becoming more seasonally specific by the 1830s and was confined chiefly to weeding and haymaking in June and July. The accounts from 1837 record only a very minor presence of women in the harvest fields. The extent of women's harvest work in Norfolk had contracted since the turn of the nineteenth century and certainly since the late sixteenth century. The small role played by women in the Norfolk harvest fields is confirmed by analysis of other farm accounts from the same period. At Stody Hall farm, for example, records from the 1820s show that twelve men were hired for the harvest period for the sum of £5 10s each (plus hiring money and beer), but women were engaged only for the odd day, turning barley.[69] Women were not entirely absent from the harvest

---

[65] Snell, *Annals of the Labouring Poor*, p. 52. As Sharpe points out, Snell provides little supporting evidence for this wide-scale involvement of women, citing only the work of Alice Clarke. Pamela Sharpe, 'The female labour market in English agriculture during the Industrial Revolution: Expansion or contraction?', *Agricultural History Review*, 47 (1999), pp. 161–81 (p. 167).

[66] A. Hassall Smith, 'Labourers in late sixteenth-century England: A case study from north Norfolk [Part 1]', *Continuity and Change*, 4 (1989), pp. 11–52 (p. 28).

[67] Hassall Smith, 'Labourers in sixteenth-century England', p. 29.

[68] Robert Shoemaker has also recently argued that although there were significant discontinuities in female labour by the early nineteenth century, evidence such as the 1834 Poor Law Report and the 1843 Royal Commission actually reveals many continuities in women's work. 'Important as these discontinuities are,' he writes, 'they do not represent any fundamental structural transformation in the sexual division of labour in agriculture. Rather, this period witnessed some accentuation of differences which had already existed in the seventeenth century.' Robert B. Shoemaker, *Gender in English Society, 1650–1850: The Emergence of Separate Spheres?* (Harlow, 1998), p. 159.

[69] NRO, MC 3/89 400x, Stody Hall farm accounts, 1827 to 1829.

process though. It has already been shown that where the harvest was let by the task to family groups, women's labour was important, but was unlikely to have been recorded by the farmer. Even where women were not involved in the cutting and gathering of the harvest in Norfolk, they were found gleaning the fields after the crop had been taken in. Gleaning was a central aspect of the non-waged economy of rural labouring families in nineteenth-century Norfolk and the task should not be dismissed as inconsequential or not constituting a useful harvest occupation. The customary role women played in gleaning was widespread across southern England. Sharpe, for example, also found that women's main role in the nineteenth-century harvest on farms in the heavy Essex clays was gleaning.[70] The significance of this task to family subsistence will be explored further in Chapter 6.

In northern England, Snell proposes that the sexual division of work was not so rigid as it was in the south-east; that 'similar work continued more noticeably into the nineteenth century'.[71] Farm records endorse the representation of women's work in the Royal Commissions by pointing to a wider range of female jobs on northern farms. In both East Yorkshire and Northumberland labour books record women's participation in the usual female tasks of planting and harvesting potatoes, swedes and turnips; weeding, hoeing and stone-picking; and haymaking. But their occupancy in the harvest was, in general, more widespread than it was in East Anglia. It is difficult to document exactly the role women performed in the harvest, as farm books rarely record the actual tasks individual labourers were paid for, but Gielgud argues that women in Northumberland sheared the corn as well as other subsidiary tasks in the nineteenth century.[72] In addition, women in the north also threshed with the machine, spread and carted dung, assisted the thatcher (preparing the straw) and performed general barn work. Yet there was still a noticeable division of tasks based on gender, and evidence again suggests that this was a long-established phenomenon. The appropriation of jobs uncovered by Elizabeth Gilboy's examination of the Thornborough estate in eighteenth-century North Yorkshire largely echoes the pattern for nineteenth-century farms across the northern counties. Thus women were employed in haymaking, harvesting (reaping), spreading manure, weeding and stone-picking, while men were found threshing (by hand), hedging and ditching, mowing, ploughing and stubbing.[73]

Unlike the south-east, Snell argues the employment of female day labourers in western England 'would be that frequently found in the rural north-west and extreme north'.[74] In the west, involvement in livestock, dairying and

---

[70] Sharpe, *Adapting to Capitalism*, pp. 80–5.
[71] Snell, *Annals of the Labouring Poor*, p. 53.
[72] Gielgud, 'Nineteenth-century farm women', ch.3.
[73] Mrs Elizabeth Gilboy, 'Labour at Thornborough: An eighteenth-century estate', *Economic History Review*, 1st ser., III (1932), pp. 388–98 (p. 391).
[74] Snell, *Annals of the Labouring Poor*, p. 46.

haymaking provided more security of employment for women and although there 'are suggestions of a distinct sexual division of labour . . . it was one which (given a relatively constant level of female activity during the year) seems to be mutually complementary'.[75] This east–west dichotomy has been questioned by Speechley. She found patterns of female agricultural employment which largely reflected those of women in the south-east. Women day labourers in Somerset, she argues, were rarely engaged in pastoral or dairying activities, with Snell's data relating to farm and domestic servants, not agricultural day labourers.[76] Women were therefore found employed to perform the familiar tasks of weeding, hoeing and stone-picking, the planting and harvesting of roots, haymaking and harvesting (not as mowers or reapers) and occasionally winnowing and threshing in the winter. These were the jobs women had been engaged to perform for 200 years or more in the south-west, suggesting the gender divide was not exaggerated by changing tools or technology in the eighteenth and nineteenth centuries.[77] Although Speechley finds a movement of female day labourers away from the corn to the hay harvest on some Somerset farms, on the whole she contends that 'the seasonal pattern of women's day labourer employment in Somerset in the mid nineteenth century differed little to that of the late seventeenth and early eighteenth century, with women still largely employed between the months of May and August'.[78]

The sexual division of labour in nineteenth-century agriculture was long established. Across the English counties women were engaged for certain tasks that were seen as suitable for female workers. Weeding, hoeing, stone-picking, planting and digging were all labour-intensive manual tasks. They were also classified as unskilled occupations. Women were sought for such work, as it required nimble fingers and an ability to concentrate on tedious, backbreaking but undemanding tasks for long periods. Women workers were also cheap labour. A significant wage gap between male and female agricultural day labourers persisted across the nineteenth century, adding to the attractiveness of women to farmers for certain tasks at certain seasons.

Table 4.4 shows the usual daily wage rates paid to female day labourers on selected farms between 1790 and 1890. These payments are interesting not least because they reveal a remarkable constancy in the level of remuneration women received for a day's work in the nineteenth century. Women employed on Earsham Home Farm in Norfolk in 1807 received 8d a day, the same amount given to women at Stody Hall Farm in the same county in 1828, Dunster Castle Farm in Somerset in 1840, Old Hall Farm in 1870s

---

[75] Ibid., p. 48.
[76] Speechley, 'Female and child day labourers in agriculture', p. 71.
[77] Speechley, 'Female and child day labourers in agriculture', pp. 93–4. See Pamela Sharpe, 'Time and wages of West Country workfolks in the seventeenth and eighteenth centuries', *Local Population Studies*, 55 (1995), pp. 66–9.
[78] Speechley, 'Female and child day labourers in agriculture', p. 73.

FEMALE DAY LABOURERS

Table 4.4 Female day wage rates on selected farms in the nineteenth century

Farm	Year	Female day rate
Holme-on-Spalding-Moor, East Yorkshire	1796	6d
Earsham Home Farm, Norfolk	1807	8d
Poulett estate, Somerset	1810	8d
John Lockwood's farm, East Yorkshire	1818	10–12d
Stody Hall Farm, Norfolk	1828	8d
Saltmarshe Home Farm, East Yorkshire	1836	8d
Hutton John Farm, Cumbria	1837–8	12d–15d
Dunster Castle Farm, Somerset	1840	8d
Breeks Farm, East Yorkshire	1851	12d
Chilcot Manor Farm, Somerset	1860	10d
Sewerby Home Farm, East Yorkshire	1861	10d
Hailes, Gloucestershire	1870	8d
Old Hall Farm, Norfolk	1871	8d
Laxton Manor Farm, East Yorkshire	1882–3	12d
Snowshill, Gloucestershire	1890	8d

Sources: Gielgud, 'Nineteenth-century farm women in Northumberland and Cumbria'; Speechley, 'Female and child day labourers in agriculture'; Verdon, 'Changing patterns of female employment'.

Norfolk and Snowshill in Gloucester in 1890. There is some evidence for a north–south divide in day labour rates. Women working on the Poulett estate in Somerset received 2d to 4d a day less than females engaged by the day on John Lockwood's East Yorkshire farm in the same decade. Similarly, at Hutton John Farm in Cumbria, women were paid 4d to 7d more in the late 1830s than women at Dunster in Somerset in 1840. The day rates on Laxton Manor Farm in East Yorkshire were also higher than female day wages in Norfolk and Gloucestershire in the latter part of the century. Yet this highland–lowland distinction was not uniform. Women in East Yorkshire in 1836 (Saltmarshe) received the same day rate as their counterparts at Dunster in 1840. The same pattern is repeated at Sewerby and Chilcot in the early 1860s. However, these day rates do disguise the higher wages women could be paid for working in specialist crops or in the harvest. At Holme-on-Spalding-Moor, the female harvest day wage rose to 15d in August 1796, and women at Saltmarshe Home Farm received 1s 4d to 2s a day for flax-pulling in the 1830s. Women in the south could also be better paid during the harvest: on the Poulett estate women received 2d a day more, and in 1870s Gloucestershire, female harvest workers were engaged for 12d per day. While the upward movement of the female day wage at certain tasks should not be overlooked, evidently on many farms in the nineteenth century, women's rates remained the same across the year. Moreover, on all the farms highlighted here, a wage gap between male and female labourers endured. How can we account for this discrepancy?

Burnette has argued that the difference between female and male wages reflects the disparity in the productivity rates of the two sexes. Women's productivity in agriculture was marginal and dependent on age, marital status and family circumstances. Women labourers tended to work fewer hours than men (because of household duties), were unreliable (moving in and out of the labour market due to childbirth) and were physically weaker. According to Burnette, 'differences in strength led to differences in productivity, and thus differences in market wages'.[79] She also highlights the distinction between piece-rate wages (by the task) and time-wage rates (by the day).

Table 4.4 represents time-wage rates. If we compare male and female average day rates in nineteenth-century agriculture, women usually earned between one-third and a half of the male day rate. Certain male-only jobs such as ploughing were paid at a higher day rate, but even when working on comparable tasks – hoeing, for instance – men normally received a higher day wage. Burnette may be correct to link this to the length of the working day. There is plenty of evidence to indicate that female agricultural day labourers did work shorter hours than men in the nineteenth century. The curtailment of the female working day was largely aimed at married women who had household duties to fit around their day's labour in the fields. Although some single and widowed women worked longer hours, nineteenth-century evidence suggests that most female agricultural workers followed the arrangement made for married women. Burnette calculated that in 1843 women on average worked 9.66 hours a day, whereas men laboured for 12 hours.[80] Other nineteenth-century commissioners verify this pattern: Edward Stanhope reported in the 1860s that women in the East Midlands worked from 8 a.m. to 5.30 p.m., while men laboured from 6 a.m. to 6 p.m., or from light to dark.[81] Taking the difference in the length of the male and female working day into account the wage gap in agriculture lessens, although it does not entirely dissipate.

Piece-rate wages show less discrimination than day rates. Speechley found that no distinction was made between piece-rate payments for men and women on any tasks in Somerset. Lower wages received by women for work on piece-rate therefore point to their lower productivity rate: men were physically stronger and were able to complete tasks far more quickly than women.[82] Farm account books are not ideal sources when attempting to

---

[79] Joyce Burnette, 'An investigation of the female–male wage gap during the industrial revolution in Britain', *Economic History Review*, L (1997), pp. 257–81 (p. 275).
[80] Burnette, 'Female–male wage gap', pp. 268–9.
[81] PP 1867–8, XVII, Report by Hon. E. Stanhope on the counties of Lincoln, Nottingham and Leicester, p. 81.
[82] Speechley, 'Female and child day labourers in agriculture', p. 129. Burnette quotes the evidence of a Kent farmer to reinforce this point: 'a man would be reaping three-quarters of an acre in the same time [two days], and a woman half an acre, if she worked as many hours as the man.' Burnette, 'Female–male wage gap', p. 275.

unravel the relationship between male and female rates on piece-work. Most accounts record only the task performed and the sum paid for the job. They do not indicate the length of time taken over the work. Thus, despite the availability of persuasive data to indicate the link between lower productivity and lower female wage rates, the evidence is not wholly convincing. The constancy of the female day wage over the nineteenth century, and across counties, implies that there was still a customary element to women's earnings. As a woman's main responsibilities were seen as being to the home and family, her earnings in the nineteenth century were viewed as supplementary or incidental to the male wage. This ideology is reflected in the persistently low wages paid to women, although disentangling the exact relationship between women's work, labour productivity and ideological considerations remains a notoriously difficult exercise.

Lifecycle changes and women's agricultural employment

It was shown in Chapter 3 that farm service, where it survived in the nineteenth century, represented a specific phase in the lifecycle of rural women. Young, single girls entered service in their early teens and left on marriage. The familial circumstances of women employed in agriculture recorded in census enumerators' books indicate that the vast majority of female day labourers were married. Girls and unmarried women were not excluded from agricultural work and certainly entered the day labour force when necessity called. But agricultural labour was seen to corrupt young girls and women, as Fraser's report on Norfolk in the late 1860s illustrates. The farmers, he argues, 'almost to a man ... express the opinion that the proper place for a young single girl is in a household, and not upon the land'.[83] Evidence suggests that most farmers in the nineteenth century preferred to engaged married women and use the labour of their children, when required, in a family context. Indeed, labour was often hired implicitly or explicitly on a family basis, as Edwin Portman pointed out in 1867:

> in a few instances there is, I fear, a tacit understanding between the employers and the labourer that in consideration of yearly and permanent employment for the father of the family, the labour of the wife and children shall be placed at the employer's disposal if required at any particular season.[84]

An analysis of the marital status of women engaged on some of the farms discussed in this chapter confirms this contention. All the regularly employed

---

[83] PP 1867–8, XVII, Report by Fraser, p. 16.
[84] PP 1867–8, XVII, Report by E. B. Portman on the counties of Cambridge and Yorkshire, p. 99.

women – and most of those more casually engaged – on Saltmarshe Home Farm in the late 1830s were, according to the census of 1841, married. Many were married to labourers who worked on the same farm. Those women who were unmarried tended to be widows. Speechley also found that of the regular female labourers employed at Dunster Castle Farm in the 1840s, only two were unmarried (and these worked alongside their mothers), while only one casually engaged woman was single (a widow).[85] This pattern is repeated again and again. At both Flitcham Hall Farm in 1851 and Old Hall Farm, Hoverton St Peter in 1871, all women who worked on these Norfolk farms were married to labourers on the same farm, with the exception of one widow in each case.[86] Looking again at Laxton Manor Farm (Table 4.3), these findings are largely duplicated. Harriet Marshall, Dinah Poole and Jane Marshall were all married to permanent male workers on the farm. However, a significant proportion of spouses did not work on the land: the Doncaster to Hull railway line passed through the edge of the village and provided work for local men such as William Briggs, Edward Steels and George Morton.

That childbearing and rearing had a palpable effect on when and how much agricultural work women could perform was recognised by many contemporary writers. David Davies' report of the 1790s notes the correlation between the presence of young children and the inability of mothers to engage in productive labour. Commenting on budgets from families living in Durham he writes: 'In Nos 1,3,4,5, the woman can earn nothing, as she will have enough to do to keep the family clean, and clothes whole: the youngest, being infants, will live mostly on breast milk.'[87] Respondees to the 1834 Poor Law Report were also conscious that a wife with four children was frequently kept from the labour market by family commitments. The return from Hackthorn in Lincolnshire stated, 'A Woman with four Children cannot work for her employer more than four months in the year, in consequence of bad weather and her necessary attention to the family.'[88] Women with young children were seen as being less productive and less reliable than those without. Burnette contends that childbearing 'encouraged women to remain out of the labour market' and 'affected women's productivity mainly through discouraging investment in human capital'.[89] But farmers were evidently willing to make allowances for women with children in order to secure their labour, and we need to assess how the age and number of children in a family influenced women's agricultural work. In order to do this, the information

---

[85] Speechley, 'Female and child day labourers in agriculture', p. 135.
[86] See Verdon, 'Changing patterns of female employment', pp. 143–9.
[87] David Davies, *The Case of Labourers in Husbandry, Stated and Considered* (London, 1795), p. 159.
[88] PP 1834, XXX, Report from His Majesty's Commissioners for Inquiring into the Administration and Practical Operation of the Poor Laws. Appendix (B.1). Answers to Rural Queries in Five Parts. Part 1, p. 293a.
[89] Burnette, 'Female–male wage gap', pp. 273–4.

recorded by the census enumerator about women employed on Laxton Manor Farm will be analysed more closely.

Was agricultural labour incompatible with having young children? This stage in the lifecycle, with 'many mouths to feed, and no child yet old enough to earn as much as fourpence a day on the farm', was described by one commentator as the time of 'greatest pressure' on the rural family in the nineteenth century.[90] At Laxton, Alice Marshall seems to fall into this category. She was a young mother with two boys under the age of 4 and worked only a few days over the year, earning just 12s 6d. But both Elizabeth Waterland and Jessy Steels also had very young children and they worked for over fifty days in that year. These latter examples suggest that women with very young children did not necessarily cease agricultural work; indeed, the pressure of additional mouths to feed may have rendered their labour more expedient. In cases where there were no older siblings to care for young children, the services of neighbours or other relatives would have been called upon. Very occasionally, when no other childcare opportunities existed, young children were taken to work by their mothers.

The evidence from Laxton indicates that where a number of older, economically active children resided in the family, women had a couple of options open to them. First, if the earnings of the children were substantial and represented a significant proportion of the family income, women could be released from the necessity of working on the farm. Mary Wilson and Dinah Poole are examples of such women. Mary's sons George (aged 13) and John (aged 12) together worked just under 300 days on Laxton Manor Farm, earning over £14. Similarly, Amos Poole (aged 14) worked nearly half the year on the same farm, receiving over £7 for his efforts. On the other hand, with working teenagers in the family, childcare became less of a barrier to female agricultural work, enabling women to work more days themselves. Hannah Morley and Hannah Briggs both had older working children but added over £3 to the family exchequer through their own labour on the farm. Again, the necessity of women's earnings is exposed.

The limitations placed by childcare on women's work receded with age. At Laxton a number of older women with no children living at home worked on the farm. Hannah Marshall worked seventy-nine days, earning £4 12s 3d. Her husband William earned £34 15s 9d on the same farm. Jane Marshall worked sixty-eight days, with her husband John earning £35 4s. Agricultural work remained attractive for women into their old age. With no children contributing to the family income and no pension schemes to fall back on, the inducement to work was still largely financial. But an element of routine and habit, and also companionship, underpinned the continued involvement of women in farmwork into their sixties, seventies and eighties. Two descriptions of the late nineteenth-century female labour force succinctly sum

---

[90] Anon, 'The life of a farm labourer', *Cornhill Magazine*, 9 (1864), pp. 178–86 (p. 181).

up this trend. The first is from Flora Thompson, who claims that although most women in her Oxfordshire village in the 1880s had 'a distaste for "goin' afield"',

> about half a dozen of the hamlet women did field work, most of them being respectable middle-aged women who, having got their families off hand, had spare time, a liking for an open-air life, and a longing for a few shillings a week they could call their own. ... Strong, healthy, weather-beaten, hard as nails, they worked all through all but the very worst weathers and declared they would go 'stark staring mad' if they had to be shut up in a house all day.[91]

The following quote is from an employer, Arthur Savory, who owned a 300-acre mixed farm in the Vale of Evesham. His description of his female workforce is interesting for several reasons: it highlights the number of hours women worked, the customary aspect of women's wages, but also the social relationship the workers formed:

> I began my farming with four dear old women, working on the land, when wanted for light jobs; the youngest must have been fifty at least. They received the time-honoured wage of tenpence a day, and worked, or talked, about eight hours. They loved to work near the main road, discussing the natural history of the occupants of passing carts or carriages. They knew something comic, tragic, or compromising about everybody, and expressed themselves with epigrammatic force.[92]

The impact of lifecycle changes on female agricultural labour cannot be summarised from just one farm in England. This topic warrants more detailed research in the future, as does the position of single, childless and widowed women in rural society. However, this examination of the women employed on Laxton Manor Farm in the early 1880s discloses one axiom: female earnings, no matter how small, remained important to most rural family incomes, even in the last quarter of the century. In East Yorkshire male day wages in agriculture rose by 20 to 25 per cent between the early 1850s and the mid-1870s, with general price levels increasing by only 5 to 10 per cent.[93] However, it seems unlikely that this improvement in real wages was sizeable enough to make labourers markedly less dependent on the intermittent earnings of their family. It was estimated in the 1890s that rents in the county ranged from £1 14s 8d to £2 12s for a one-storey, two-roomed cottage without much garden, up to £5 4s a year for a four- or five-roomed house with a large garden.[94] Thus the

---

[91] Flora Thompson, *Lark Rise to Candleford*, 1st edn 1939 (Harmondsworth, 1984), p. 58.
[92] Arthur H. Savory, *Grain and Chaff from an English Manor* (Oxford, 1920), p. 74.
[93] M. G. Adams, 'Agricultural change in the East Riding of Yorkshire, 1850–1880: An economic and social history' (Ph.D. thesis, University of Hull, 1977), p. 348.
[94] PP 1893–4, XXXV, Report by Mr Edward Wilkinson on the Poor Law Union of Driffield, p. 55.

earnings of women such as Emma Wainman, Hannah Marshall and Harriet Marshall from Laxton Manor Farm represented the yearly rent on an average cottage in the East Riding. This was no inconsiderable contribution.

Although women's labour in nineteenth-century English agriculture exhibited certain universal characteristics, the persistence of regional distinctions in the amount and type of work performed and the level of payment received renders any all-encompassing conclusions difficult to reach. Future research on other counties can only augment our understanding of this topic, but the nature of surviving farm records, as we have seen, inhibits the passage to a complete picture of the female day labourer in agriculture. But seeking fresh approaches enables us to move away from the repetition of long-established generalisations on women's day labour towards a more critical and sophisticated analysis of the impact on women workers of regional, social, economic and cultural change.

5

Alternative employment opportunities

Domestic industries

The availability of an alternative form of female employment could have far-reaching repercussions not only on women's work patterns, but also on the agricultural labour market and the general milieu of nineteenth-century village life. In this chapter the significance of cottage industries will be addressed. Although the fortunes of domestic industries were susceptible to seasonal and trade fluctuations in the nineteenth century, the important contributions these industries made to the subsistence of rural labouring families was widely recognised by contemporary social observers. Frederick Morton Eden attributed the low poor rates at Dunstable in the last decade of the eighteenth century to the widespread employment of 'every woman, who wished to work' in straw manufacture.[1] William Bennett, writing in 1857, acknowledged that the employment of women and children in the straw-plaiting districts of south Bedfordshire was a 'most welcome addition to the income of the household'.[2] At the close of the century, William Bear, reporting for the Royal Commission on Labour, lamented the decline of rural industries in the same county, arguing that

> the total money earnings of the labourers and their families are certainly much less than they were in the times when plaiting and lace-making were fairly remunerative and when every member of a family not a mere infant contributed to the total takings.[3]

Historians too have been aware that cottage trades affected female employment patterns in certain rural areas. Notwithstanding this recognition however, there has been little recent debate on the position of women working in rural industries in the nineteenth century, or the consequences a viable alternative employment opening had on female choice. The purpose of

---

[1] Sir Frederick Morton Eden, *The State of the Poor*, 3 vols (London, 1797), vol. 2, p. 2.
[2] William Bennett, 'The farming of Bedfordshire', *Journal of the Royal Agricultural Society*, 18 (1857), pp. 1–29 (p. 26).
[3] PP 1893–4, XXXV, Royal Commission on Labour. The Agricultural Labourer. Report by Mr William Bear on the Poor Law Union of Woburn, p. 25.

this chapter is to re-evaluate such issues. Given restrictions on space, the following discussion will concentrate principally on the south Midland county of Bedfordshire and consider the value of the two dominant cottage industries of the region – lace-making and straw-plaiting – to nineteenth-century women workers.

Prosperity and pauperism

Chapter 2 acquainted us with the range of cottage industries that drew on the labour of women in the early nineteenth-century countryside. The regional distribution of the major surviving trades is well documented: pillow lace-making in the south Midlands and Devon; glove-making in Oxfordshire and areas of the south-west; straw-plaiting in the south Midlands and Essex; hosiery and lace work in the East Midlands and button-making in Dorset.[4] Some of these industries were long established. Joan Thirsk argues that rural industries began originally in regions of pastoral farming, providing work for cottagers who did not find full-time employment in the dairying and livestock agricultural economy. She cites the example of the cloth-making industry of Wiltshire, which developed in the period after 1450.[5] But as industries also evolved in arable-dominated areas, other factors have been proposed to account for their foundation. Accessibility to raw materials and proximity to a ready market were important to some industries such as straw-plaiting.[6] However, the expansion of cottage industries in the late eighteenth century – particularly lace, straw and gloving – was mainly connected to necessity and may be seen as an attempt to mitigate the distress caused by the irrevocable collapse of the hand-spinning industry across the English countryside.[7] According to William Cobbett, the '*Lords of the Loom*' had taken away 'a great part of the employment of the country *women and girls*'. He championed the development of straw work into more areas of the countryside to restore female and child work opportunities:

> It will be impossible for any of the '*rich ruffians*'; any of the horse-power or steam-power or air-power ruffians; any of these greedy, grinding ruffians, to draw together bands of men, women and children, and to make them slaves, in the working of

---

[4] See Ivy Pinchbeck, *Women Workers and the Industrial Revolution, 1750–1850*, 1st edn 1930 (London, 1981), p. 202.
[5] Joan Thirsk, 'Industries in the countryside', in F. J. Fischer, ed., *Essays in the Economic and Social History of Tudor and Stuart England* (Cambridge, 1961), pp. 70–88.
[6] Pamela Horn, *Victorian Countrywomen* (Oxford, 1991), p. 167.
[7] Deborah Valenze, *The First Industrial Woman* (Oxford, 1995), p. 117; G. F. R. Spenceley, 'The origins of the English pillow lace industry', *Agricultural History Review*, 21 (1973), pp. 81–93 (pp. 90–1).

straw. The raw material *comes of itself*; and the *hand*, and the *hand alone*, can convert it to use.[8]

However, Maxine Berg has warned that these newer industries should not be seen as direct replacements for the old cloth industries: 'they were smaller and poorer than their great predecessors', she maintains, and some, such as shoemaking in Northamptonshire, were 'sometimes not real replacements at all', being made in different areas by different sections of the rural population than cloth had been.[9]

There is a large canon of literature on rural industries, including the lace-making and straw-plaiting trades of Bedfordshire, and the need for adding to this collection may be questioned. The choice is tenable for several reasons. Historical research has tended to focus on certain aspects of the two trades. Early histories, published in the late nineteenth and early twentieth centuries, were written as the industries were entering the final stages of a prolonged decline, and these studies provide a nostalgic and romantic vision of disappearing rural crafts.[10] Another branch of scholarship has furnished us with broad overviews of the history of certain rural industries.[11] More recently, the teaching of craft skills in rural schools, the role of dealers and middlemen, and the foundation of philanthropic associations to promote the survival of domestic industries in the late nineteenth century have been addressed.[12] The exploitation of child workers, and the physical and moral

---

[8] William Cobbett, *Rural Rides*, 1st edn 1830 (Harmondsworth, 1985), p. 118. Cobbett saw straw-plaiting as a useful female employment and ideally suited to the cereal counties of south-eastern England. See Pamela Sharpe, 'The women's harvest: Straw-plaiting and the representation of labour women's employment, c.1793–1885', *Rural History*, 5 (1994), pp. 129–42 (p. 133).

[9] Maxine Berg, *The Age of Manufacturers, 1700–1820: Industry, Innovation and Work in Britain* (London, 1994), p. 110.

[10] See e.g. Thomas Austin, *The Straw-Plaiting and Straw Hat and Bonnet Trade* (Luton, 1871); C. Channer and M. E. Roberts, *Lacemaking in the Midlands* (London, 1900); Alice Dryden, 'Pillow lace in the Midlands', *Pall Mall Magazine*, 8 (1896), pp. 379–91; Elizabeth Mincoff and Margaret S. Marriage, *A History of Hand-made Lace* (London, 1900); Mrs Bury Palliser, *A History of Lace* (London, 1875); M. Sharpe, *Point and Pillow Lace* (London, 1899); Thomas Wright, *The Romance of the Lace Pillow* (London, 1900).

[11] See e.g. Charles Freeman, *Luton and the Hat Industry* (Luton, 1953); Charles Freeman, *Pillow Lace in the East Midlands* (Luton, 1958).

[12] Anne Buck, 'The teaching of lacemaking in the east Midlands', *Folk Life*, 4 (1966), pp. 39–50; David Bushby, 'The Bedfordshire schoolchild', *Bedfordshire Historical Record Society*, 67 (1988); Dave Thorburn, 'Gender, work and schooling in the plaiting villages', *The Local Historian*, 19 (1989), pp. 107–13. On the role of dealers and middlemen see Anne Buck, 'Middlemen in the Bedfordshire lace industry', *Bedfordshire Historical Record Society*, 57 (1978), pp. 32–58. On the lace associations see G. F. R. Spencerley, 'The lace associations: Philanthropic movements to preserve the production of handmade lace in late Victorian and Edwardian times', *Victorian Studies*, 16 (1973), pp. 433–52.

consequences of their work, has formed another area of interest.[13] Within this literature, the employment of women is often a peripheral interest. Moreover, few studies have assessed the role and status of women workers in rural industries across the whole of the nineteenth century. Accounts often suspend their analysis in the mid-nineteenth century, which may have led to an unrepresentative picture of female involvement in some industries.

Once more, for the classic description of rural women's industrial employment in the period between 1750 and 1850, we must consult Ivy Pinchbeck. She shows how the pinnacle of prosperity coincided with the French Revolutionary Wars, as an embargo on foreign imports aided the production of British goods. Thereafter, prices fell rapidly and by the early 1830s all trades were severely depressed. The following depiction of the demise of the handmade lace industry is typical of Pinchbeck's view:

> The period of high wages did not last long; prices dropped with the peace in 1815, and from then onwards until the complete decline of the trade in the 'eighties, lace makers dwindled in number as their condition went from bad to worse.[14]

More recent writers have appropriated this trajectory. George Boyer argues that while the decline of wool-spinning was offset by employment in other industries such as lace, straw and gloving, the affluence of these trades was temporary, with female wage rates and work levels dwindling after 1815. The responses to the 1834 Poor Law Report 'make it clear that employment in cottage industry was declining throughout the south of England', leading to widespread underemployment, a fall-off in family income and increased demand for poor relief.[15] Robert Allen repeats a similar chronology of decline.[16] Deborah Valenze suggests that although their significance as wage-earners could enhance women's role in the family and wider community, women's work in cottage industries in the early nineteenth century 'contributed to a long-term erosion in the status of labouring women'.[17] Because cottage industries were low-paid, categorised as low-skilled, subject to seasonal booms and slumps as well as wider changes in

---

[13] G. F. R. Spencerley, 'The health and disciplining of children in the pillow lace industry in the nineteenth century', *Textile History*, 7 (1976), pp. 154–71; László L. Gróf, *Children of Straw: The Story of a Vanished Craft and Industry in Bucks, Herts, Beds and Essex* (Buckingham, 1988); Pamela Horn, 'Child workers in the pillow lace and straw plait trades of Victorian Buckinghamshire and Bedfordshire', *Historical Journal*, 17 (1974), pp. 779–96.
[14] Pinchbeck, *Women Workers*, p. 208.
[15] George R. Boyer, *An Economic History of the English Poor Law, 1750–1850* (Cambridge, 1990), pp. 40–2.
[16] R. C. Allen, *Enclosure and the Yeoman: The Agricultural Development of the South Midlands, 1450–1850* (Oxford, 1992), pp. 247–8.
[17] Valenze, *First Industrial Woman*, p. 116.

the industrial economy, at the mercy of various underhand practices of manufacturers and dealers, they came to be associated by contemporaries 'with the very margins of survival'.[18] Yet this picture of decay across the English countryside by the late 1830s is at variance with Pamela Horn's study of the nineteenth-century census returns. Official figures indicate that the number of female straw-workers (of all ages) in Buckinghamshire – one of the centres of the industry – actually increased by over 60 per cent between 1851 and 1871.[19] Similarly, the number of female lace-makers in Buckinghamshire rose by 59 per cent between 1841 and 1851; in Northamptonshire the increase was 74 per cent and in Bedfordshire there were 55 per cent more women engaged in the industry in 1851 than ten years earlier.[20] Berg recognises that the handmade lace and straw-plaiting industries continued to be viable until the 1870s and 1880s.[21] Pamela Sharpe also points out that high earnings could be gained by women in the straw-plaiting industry of Essex outside the artificial conditions of wartime.[22] These studies suggest, then, that some domestic industries continued to have a meaningful presence in various rural localities beyond the 1830s and merit further research.

The fact that our understanding of rural industries is based on a restricted number of familiar sources goes some way towards explaining the lack of theoretical analysis of women's work and wages in these trades. Duncan Bythell argues that the records of manufacturers and dealers are difficult to uncover since many firms were small, ephemeral and went out of business in the nineteenth century.[23] Wage datasets are exceedingly uncommon and it is

---

[18] Ibid., p. 117.
[19] Horn, 'Child workers', p. 796.
[20] Pamela Horn, 'Pillow lacemaking in Victorian England: The experience of Oxfordshire', *Textile History*, 3 (1972), pp. 100–15 (p. 113).
[21] Berg, *Age of Manufacturers*, p. 111.
[22] Pamela Sharpe, *Adapting to Capitalism: Working Women in the English Economy, 1700–1850* (Basingstoke, 1996), p. 59.
[23] Duncan Bythell, *The Sweated Trades: Outwork in Nineteenth-Century Britain* (London, 1978), p. 20. Bedford and Luton Archives and Records Service (hereafter BLARS) maintain the records of the Willis Brothers, straw hat and bonnet manufacturers of Luton, and John Eyles, straw-plait manufacturer of Luton. See BLARS M15/32–4, Statement of affairs and list of creditors of Willis Brothers, straw hat and bonnet manufacturers of Luton, 1873; BLARS M15/35, List of creditors and accounts of John Eyles, straw-plait manufacturer, Luton, 1879. Both went out of business in the 1870s and list creditors, assets and liabilities but reveal nothing on labour employed at the firms. The accounts of Mrs Rachael Read, pillow lace manufacturer of Cranfield, also survive, but are sketchy notebooks of orders and customers, and again shed no light on women workers employed in the trade. See BLARS X259/1–4, Pillow lace books and photographs of Mrs Rachael Read, Pillow lace manufacturer, Cranfield, 1886. Luton Museum's collection includes the account books of Henry Horn, a Dunstable plait dealer in the late nineteenth century. Again the information they contain on women workers is limited. See M8/6–8, Account books of Henry Horn, plait dealer, Dunstable, 1870s.

tricky to determine annual earnings of individuals: women's work was paid by the piece and we do not know precisely how many hours it took the average worker to complete different tasks.[24] What we are left with as the major points of reference are official parliamentary commissions and census data. Looking specifically at the lace and straw-plait industries, there were three major reports pertaining to the conditions of work in these trades in the nineteenth century (published in 1843, 1863 and 1864).[25] All were written under the auspices of the Children's Employment Commission. In addition, other nineteenth-century reports make reference to the industries in their voluminous pages.[26] Recourse to these sources has resulted in a retelling of 'familiar facts without adding much to our knowledge'.[27] The need to assess in more detail the position of women workers in nineteenth-century rural industries is clearly warranted, and the examination of one county as a case study is one way to regenerate and open up the debate. In order to do this, a number of questions will be addressed here: what was the relationship between agricultural work and domestic industries and did women move between the two on any occasions? What was the exact nature of women's contribution to lace-making and straw-plaiting, and what changes occurred in female employment patterns across the nineteenth century? Were women better off in regions where domestic industries persisted than in other counties where female productive roles were essentially restricted to agriculture? Did the existence of domestic employments mean that local women made a conscious choice about what type of work they engaged in?

---

[24] Joanna Bourke, '"I was always fond of my pillow": The handmade lace industry in the United Kingdom, 1870–1914', *Rural History*, 5 (1994), pp. 155–69 (p. 159).

[25] PP 1843, XIV, Children's Employment Commission (Trades and Manufactures). Report by Major J. G. Burns on the Employment of Children and Young Persons in Paper-Mills, etc., in the South-eastern Counties of England and on the State, Condition, and Treatment of such Children and Young Persons; PP 1863, XVII, First Report of the Children's Employment Commission. Report upon Lace Manufacture by Mr J. E. White; PP 1864, XXII, Second Report of the Children's Employment Commission. Report upon the Straw Plait and Bonnet Manufacture by Mr J. E. White.

[26] See, for instance, PP 1867–8, XVII, First Report from the Commissioners on the Employment of Children, Young Persons and Women in Agriculture. George Culley Esq., Report on the Counties of Bedfordshire and Buckinghamshire; PP 1893–4, XXXVII, Royal Commission on Labour. The Employment of Women by Clara Collett; PP 1893–4, XXXV, Report by Bear.

[27] Pamela Sharpe, 'The organisation of the lace industry in England and Ireland', in Anne Devonshire and Barbara Wood, eds, *Women in Industry and Technology* (London, 1996), pp. 179–83 (p. 182).

Lace-making and straw-plaiting in Bedfordshire: an overview

In rural Bedfordshire, the domestic industries of lace-making and straw-plaiting co-existed alongside agriculture. Continental refugees escaping persecution in the second half of the sixteenth century introduced the manufacture of pillow lace into England.[28] By the early decades of the seventeenth century it was firmly established on a commercial basis and was carried out over a wide area of Britain, partly at the initiative of Poor Law overseers who were anxious to increase the employment of paupers in their villages.[29] When Daniel Defoe visited Bedfordshire in the 1720s he discovered a flourishing trade:

> From hence, thro' the whole Part of this County, as far as the Border of Buckinghamshire and Hertfordshire, the People are taken up with the manufacture of Bone-Lace, in which they are wonderfully encreas'd and improv'd within these few Years past.[30]

The closure of the American market during the War of Independence severely disrupted the industry, causing the decline of lace manufacture in many outlying districts of England. As a result of this contraction, by the late eighteenth century lace-making was firmly concentrated in two regions of the country: the south Midland counties of Bedfordshire, Buckinghamshire and Northamptonshire, and the Honiton region of Devon. In 1780 it was estimated that the industry employed over 140,000 people in the three Midlands counties alone.[31] The value of lace-making to rural society became apparent during the 1790s. High food prices and poor harvests were instrumental in pushing up poor rates throughout the English countryside, but in the Bedfordshire lace villages female wages maintained stability. Arthur Young observed this circumstance on his visit to the village of Shefford at the turn of the nineteenth century. 'It is remarkable that poor rates at Shefford are at present in this severe scarcity only five shillings in the pound, not having been raised by these bad times above sixpence', he wrote.[32] Prosperity continued throughout the period of the French Revolutionary Wars, as imports of foreign lace were blocked.

---

[28] Freeman, *Pillow Lace*, pp. 10–11.
[29] The earliest reference to the teaching of lace-making to pauper children in Bedfordshire comes from Eaton-Socon in 1596. See Buck, 'Teaching of lacemaking', p. 39. See also David H. Kennett, 'Lacemaking by Bedfordshire paupers', *Textile History*, 5 (1975), pp. 111–18.
[30] Daniel Defoe, *A Tour Through the Whole Island of Great Britain*, 2 vols, 1st edn 1726 (London, 1962), vol. 2, p. 114.
[31] Pinchbeck, *Women Workers*, pp. 203–204.
[32] Arthur Young, 'Lace-making', *Annals of Agriculture*, 37 (1801), pp. 448–50 (p. 448).

DOMESTIC INDUSTRIES

After 1815 two factors converged to halt the good times. Renewed imports from Europe coincided with the rise of British machine-made lace, severely curtailing the wages of female lace-makers. By the 1830s and 1840s, contemporaries conveyed a picture of a pauperised industry in the Bedfordshire countryside.[33] Major Burns, reporting to the 1843 Children's Employment Commission, found the trade in a 'depressed state', the numbers learning the trade 'very much diminished'.[34] The industry attempted to compete with machine-made lace by adopting repetitive patterns and coarser thread. This partly succeeded in the 1850s and 1860s when Maltese lace was in vogue, resulting in a mid-Victorian boom for the English handmade lace industry. However, in the long term these changes lowered the standards of the lace product and diminished the skills of workers. Ultimately the decline of handmade lace in the face of machinery competition could not be prevented. Lace schools also died out in the 1870s under pressure to reform after the passing of the 1867 Workshop Act and the 1870 Education Act.[35] The decline of the trade caught the attention of local authorities and philanthropists, and, in the general revival of interest in rural life and handicrafts at the end of the century, a number of Lace Associations were established to secure a market for the production of better quality lace.[36] One of these, the Midlands Lace Association, was formed in 1891 and covered the counties of Bedford, Buckingham and Northampton. The impact of such organisations was negligible however. At its peak, the Midlands Association had no more than 400 lace-makers on its records.[37] Thus, in 1893 Bear characterised the industry as 'nearly extinct' in Bedfordshire, with few women, 'who injure their health by stooping over this monotonous and tiresome work'.[38]

The straw-plaiting trade originated in Tuscany in the fourteenth century and, like lace-making, was introduced into Britain by sixteenth-century refugees.[39] By the late seventeenth century the industry was firmly localised in the south Midlands region, although it did not become a significant employer until the end of the eighteenth century. The light, chalky soils of

---

[33] Following the French Wars, import duties were lowered in 1826, 1842 and 1846 but were not removed altogether until 1860. See Patricia Wardle, *Victorian Lace* (London, 1968), p. 136. Heathcote patented his improved machine for bobbin net in 1809 and the manufacture of machine lace spread thereafter. See Pinchbeck, *Women Workers*, p. 209.

[34] PP 1843, XVI, Report by Burns, p. 12.

[35] Under the 1867 Act, no child under 8 could be employed. Between the ages of 8 and 13, children were to attend elementary school for at least ten hours a week under the half-time system. Regulations were notoriously difficult to enforce. Horn, *Victorian Countrywomen*, p. 181.

[36] Spencerley, 'The lace associations'.

[37] Horn, *Victorian Countrywomen*, p. 172.

[38] PP 1893–4, XXXV, Report by Bear, p. 24.

[39] Freeman, *Luton and the Hat Industry*, p. 8; C. M. Law, 'Luton and the hat industry', *East Midland Geographer*, 4 (1968), pp. 329–41 (p. 329).

the Chilterns were essential to the growth of good-quality wheat, and along with easy access to local and national markets (Luton, Dunstable and London), explained the establishment of the straw industry in this particular area of England. By 1860 one local observer could write:

> Bedfordshire has long been celebrated for the production of beautiful wheat straws, suitable for the purpose of plaiting. . . . Straw growing now extends throughout the southern part of the country, in the valleys and along the slopes of the Chiltern hills, and also in parts of Hertfordshire, Buckinghamshire, Oxfordshire and Berkshire.[40]

The suitability of the Midlands product was reflected in the fact that Essex and Suffolk dealers purchased straw in Hitchin market and transported it back to their localities.[41] The industry grew rapidly during the Napoleonic War period – both geographically and in terms of the numbers it employed – as the import of superior Italian goods was halted. Thomas Batchelor noted the expansion of the plaiting district in Bedfordshire in 1808:

> Straw-plaiting was formerly confined to the chalky part of the county; but has been so much encouraged within the last few years, that it has spread rapidly over the whole southern district, as far as Woburn, Ampthill, and Shefford.[42]

As a result, areas previously noted for lace-making gave way to straw-plaiting under the inducement of higher wages.[43] The introduction of the straw-splitting machine in 1800, making a finer and fancier plait possible, further aided the growth of the industry.[44] The presence of renewed imports from Italy and Switzerland after 1815 depressed the straw-plait trade, but it was only after the importation of cheap plait from the Far East in the 1870s that the collapse of the English industry began in earnest. The wave of cheaper goods from Asia appeared at the same time as the sewing machine in the bonnet industry. The home-plaiting industry was simply unable to meet the increased demand of the bonnet trade. In 1893 it was estimated that less than 5 per cent of the plait sold at Luton market was English, and around the

---

[40] A. J. Tansley, 'On the straw plait trade', *Journal of the Society of Arts*, 9 (1860), pp. 69–77 (p. 69).
[41] Law, 'Luton and the hat industry', p. 332; Sharpe, 'The women's harvest', p. 130.
[42] Thomas Batchelor, *General View of the Agriculture of the County of Bedford* (London, 1808), p. 594.
[43] At Northill, originally at the centre of the lace-making district, it became impossible to find applicants for Hutchinsons' Charity for educating and apprenticing fatherless girls 'in consequence of their preferring the home industry of plaiting, at that time very flourishing'. Quoted in John G. Dony, *A History of the Straw Hat Industry* (Luton, 1942), pp. 32–3.
[44] Sharpe, *Adapting to Capitalism*, p. 57.

Woburn district it was noted that the 'plaiting industry once hardly inferior to that of agriculture as the mainstay of the working class in the district, is all but extinct'.[45]

Agriculture, lace and straw: competing industries

The portrayal of Bedfordshire agriculture in the nineteenth century is an overwhelmingly male one. Batchelor wrote in 1808 that 'very few women attend to any of the business of agriculture'.[46] We saw in Chapter 2 how parish replies to the Rural Queries in the early 1830s depict an absence of women engaged in agricultural labour in regions where domestic industries were situated. George Culley, reporting on Bedfordshire for the 1867 Royal Commission on Children, Young Persons and Women in Agriculture, confirms this pattern:

> It is not, however, the custom to employ women in farm labour in Bedfordshire. In the north of the county the females of the labouring class are engaged in lace-making, and in the south and more populous part of the county in plaiting straw.[47]

A fixed dichotomy between male outdoor agricultural activity and female indoor work in cottage industries in Bedfordshire is firmly entrenched in the literature. This sharp distinction does not allow for any possible links between the industries. An exploration of this issue will help us to understand how these industries competed for male, female and child labour, and the impact rival trades had on local wage and family work patterns in the nineteenth century.

An analysis of farm records substantiates the view that agriculture in Bedfordshire was a male-dominated operation. Table 5.1 shows the annual expenditure on male, female and child day labourers – as well as task work operations – on eleven farms in the county. Women workers feature in the labour books of only four farms throughout the century: Podington in 1795, Eversholt in 1811, Luton in 1835 and Shillington in 1894. On no farms do women account for more than 3 per cent of annual expenditure on labour. The relative invisibility of women, and the points where they are present in the fields, is revealing, and discloses much about the interrelationship between agricultural and domestic industries in the regional economy of Bedfordshire. How this association functioned and changed over

---

[45] Horn, *Victorian Countrywomen*, p. 169; PP 1893–4, XXXVII, Report by Collett, p. 24.
[46] Batchelor, *General View . . . of Bedford*, p. 597.
[47] PP 1867–8, XVII, Report by Culley, p. 124.

Table 5.1 Annual farm expenditure on male, female and child labour in nineteenth-century Bedfordshire

Farm	Year	% Men	% Women	% Children	% Task
Podington Manor Farm	1795	82	1	3	14
	1841	78	0	8	14
	1885	78	0	6	16
Eversholt	1811	77	3	1	19
Birchfield	1818	55	0	6	39
Manor Farm, Upper Stondon	1832	61	0	8	31
	1862	85	0	4	11
Rameridge End Farm, Luton	1835	87	1	12	*
Cardington	1848	88	0	10	2
Chalgrave Manor Farm	1848	86	0	10	4
Chawston Manor Farm	1869	90	0	10	*
Manor Farm, Stevington	1875	93	0	7	*
Duck End Farm, Wilstead	1881	83	0	17	0
Parsonage Farm, Shillington	1894	93	2	5	*

Note: * On these farms it was impossible to distinguish task work payments from ordinary weekly wages.

Sources: BLARS, OR 1370–81, Farm and estate accounts of Richard Orlebar, Podington, 1792 to 1888; University of Reading Library (hereafter URL), BED P245/1, Farm accounts, Eversholt, 1802 to 1817; BLARS, X 297/81, Farm accounts, Birchfield farm, Howbury estate, 1817 to 1819; BLARS, X 159/1–3, Wages books of the Long family, Manor Farm, Upper Stondon, 1817 to 1887; BLARS, Z 600/2, Farm accounts of William Barber of Rameridge End farm, Luton, August 1833–August 1837; BLARS, MIC 85, J. Newman's account books, Cardington, 1839 to 1848; BLARS, X 52/70, Labour book, Chalgrave Manor Farm, 1847 to 1857; BLARS, Z 512/1, Chawston Manor Farm, Labour books of John Wilkinson of Roxtow, 1868 to 1885; BLARS, X 117/22, Farm account book, Manor Farm, Stevington, 1875 to 1876; BLARS, MIC 85, J. Newman's account books, Duck End Farm, Wilstead, 1875–1891; BLARS, X 230/6, Parsonage farm, Shillington. Accounts, 1893 to 1898.

the course of the nineteenth century will be explored in the remainder of this chapter.

The early nineteenth century

Labour shortages during peak seasons in the agricultural year were apparent in Bedfordshire during the Napoleonic War period. A local doctor alluded to this state of affairs in 1797, arguing that harvest wages had been forced up to an unprecedented level due to the lack of workers:

> Our harvest is very promising, but the price of labour is enormous. What we used to pay 5 shillings an acre for reaping, is now 15s to a guinea which will make

DOMESTIC INDUSTRIES

Table 5.2 Nineteenth-century weekly wages in lace-making, straw-plaiting and agriculture

Year	Women in lace	Women in straw	Men in agriculture
1808	5s–9s	Up to 21s	8s–10s
1834	1s 6d–3s	5s–10s	9s–12s
1843	3s 6d	3s–4s	8s–12s
1867–8	2s 6d–3s	2s 6d	11s–14s
1893–4	6d	6d–1s	12s–16s

Sources: Batchelor, *General View . . . of Bedford*, p. 596, p. 594, p. 582; PP 1834, XXX, Report from His Majesty's Commissioners for Inquiring into the Administration and Practical Operation of the Poor Laws. Appendix (B.1). Answers to Rural Queries in Five Parts. Part 1, p. 3a, p. 7a, p. 8a; PP 1843, XVI, Report by Burns, p. a11, p. a12; PP 1867–8, XVII, Report by Culley, p. 134, p. 136; PP 1893–4, XXXV, Report by Bear, p. 24.

considerable difference in regard to the profits on the produce. Thanks to Mr. Pitt for having been the cause of destroying so many of our fellow countrymen and of making of those few that remain at home soldiers.[48]

Yet, even in those extraordinary times, farmers in the county did not secure the assistance of female workers to satisfy labour demands. At Podington Manor Farm, a 215-acre farm situated in north Bedfordshire, three women were very casually employed for a few days weeding barley in June, haymaking in late July and raking barley in October 1795. The three women were paid £2 11s 10d in total, or 1 per cent of farm outgoings in that year.[49] At Eversholt in 1811 women were employed for a number of days between May and August, and although tasks were not recorded in this account, the pattern of work is likely to replicate that at Podington. This was a small farm employing two to four male labourers in this year with total labour outgoings of £91 17s 8d.[50] Like other southern counties, these two farms in Bedfordshire continued to rely on a core male workforce during the Napoleonic Wars.

The absence of women farmworkers during the French Wars is more easily explained for Bedfordshire than for other counties where no alternative employment opportunities existed outside the agricultural market. The remunerative value of both lace-making and straw-plaiting largely kept women from agricultural labour. Table 5.2 illustrates the level of weekly wages obtained by women working in the two domestic industries in the nineteenth century, and males engaged in agricultural labour. The peak in female earnings in the first decade of the century is clear. Straw-plaiting was by far the most lucrative trade: weekly earnings of a guinea were reported

---

[48] BLARS, BS 2094, Letter from William Lee Antoine to Lawer, 20 August 1797.
[49] BLARS, OR 1370. Women may also have worked alongside their husbands at task work in the harvest though.
[50] URL, BED P245/1.

in some regions of the county. Batchelor was somewhat sceptical about this amount, speculating that some workers would 'boast of their earnings', but he believed it was 'an undoubted fact, that straw-plait to the value of a guinea, and upwards, has been sometimes manufactured in one week by a single person'.[51] It is not surprising that straw-plaiting ousted lace-making as the dominant occupation of women in the southern region of Bedfordshire at this time, but even those districts entirely reliant on lace prospered. An experienced lace-maker could earn up to 9s a week, the equivalent of an average weekly male wage in agriculture. 'The families of those women who do not understand this useful art', Batchelor complained, 'are often extremely troublesome to the parishes.'[52]

The affluence of these domestic industries and the effect on local agriculture is shown clearly by comments made by the authors of the General Views of the neighbouring county of Buckinghamshire. In 1794 it was noted that rural industries did 'not employ so great a number of hands as to produce any particular effect upon the agriculture of the district'.[53] By 1813 however, employment in lace and straw manufacture was so 'advantageous . . . that the farmer suffers: no women nor young persons will work in the field'.[54] As Sharpe points out, the main seasons for plaiting – spring and summer – overlapped with the peak times for the employment of women in agriculture for tasks such as weeding and hoeing.[55] The high earnings in straw work would have therefore dissuaded women from participation in agricultural labour. Lace-making was less interwoven with the agricultural calendar but was still essentially incompatible with agricultural work. This is illustrated by Joanna Bourke's research on the Irish lace-making industry. In some regions attempts were made to establish lace-making as a supplementary form of labour for the wives and daughters of labourers in slack agricultural seasons when their labour on farms was not required. A number of problems resulted from this experiment. Lace output in these areas dropped in the spring and autumn seasons when women's work in agriculture peaked, an interruption in production not appreciated by lace dealers. In addition, higher wages had to be paid to try and retain lace workers during the harvest period, and women found their coarsened hands clumsy for detailed lace work.[56]

Statements of high female earnings are plentiful but should not obscure characteristics of the two industries that impeded women's potential income. Even though the general economic conditions were favourable in the early

---

[51] Batchelor, *General View . . . of Bedford*, p. 594.
[52] Ibid., p. 596.
[53] William James and Jacob Malcolm, *General View of the Agriculture of the County of Buckinghamshire* (London, 1794), p. 46.
[54] Revd St John Priest, *General View of the Agriculture of Buckinghamshire* (London, 1813), p. 81.
[55] Sharpe, 'The women's harvest', p. 134.
[56] Bourke, '"I was always fond of my pillow"', p. 162.

nineteenth century, the straw-plait industry still experienced great seasonal fluctuations. Plaiting was essentially a springtime occupation, with the peak in demand and wages between April and June.[57] The spring and early summer price of plait was double that of autumn and winter. Lucy Luck, a plait worker from Hertfordshire, wrote in her autobiography, 'The straw work is very bad, as a rule, from July up to about Christmas'.[58] Moreover, as Batchelor noticed, expedients such as the expense of the straw and the time occupied in sorting and bleaching the article were often 'overlooked in those high-sounding calculations'.[59] In the late eighteenth and early nineteenth centuries, the plaiters bought straw bundles direct from local farmers, cut into lengths and split ready for plaiting at home. As the trade increased, dealers quickly moved in, purchasing the straw from farmers, then sorting it and selling it to women in smaller quantities and at higher prices. The finished plait was coiled into scores (twenty yards) ready for sale. The poorest women sold to the village dealers, often at lengths of less than twenty yards: the need was the greatest but the prices paid were the lowest. It was far more advantageous for women to sell at market themselves, vying for the highest price alongside other sellers and dealers. Edwin Grey, who grew up in the Hertfordshire village of Harpenden, describes this process:

> Many of the women preferred to sell their plait at greater advantage in the open market at St. Albans, than to any of the merchants calling and collecting locally, also at the same time the money obtained could be spent more advantageously at the large shops in the town.[60]

Lace-makers were less affected by dramatic seasonal fluctuations but were more dependent on dealers, whose exploitative tactics could significantly affect the remuneration women received for their work. Lace workers were dependent on dealers for thread, patterns, orders and payments on completion. They were under an obligation to sell lace made from a buyer's pattern to that buyer alone. In the lace villages there was a 'cut-off' day every four to five weeks, where lace was removed from the pillow and sold. The lace dealers were either independent salesmen who bought lace from workers and resold it to merchants, or they were agents for a merchant. The latter type of middlemen took over much of the business of sale in the nineteenth century and conducted it without an in-depth knowledge of the craft, concerned only

---

[57] The records of the Dunstable plait dealer illustrates this seasonal pattern. The number of women he employed, and total outgoings were lowest in August to October, picking up in November and December for the spring market. See Horn, *Victorian Countrywomen*, p. 177.
[58] John Burnett, ed., *Useful Toil: Autobiographies of Working People from the 1820s to the 1920s*, 1st edn 1974 (London, 1994), p. 63.
[59] Batchelor, *General View . . . of Bedford*, p. 595.
[60] Edwin Grey, *Cottage Life in a Hertfordshire Village* (St Albans, 1935), p. 78.

with buying and selling at the best prices. Sometimes the agent was a village shopkeeper who paid women in kind, with food and candles exchanged at greatly inflated prices. This was an enormous grievance to lace-makers, and government legislation in 1831 was aimed at outlawing the operation of the truck system. It was largely unsuccessful. In 1863, White found that the system, 'either entire or partial, is the rule, though I am told not the universal rule, of the pillow lace manufacture. The small manufactures or buyers have shops of grocery and drapery, etc., which must be taken in payment.'[61] Dealers also charged women exaggerated sums for thread and other essential equipment. Batchelor estimated that such expenses totalled one-eighth of the gross value of the lace, while White believed the total outlay on 'thread, silk, patterns etc' from buyers could amount 'to a third or more of the entire cost, from the price paid'.[62] These charges are overlooked in most wage estimates. Joseph Bell writes lucidly of how the relationship between his mother and sister and the lace dealer in the village of Turvey in the first half of the nineteenth century was extremely disadvantageous to the workers:

> For all their labour and contrivance they were very badly paid. They had to work long days to earn a few pence . . . by the time they had paid for the hire of their parchment and the cotton they had the handling of very little money indeed but were often in debt – which was often much to their disadvantage, which made them feel very humble and submissive . . . many of these lace dealers were what are called 'Tallymen'. In this way they would get this beautiful lace out of these poor people for a mere nothing. . . . This goes to show how these commercial capitalists had battered and fattened on these poor people.[63]

Seasonal fluctuations and the exploitative tactics of the dealer were exacerbated by changes in fashion. Both lace-making and straw-plaiting were at the mercy of taste. Because of this, as Sharpe points out, the amount of employment and level of wages obtained by rural women working in such trades was dictated by the urban market.[64] Village women were in no position to rally against these conditions.

Did the presence of remunerative domestic industries have an impact on the level of male earnings in agriculture in the early nineteenth century? Previous studies have suggested that they did, with men being paid less than in parishes where no alternative female employment opportunities existed. In Essex, Sharpe found that 'male wages were noticeably lower in parishes with female work of any type, including straw-plaiting'.[65] The basis of poor

---

[61] PP 1863, XVII, Report by White, p. 185

[62] Batchelor, *General View . . . of Bedford*, p. 596; PP 1863, XVII, Report by White, p. 185.

[63] BLARS, FAC 129, The autobiography of Joseph Bell of Turvey. The story of twelve years in the life of a village orphan, 1846 to 1858 told by himself, pp. 14–15.

[64] Sharpe, 'The women's harvest', p. 134.

[65] Sharpe, *Adapting to Capitalism*, p. 59.

male earnings, according to Pinchbeck, was 'the assumption that wives and children by some means or other, earned their own keep'.[66] This supposition does not fully tally with the evidence from early nineteenth-century Bedfordshire, where there was a demarcation between agricultural wages in the northern and southern districts of the county. In the straw-plaiting districts, the buoyancy of female wages in that trade raised the wages of all classes of agricultural workers. Thus, whereas male weekly wages in agriculture were recorded at 8s to 9s in the west and northern villages, 'in the south and eastern district, the wages are in general rather higher; as from 9 to 10 shillings in the greater part of the district included between Eaton-Socon, Dunstable and Luton'.[67] Similarly, the average annual wage of female servants in 1808 was said to be five guineas, although that sum was 'rather below the average of the straw-plait district in the south-east of the county'.[68] The female servants most coveted by farmers were dairymaids. Farmers were forced into elevating payments to certain classes of male and female agricultural workers in order to secure their labour in the face of vibrant industrial competition. As we have seen, they were largely unsuccessful in procuring women for casual work and 'did not find it profitable enough to retain women as day labourers'.[69]

While the benefits of female employment were recognised in the early nineteenth century, the possibility of women earning very high wages drew much condemnation from observers. To many, the very foundations of patriarchal family life were being undermined by the presence of high-earning females. There were frequent reports that women and children gained more from their work than the male head of the household. Certainly in prosperous years men were drawn into straw and lace work, although it was most likely to have been looked upon as a secondary occupation in times of bad weather or underemployment, rather than as a permanent substitute for agricultural work.[70] In 1815 it was noted that across the south Midlands counties 'Lace-making is the employment not only of nearly all the adult and unmarried Females but of Mothers of Families'. In addition, 'Children of both sexes and some cases of Men especially of the aged and infirm and others who are unfit for Laborious occupations' were also engaged in the trade.[71]

---

[66] Pinchbeck, *Women Workers*, p. 202.
[67] Batchelor, *General View . . . of Bedford*, p. 582.
[68] Ibid., p. 581.
[69] Allen, *Enclosure and the Yeoman*, p. 256.
[70] In Ivinghoe, Buckinghamshire, it was found that seventy-six males in 1871 still earned a living as plaiters according to the census of that year. In addition, three men worked as dealers, one man as a straw-cutter and two men as plait dealers in the village. See C. A. Horn and P. Horn, 'The social structure of an "industrial" community: Ivinghoe in Buckinghamshire in 1871', *Local Population Studies*, 31 (1983), pp. 9–20 (p. 10).
[71] Newton and Cowper Museum, Olney, The Proceedings of the Committee of Lace Manufacturers for the Counties of Buckingham, Bedford and Northampton, 1814 to 1815.

Commenting on the straw-plait industry, Grey claimed that 'some of the men and the lads were also good at the work, doing it at odd times, or in the evening after farm work, but this home industry was always looked upon really as women's work'.[72] Other commentators believed men were discouraged from seeking continuous employment, or fully contributing to the family income, allowing their wives and children to become the chief breadwinners of the family. Burns claimed that 'it is too much the case that married men, knowing their wives and families earn enough to support themselves by plaiting, take no care about them, and spend all their own earnings at the beer-houses'.[73]

The productive role bestowed on women through their work in domestic industries had the potential to disrupt traditional patterns of work and divisions of labour.[74] Married female wage-earners were criticised for abandoning their domestic duties in the home; single women were perceived as being too independent due to their financial gains. This not only encouraged young women to turn their backs on service, but also freed them from the constraints of parental supervision and led them into some apparently morally dubious liaisons.[75] Thomas Bennett, Steward to the Duke of Bedford, highlights this viewpoint. Writing on a scheme to pay labourers part of their wages in wheat, Bennett argued that this would 'enable the labourers to grind their own Wheat and make their own Bread':

> The labourers families would also profit by this as it wd accustom them to more domestic work and fit them better for going in Farm Houses etc instead of learning nothing at home but the lace pillow and straw-plaiting, the fertile source of prostitution and other depraved habits, which our villages are become most notorious for.[76]

Batchelor was also condemnatory of the frivolous lifestyle that resulted from sizeable earnings:

> The female sex are fond of the luxury of dress; the lace-makers and female servants, who receive from four to seven guineas per annum, can afford to purchase a pair of shoes every three or four months, and other apparel not much inferior to that of their employers; in consequence of which, in a few years after marriage,

---

[72] Grey, *Cottage Life*, p. 68.
[73] PP 1843, XIV, Report by Burns, p. a50.
[74] Valenze, *First Industrial Woman*, p. 115.
[75] Young commented on the straw-plait trade: 'The farmers complain of it doing mischief, for it makes the poor saucy, and no servants can be procured, or any field work done, where this manufacture establishes itself.' Arthur Young, *General View of the Agriculture of the County of Hertfordshire* (London, 1804), pp. 222–3.
[76] BLARS, R3 4739, Correspondence of the Russell estate. Duke of Bedford's Steward's correspondence. Thomas Bennett to C. Haedy, 1843.

they become dependent on their parish for food and clothing, household furniture, and even rent.[77]

The ability of rural women to earn money was vital to family subsistence in the early nineteenth century. However, women working in the Bedfordshire domestic industries crossed an undefined boundary between earning wages which contributed to family survival, and earning wages which represented undesirable and disruptive qualities: authority, autonomy and extravagance.

1815–1870

After 1815 the correlation between high agricultural wages and the presence of domestic industries decreased. Table 5.2 indicates the collapse in wages in both lace-making and straw-plaiting when peacetime conditions were restored. Wages in the plaiting trade held up better than those in lace in the 1820s and 1830s, although the sense of depression was all-consuming in the observations of commentators like Cobbett. He suggested that domestic manufacture had, by the 1820s, 'greatly declined, and has left in poverty and misery those whom it once well fed and clothed'.[78] The post-war state of agriculture was also depressed. The high ratio of corn-growing land in Bedfordshire, and the seasonal input of labour that this needed, combined with a general shortage of capital for farming improvements after 1815, resulted in 'extreme seasonality' in local labour demands, especially in the Woburn and Ampthill regions of south Bedfordshire.[79] Farm servants were dismissed in large numbers after the end of the French Wars. Thus the attractiveness of women workers for agricultural labour receded in the post-war period. Farm accounts from this period show 'roundsmen' employed on local farms in trivial or inessential work, and paid less than ordinary day or weekly labourers.[80] This surplus labour problem constantly troubled

---

[77] Batchelor, *General View . . . of Bedford*, pp. 607–8.
[78] William Cobbett, *Cottage Economy*, 1st edn 1822 (Oxford, 1979), p. 154.
[79] William Apfel and Peter Dunkley, 'English rural society and the new poor law: Bedfordshire, 1834–1847', *Social History*, 10 (1985), pp. 37–68 (p. 59). Like other south-east counties, the conversion of land to arable production had been rapid during the Napoleonic period, under the inducement of high corn prices. By the mid-nineteenth century, 70 per cent of land in Bedfordshire was under arable cultivation. Bennett, 'Farming of Bedfordshire', p. 18.
[80] Under the roundsmen system, labourers were taken on by the farmers in the village in proportion to each farm's rateable value. The farmer received back from the poor rate part or all of the money given as wages to labourers. See A. F. Cirket, 'The 1830 riots in Bedfordshire: Background and events', *Bedfordshire Historical Record Society*, 57 (1978), pp. 75–112 (p. 75). Farm accounts which record this system in operation include Podington Manor Farm, BLARS, OR 1370, 1792 to 1802 and Birchfield farm on the Howbury estate, BLARS X 297/82.

landowners and poor law officials in the 1820s and 1830s. Another letter penned by the Duke of Bedford's Steward is illustrative of this concern:

> Men have been then to spare in every parish round about us during Harvest, a striking proof that the population is overabundant: we have made no arrangements as yet; but there are so many out of work, in Ridgemont, Crawley and Eversholt, that we must do something this Week.[81]

Poor relief in the county doubled in the first two decades of the century, peaking in 1830.[82] By 1834 men working on farms could expect to earn between 9s and 12s a week. By this date the trade in lace was described as being in a 'very bad state',[83] with earnings of 1s 6d to 3s a week reported.[84] Straw work was still held to be profitable in some parishes. At Caddington it was claimed that single women could earn from 7s to 10s per week and married women from 5s to 7s, according to the size of their family.[85] Across the rest of the county, wages ranging from 1s to 6s per week 'according to the work' were declared.[86] The 'very depressed state' of business persisted into the 1840s: women were found to be working up to fourteen hours a day in order to earn a maximum sum of 4s a week: 'the earnings now of the plaiters at least a third less than they were in former years.'[87] The situation for lace-makers was much the same: 'A young woman must work hard for 14 or 15 hours a day to earn 3s 6d a week, who formerly could easily have made 8 or 9s.'[88] By the time Culley reported in the 1860s, male agricultural wages in the plait districts were the lowest in the county; 11s per week before extras.[89] In the early years of the century the lace, straw and agricultural industries had competed for the services of Bedfordshire workers; by the mid-nineteenth century the domestic industries had only a limited effect on the agricultural labour market. John Howlett, writing in the late eighteenth century, had noted the correlation between flourishing industry and high agricultural wages. He also correctly predicted the fate of the latter when the former declined:

> the fluctuation of manufacturers themselves will greatly affect the earnings of the husbandmen and his family. While manufacturers are flourishing and increasing,

---

[81] BLARS, R3 3772, Correspondence of the Russell estate. Duke of Bedford's Steward's correspondence. Thomas Bennett, August, 1833.
[82] Apfel and Dunkley, 'English rural society', pp. 39–40.
[83] PP 1843, XVI, Report by Burns, p. 7a.
[84] PP 1834, XXX, p. 8a.
[85] Ibid., p. 3a.
[86] Ibid., p. 8a.
[87] PP 1843, XVI, Report by Burns, p. a11. The depression was caused by the removal of protection tariffs in 1842.
[88] Ibid., p. a12.
[89] PP 1867–8, XVII, Report by Culley, p. 124.

the price of agricultural labour in the immediate vicinity will flourish and increase too; but the decline of the former will soon be followed by the decline also of the latter.[90]

Despite the downturn in the prosperity of the domestic industries after Waterloo, there is little evidence to suggest that women sought to supplement or supplant their more modest earnings in lace and straw by agricultural employment. Women are virtually absent from all Bedfordshire farm accounts from the 1820s down to the 1890s. At Podington Manor Farm in 1841 Hannah and Bet Lovell, Hannah and Lucy Brown and Sarah Clark were employed for weeding in June and shocking oats and barley in September, but payments made to these women represented less than 1 per cent of the farm's labour expenditure in that year.[91] At Rameridge End Farm near Luton, one solitary woman was engaged at harvest time according to the accounts of 1835, earning £1 for her work.[92] The presence of the women on these farms was exceptional and not their usual employment: the women from Podington were all described as lace-makers by the occupational census of 1851. Given the incompatibility of agricultural employment and work in the domestic industries, these findings are not unexpected.

In the absence of female labourers, who carried out the tasks typically labelled 'women's work' in agriculture? Weeding, stone-picking and hoeing, haymaking and cultivating root crops were performed by boys and male teenagers working with adult men. Female child labour was practically unheard of in Bedfordshire: the expenditure for all farms on child labour in Table 5.1 went on male children. In the 1860s Culley suggested that 'Where females are not employed the ordinary staff per 1,000 acres would be increased by as many lads between 10 and 18 as would represent 5 women'. Thus on a large arable farm, the usual staff included eight lads between the ages of 13 and 18, nine boys aged 10 to 13 and three boys aged 8 to 10.[93] Boys were largely employed on the same farms as their fathers, often working in teams. At Podington in 1795 'Brown and 2 sons' were recorded in the accounts. At Eversholt in 1811 'Valentine and boy' worked year round, as did 'Whitbread and his three sons' at Upper Stondon in the early 1860s.[94] Payments in all these cases went to the father of the group; the total amount of expenditure on child labour in Table 5.1 is therefore an underestimate of the true total.

Boys were expected to attend village schools to learn the rudiments of lace-making and straw-plaiting until the age of 8, after which they were

---

[90] Revd John Howlett, 'The different quantity and expense of agricultural labour in different years', *Annals of Agriculture*, 18 (1792), pp. 566–72 (p. 571).
[91] BLARS, OR 1370–81. See 1376 which covers the years 1835 to 1850.
[92] BLARS, Z 600/2.
[93] PP 1867–8, XVII, Report by Culley, p. 126.
[94] URL, BED P245/1; BLARS, OR 1370; BLARS, X 159/3.

engaged on farms as ploughboys or teamboys, their services required year round. Surviving daily diaries of work done and numbers of men and boys employed on the Woburn estate highlight the reliance on the labour of boys in that area. In 1806 to 1807, Park Farm employed twenty-six male labourers, rising to thirty-one at harvest. Twenty-two boys worked alongside them, with twenty-eight employed in August. No women worked on this farm.[95] According to Culley, a gang of boys was still employed on the same farm in the 1860s: the heavy reliance on male children had not lessened.[96] The accounts from Podington Manor Farm in the early 1840s tell a similar story. In 1841 up to ten ploughboys were employed all year, with extra boys used in May and June to weed and gather twitch, and in July for haymaking.[97] Robert Long, the farmer at Upper Stondon, kept a detailed dairy of daily farm labour in the 1860s, indicating the employment of men and boys for those arable jobs usually performed by women. This is particularly clear in entries from the spring and early summer months when men and boys were engaged in weeding, hoeing and haymaking tasks alongside their other jobs. On 3 May 1862, for example, he wrote, 'The men have been hoeing in Debditch since the Dung carting was finished'; on 31 May, 'The men have been hoeing the winter beans again, and the Mangold Wurzel and two day weeding the wheat in Chibley Meadow'. In June, the men and boys 'when not at the Hay have been hoeing the Beet plants in Rye close', and on 12 July 'The company of men and boys have been hoeing out the weeds between the Beans this week since finishing the Beet'.[98] Women agricultural workers were seen as being particularly suited to cleaning and planting tasks in nineteenth-century arable cultivation. The scarcity of women available for farm labour in Bedfordshire caused farmers to rely on a male workforce. To those who had been so shocked by the conditions encountered by female agricultural workers in other counties of England, this was a welcome change.

Why did women not seek more farmwork after depression hit the domestic industries? It has already been shown that the demand for female agricultural labour had contracted during the post-war years of depression, as farm service declined and surplus male workers saturated the labour market. Another explanation pertains to female earnings in the domestic industries. The Royal Commissions of the 1830s, 1840s and 1860s investigated the industries at downturns in trade. But even in these circumstances female wages could be fairly substantial: replies to the 1834 Poor Law Report indicated that women in Bedfordshire were still contributing around 13 per cent of the total annual family income through their work in the domestic industries.[99] In other years

---

[95] BLARS, R3 2114/264–316, Woburn estate accounts. Park Farm, Priestly Farm and Speedwell Farm, daily diaries of work done, 1806 to 1808.
[96] PP 1867–8, XVII, Report by Culley, p. 125.
[97] BLARS, OR 1376.
[98] BLARS, X 159/1–3. See X 159/3 for the years 1861 to 1887.
[99] See Chapter 2, Figure 2.2.

DOMESTIC INDUSTRIES

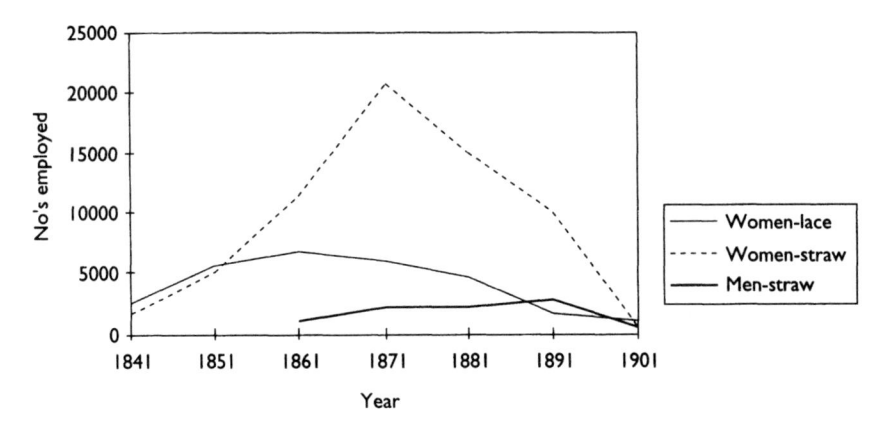

Figure 5.1 Numbers employed in lace-making and straw-plaiting in Bedfordshire, 1841 to 1901

Source: Census Reports of Great Britain, 1841 to 1901

lace-making and straw-plaiting were still lucrative enough to be an attractive employment option. In the late 1840s and 1850s the price and demand for lace reached their highest since 1815, with a large market in America, and continued to strengthen into the early 1860s.[100] The impact of trade fluctuations was recognised by Culley in his report of the late 1860s. When he visited Bedfordshire he found the straw trade to be 'very "bad", and many families were in consequence in great distress'.[101] But he also noted that in better years women and men were still able to earn higher wages in the domestic industries 'than persons of the same sex employed in agriculture'.[102] Tansley made the same point. In the 1850s he discovered the earnings of a good plaiter, after deductions, to be between 5s and 7s 6d a week 'in a good state of trade'. From this, 'a well-ordered family will obtain as much or more than the husband who is at work on the neighbouring farm'.[103]

Looking at the census figures, female employment in both lace-making and straw-plaiting in the county actually increased across the middle decades of the nineteenth century. The figures may not duplicate those of the late eighteenth and early nineteenth centuries, but they show that thousands of women continued to be engaged in domestic industries. According to the census data, the number of female lace-makers (of all ages) in Bedfordshire peaked in 1861 at 6714 and remained stable in 1871 at 6051 (see Figure 5.1). White outlines this trend in his report of 1863:

---

[100] G. F. R. Spencerley, 'The English pillow lace industry, 1840–1880: A rural industry in competition with machinery', *Business History*, 19 (1977), pp. 68–87 (p. 71).
[101] PP 1867–8, XVII, Report by Culley, p. 124.
[102] Ibid.
[103] Tansley, 'On the straw plait trade', p. 72.

In some parts the pillow lace employment has much declined, and as it seems permanently, probably, from the improvement of machine-made lace; in all it is depressed from the state of fashion and temporary causes. Still the number of persons employed, and the amount paid for labour, are very large. One manufacturer alone employs 3,000 people, and others spoken of as in the same rank of business.[104]

The number of female plaiters in the county peaked in 1871 at 20,701. The trade was still prosperous enough to employ over 2000 men in Bedfordshire until the 1890s. The number of men recorded as lace-makers in the nineteenth-century censuses was tiny however. In 1851 only thirty-two males were classified in this occupation, and nineteen of these were under 15 years of age. How reliable are these census figures? Although there was still likely to be some under-enumeration, on the whole census enumerators seemed much more willing to record women engaged in domestic industries as occupied than women working in agriculture. While female agricultural labour was seasonal and intermittent, lace-making was a year-round occupation and therefore fitted more closely to the designations followed by enumerators. However, this does not explain fully the discrepancy in recording different types of rural female work, as straw-plaiting was also seasonal. The readiness to recognise female labour in domestic industries may be linked to the fact that lace-making and straw-plaiting were more closely connected to the household and were therefore viewed as a more suitable occupation for women.

The dominance of domestic industries in mid-nineteenth-century village occupational structures may be assessed by more detailed analysis of the census at parish level. A useful way to show this is to look at villages we have already encountered in the farm records. It has been shown that at Podington in north Bedfordshire, few women were employed in the fields. This did not mean they were not working: of women aged 15 and over, 55 per cent were classified as lace-makers in 1851. In addition, twenty-seven girls under age 15 were also engaged in the trade. Of those lace-makers aged 15 and over, half were married, over one-third were unmarried and 12 per cent were widows. These women were spread fairly evenly over the age range: 18 per cent were aged 15 to 18 years; 28 per cent between 19 and 30; 26 per cent between 31 and 49 and 28 per cent aged 50 and over. The trade, then, was still attractive to women of all ages in 1851, and there is little indication that younger women were seeking alternative occupations in this village in the mid-nineteenth century. The majority of married women lace-makers in Podington were betrothed to agricultural labourers (76 per cent), but others were married to tradesmen such as shoemakers, carpenters, sawyers and woodmen. One female lace-maker – Sussanah Knowlton – was married

[104] PP 1863, XVII, Report by White, p. 125.

to the parish clerk, and Sarah Tye's husband was returned as a farmer. No boys or men were classified as being involved in the lace-making industry in this village. The availability of remunerative employment in the home resulted in a high number of Podington households with older children still living at home: in nearly a quarter of homes the residing children were aged 16 and over. The composition of labouring households in Bedfordshire therefore stood in contrast to counties such as the East Riding of Yorkshire, where the majority of children left home before they were 14 years of age to go into farm service. Podington was not a unique parish in Bedfordshire. Osamu Saito has analysed census returns for the village of Cardington in the centre of the county, and found a similar concentration of employment. Moreover, the existence of a population listing in Cardington for 1782 has made analysis over time possible. Saito found that the proportion of Cardington women in the labour force hardly changed between 1782 and 1851, and argues that the effect of lace-making on the labour force participation profiles of females was remarkable, with around 65 per cent of married women in the village occupied in the trade in 1782 and 1851.[105]

A similar concentration of employment was to be found in the plaiting villages of south Bedfordshire in the second half of the nineteenth century. In Upper Stondon the number of women engaged in straw-plaiting in 1861 was high. Although only a small parish, 55 per cent of women aged 15 and over were classified as plaiters. The only alternative employments recorded in the census were house servants at the two village farms. The age range of women engaged in straw-plaiting in Upper Stondon in 1861 shows a slight concentration in the older age groups: 33 per cent of women were aged between 20 and 39 years and 42 per cent aged 40 and over. This parish does not show a predominance of child plaiters as Sharpe found in Essex in the second half of the nineteenth century.[106] Fifty-eight per cent of female plaiters (aged 15 and over) in Upper Stondon were single women. These, Tansley argued, being 'skilful and quick, earn the most'. But one-third of women plaiters were married, and despite the burden of domestic responsibilities, they could still 'contrive to do pretty well' by the trade.[107] Nigel Goose has also uncovered high female employment rates in plaiting villages in his analysis of the 1851 census for the Berkhamstead region of Hertfordshire, where 57 per cent of women aged 15 and over were employed

---

[105] Osamu Saito, 'Who worked when: Life-time profiles of labour force participation in Cardington and Corfe Castle in the late eighteenth and mid nineteenth centuries', *Local Population Studies*, 22 (1979), pp. 14–29 (p. 25). The listings for Cardington have been used by other historians. See, in particular, R. S. Scofield, 'Age-specific mobility in an eighteenth-century rural English parish', *Annals de Démographic Historiqué* (1970), pp. 261–74; David Baker, 'The inhabitants of Cardington in 1782', *Bedfordshire Historical Record Society*, 52 (1973). The list is reprinted in full in the latter text.
[106] Sharpe, 'The women's harvest', p. 138.
[107] Tansley, 'On the straw plait trade', p. 72.

in the straw-plaiting trade. Thirty-five per cent of married women were engaged in the work. Thus, as Goose argues, straw-plaiting provided more work for married women than the cotton manufacturing towns of the north-west, where only 26 per cent of married women worked in 1851.[108]

Female workers in domestic industries experienced great fluctuations in wage levels and demand over time, but up to the 1870s both lace and straw work were still attractive enough to maintain large numbers of Bedfordshire women in work. Until the 1870s straw work was still a viable option for women to earn money and 'usually paid much better than farm work for women'.[109] Even lace-making paid 'sufficiently well to keep a number of women employed at it'.[110] Although the women employed at Podington in the 1840s could earn up to 1s 4d a day in agricultural work, the very casual, sporadic nature of the work meant that, over the whole year, wages earned by plaiting straw or making lace could be substantially more profitable to women workers. Moreover, both trades employed women at all stages of the lifecycle. The reasons for this are not hard to pinpoint and provide another reason why women continued to work in the domestic trades. For young, single women, they offered more freedom and independence than service or farmwork. Straw-plait in particular could be manufactured outdoors, and groups of young women and children congregating in the village lanes were a common sight. Lace-making, although more confining, could also be a social occupation. In the summer months women would sit outdoors in groups talking as they worked at their pillows. In winter, partly to economise on candles, they would work together indoors. For married women with children, both occupations could be fitted around the daily routine of household chores. Work could also be arranged around other economic activities such as taking in washing and tending gardens. Grey's description of the flexibility of women's work patterns in the plaiting villages is instructive:

> The housewife could, when wanting to go on with other household work, put aside her plaiting, resuming it again at any time. She could also do the work sitting in the garden, or while standing by the cottage door, enjoying a chat or gossip with her neighbours. The mother also could rock the cradle with her foot, while using both hands at the plaiting, and also in the summer time when strolling in the lanes or fields they would most often be plaiting. I've often seen groups of women and girls gathered in little groups round the cottage doors or on the commons, talking and laughing and all busy plaiting.[111]

Similarly, Emma Thompson of Cardington recounts how she could complete all her housework chores before bringing out the lace pillow:

---

[108] Nigel Goose, *Population, Economy and Family Structure in Hertfordshire in 1851: The Berkhamsted Region* (Hatfield, 1996), p. 36.
[109] PP 1893–4, XXXV, Report by Bear, p. 20.
[110] Ibid.
[111] Grey, *Cottage Life*, pp. 69–70.

DOMESTIC INDUSTRIES

Well in those days it didn't take long to make Jam and marmalade as we couldn't get the sugar, neither did it take long to clean our furniture, as we only got a round deal table and about three chairs and an old stool or two, and no grates... I can tell you I used to get all done and ready for the lace pillar at nine o'clock.[112]

1870–1900

The decline of the lace-making and straw-plaiting industries in Bedfordshire was a protracted affair. Only in the last quarter of the nineteenth century did a complete collapse occur. Between 1871 and 1891 the number of female lace-makers in the county fell by some 75 per cent. In 1901 there were 1144 women employed in the Bedfordshire industry. In straw-plaiting, the decline of female employment was also dramatic. In the same twenty years after 1871, the number of women recorded as straw-plaiters declined by half. In 1901 just 485 females were classified in the occupation. As we have seen, at the close of the nineteenth century both trades were depicted as pauperised and low-status occupations. Weekly wages in the early 1890s were pitiful: 6d in lace-making and 6d to 12d in straw work (see Table 5.1). Such lowly earnings were still useful to certain sections of the female labour force though. For elderly, infirm or widowed women – or those women who had little opportunity to turn their hand to anything else because of family circumstances – the persistence of domestic industries after the 1870s was appreciated. In 1900 it was noted that 'There are hundreds of women between sixty and ninety years of age quite unfit for any other kind of work who keep themselves by it in independence'.[113] The testimony of Mrs Thomson from the early twentieth century also reveals this viewpoint:

Well I am so glad there is still a laceman, as I am sure poor people were Glad of a laceman when I was a child, and since I have been a woman we were almost starved and we should have been quite if there hadn't been a laceman.[114]

As the nineteenth century wore on, younger women began to hold employment in the decaying lace and straw trades in contempt and started to move into service, a complete reversal of the Napoleonic War period. This trend was most noticeable in the lace districts of north Bedfordshire where few alternative opportunities existed. Thomas Lester, one of the main lace manufacturers of the county, gave evidence to the 1863 Children's Employment Commission and noted the beginning of this change. 'There are as many young girls employed upon lace in this district as there ever were',

---

[112] BLARS, CRT 150/121, 'The good old times', *Bedfordshire Times*, April 1910.
[113] Channer and Roberts, *Lacemaking in the Midlands*, p. 62.
[114] BLARS, CRT 150/121.

he contended, 'though the pay is much lower and consequently more of the bigger girls leave lace to go into service.'[115] Mrs Carter, who lived at Clapham, also highlights this shift in the attitude of young women in the second half of the century:

> I made lace often eight hours a day. . . . We used to have boiled onions almost every night to eat with our potatoes instead of meat, for there was eight of us to live, and I know I was glad enough to go off to a farm house at Riseley to get a good living in a farm house.[116]

In the plaiting districts, young single women were recruited into the more lucrative employment of sewing bonnets and hats in Luton and Dunstable. As a result the population of Luton trebled between 1841 and 1861.[117] By 1871 there were 125 females to every 100 males in both towns. In the age group 20 to 25, women outnumbered men by two to one.[118] Again we can turn to Grey for a clear account of the changing pattern of female employment in the late nineteenth century:

> It seemed quite a natural change over that most of the young women who were engaged in the making of straw plait should at the decline of that industry have come on to straw hat making . . . to the hat factories in the village, or maybe by train to one or other of the numerous factories in Luton and St. Albans. . . . But all were not factory hands; some clothes shop assistants etc., . . . some few of the younger plaiters also entered domestic service, but they were in the minority; many of the married women bordering on middle age, and the active of the middle age, gradually finding work as charwomen, laundry work, etc., at the many villa residences now springing up, while quite a number of the able-bodied elderly women went to work on the farms at certain seasons.[119]

Grey's portrayal is interesting, not least because he points to the possibility of older women moving into farmwork in the final decades of the century as opportunities in domestic industries diminished. There is some evidence to corroborate this opinion and we should not completely dismiss the notion that women did assist with certain agricultural operations in the late nineteenth century. Three arenas where women's presence in the fields was visible emerge from the sources. First, women may have assisted their husbands and families in certain piece-work operations. Mr Druce, Assistant Commissioner to the Royal Commission on the Depressed Condition of Agricultural Interests in the 1880s, claimed that women in Bedfordshire

---

[115] PP 1863, XVII, Report by White, p. 262.
[116] BLARS, CRT 150/121.
[117] Law, 'Luton and the hat industry', p. 337.
[118] D. J. M. Hooson, 'The straw industry of the Chilterns in the nineteenth century', *East Midland Geographer*, 4 (1968), pp. 342–50 (p. 344).
[119] Grey, *Cottage Life*, pp. 227–9.

were 'rarely employed on the farms in this county'. However, he goes on to say that the 'few that are employed help their husbands or male relatives in the harvest field'.[120] Bear, reporting a decade later, echoed these sentiments. Few women were employed in agriculture, he contended, 'unless in assisting their husbands or fathers at piece-work'.[121] Second, women also participated in gleaning the fields after the harvest, as they had done throughout the nineteenth century. The valuable contribution this source of income made to the family economy may have offset the fact that women generally could not participate in agricultural work at the same time as making lace or plaiting straw. Tansley wrote of the 'interruption of harvest time' to plaiting work, when 'plaiters do but little then, especially when the time of gleaning arrives'.[122] This operation features strongly in autobiographical writing from the area. A resident in the village of Wooton remembered 'Scores of women folk' obtaining 'enough to keep them in the winter time in flour' by their gleanings.[123] Grey's recollections are also revealing:

> The gleaning season was made the most of by many of the cottage women, for the flour obtained as a result of this wheat gleaned was a great asset to the food supply of the household during the autumn and early winter. . . . The number who did so, together with the boys and girls, was quite considerable. I should think perhaps that this time of the year must have been somewhat slack as regards plaiting, for I cannot recollect seeing very much of it being done during this period.[124]

The market gardening districts of south-east Bedfordshire represent the third instance where women were found working in agriculture. There had been a steady increase in the number of gardeners and acreage of gardening land in the early nineteenth century, but it was after the opening of the Great Northern Railway in 1851 that the industry began to assume extensive proportions, based particularly around the Biggleswade and Sandy regions.[125] Quicker journeys to London – an already established market – were now possible, new markets were opened up in the Midlands and north of England and vast quantities of horse manure were able to be transported from London to Bedfordshire by train. The depression in corn prices after the 1870s contributed to a shift in resources to market gardening, and statistics show an increase from 3885 to 7997 acres of land being used for this purpose

---

[120] PP 1882, XV, Royal Commission on Depressed Condition of Agricultural Interests. Report by Mr Druce on the East of England, p. 9.
[121] PP 1893–4, Report by Bear, pp. 19–20.
[122] Tansley, 'On the straw plait trade', p. 71.
[123] Quoted in Brenda Fraser-Newstead, *Bedford Yesteryears: The Rural Scene* (Dunstable, 1994), p. 103.
[124] Grey, *Cottage Life*, pp. 118–19.
[125] F. Beavington, 'The development of market gardening in Bedfordshire, 1799–1939', *Agricultural History Review*, 23 (1975), pp. 23–48 (p. 31).

in Bedfordshire between 1885 and 1896.[126] In addition, market gardening was more labour intensive than arable farming, and although the horsedrawn plough had replaced the spade, hand labour still dominated the industry.[127]

Several types of source highlight the appearance of female workers in this agricultural sector. Culley found private gangs of women and children peeling onions for up to twelve weeks for the market gardeners of the Biggleswade neighbourhood in the 1860s. Women earned relatively high wages for this work – 1s to 1s 6d per day (compared to around 2s 6d a week in lace-making and straw-plaiting at this time) – while children over 12 years old were paid 6d a day.[128] In the 1890s, Bear witnessed a 'few women' at work in the pea fields and fruit orchards around Toddington.[129] At St Neots though, female labour was widespread. He discovered women made up 'a good many regular workers' and at Eaton Socon '14 or 15 women, I was told, work regularly in market gardens all year round'.[130] Again turning to local reminiscences, the reliance on female labour for some types of work in the market gardens becomes clear. The following quotes relate to the villages of Stotford and Broom at the turn of the century:

> The pea-picking was in late June and early July, this was done by hand. The women would get up at four o'clock in the morning and arrive at the field with their small stools and lunches. They were paid piece-work for the number of weighed bags.[131]

> At harvest time, the onions were first hand-hoed with one blade, then pulled up and laid in rows to dry. This was done by men, local women and school-children in their summer holidays. The onions were then loaded into carts, brought back to Manor Farm where women from Biggleswade, Stanford, Clifton, Southill, Shefford, Langford (all walked, no bicycles) and Broom, peeled them. . . . The women collected the onions from the yard, then carried them inside in big round tins. . . . They loaded the trays with onions, balanced on their knees, and peeled away, putting the peeled onions in small barrels filled with water. . . . At 4pm a bell was rung and the women formed a queue when the weighing commenced. . . . For each peck and pint brass tokens were given, these were collected and come Friday at 4pm the women queued at Broom House Farm to be paid according to their tokens collected.[132]

---

[126] Beavington, 'Market gardening in Bedfordshire', p. 33.
[127] Beavington, 'Market gardening in Bedfordshire', p. 39. Bear commented in 1892 that a market gardener 'has more men in proportion to his acreage than a large farmer employs'. PP 1893–4, XXXV, Report by Bear, p. 17.
[128] PP 1867–8, XVII, Report by Culley, p. 126.
[129] PP 1893–4, XXXV, Report by Bear, p. 19.
[130] PP 1893–4, XXXV, Report by William Bear upon the Poor Law Union of St Neots, p. 38.
[131] Quoted in Christine Smith, ed., *Stotford Reflections* (Baldock, 1993), p. 72.
[132] Bedfordshire Federation of Women's Institutes, *Bedfordshire Within Living Memory* (Newbury, 1992), pp. 164–5.

Finally, going back to the archival records, the presence of women workers may be seen on some farms towards the end of the nineteenth century. At Parsonage Farm in Shillington, women were employed in 1894 for pulling peas, as well as charlocking and weeding.[133] Similarly, records from Willington Nursery in the first decade of the twentieth century record the employment of women between June and November in weeding, pea-picking and onion work.[134] Expenditure on women workers at Shillington in 1894 was just 2 per cent of total labour payments, and at Willington in 1910 it was only 4 per cent, but these accounts do indicate a trend in female employment at the end of the century. The contribution made by female labourers to the market gardens of southern England was to increase in the twentieth century and deserves greater attention.

The significance of alternative employment opportunities

The work performed by women in the nineteenth-century Bedfordshire industries of lace-making and straw-plaiting is often characterised as marginal or secondary to the male business of agriculture. Charles Freeman, writing in the 1950s, represented lace-making as 'a picturesque if sweated industry whose earnings supplemented the meagre wages of the farm population'.[135] Correspondingly, Joyce Godber states that lace-making and straw-plaiting were the 'traditional "standbys"' of the wives of agricultural labourers.[136] It is argued by Valenze that the language used to describe female employment in cottage industries has led to the reinscription of 'a historically constructed notion of "supplementary" upon the work of women' which 'impedes our understanding its meaning'.[137] This analysis of census material, contemporary literature and archival records places these industries at the centre of rural women's lives. As Robert Malcolmson suggests for an earlier period, the notion of a 'by-employment' for such female work is misleading.[138] Up to the 1870s both lace-making and straw-plaiting were still profitable enough to engage thousands of women in the county. The prosperity of the Napoleonic Wars era was never replicated, but both remained important employers of rural women until the last quarter of the century.

Throughout the century it was customary for women in Bedfordshire not to work in the fields. When the domestic industries were at their height in the

---

[133] BLARS, X 230/6. Charlock was a wild mustard – a weed with yellow flowers. The women on this farm were aided by girls, one of the few instances of female children being employed by farmers in the county.
[134] BLARS, X 342/5, Willington Nursery records, 1910.
[135] Freeman, *Pillow Lace in the East Midlands*, Preface.
[136] Joyce Godber, *History of Bedfordshire, 1066–1888* (Bedford, 1969), p. 479.
[137] Valenze, *First Industrial Woman*, p. 115.
[138] Robert Malcolmson, *Life and Labour in England, 1700–1780* (London, 1981), pp. 38–9.

early years of the nineteenth century, farmers could not compete with the wages women received for lace and straw work, and complained they could not find women willing to engage in farm labour. Even after the remunerative value of the rural industries abated, women stayed out of the fields except perhaps for gleaning, piece-work at harvest time and some tasks in the market gardens of south-east Bedfordshire. Did women therefore pursue a conscious decision to refuse field labour? While, as Grey argues, there were always some women who 'did not care' for plaiting (or lace) work, preferring 'outdoor work', there is no evidence to indicate that women themselves wished to engage more in agricultural labour.[139] Work in the lace and straw industries was synonymous with long hours, health problems and manipulation by employers. Both trades were classified as unskilled, with the concentration and handiwork needed for intricate lace work in particular, dismissed or unrecognised. These industries, therefore, 'represented an extension of exploitative town-based trades into the countryside to tap into cheap labour supplies – a classic case of outwork'.[140] But women still perceived working in domestic trades as more advantageous to their circumstances than agricultural labour. Charlotte Humhries, a lace worker interviewed in 1843, stated: 'Been in the trade all my life . . . I have four children in the work, and consider it as healthy as any other; think it as healthy, yes, sir, more so than picking stones and working in the fields.'[141] Bear, reporting in the 1890s, certainly understood 'why it has not been customary in the past for women to work on the land' in Bedfordshire, as 'they had something better to do'.[142] However, he was more perplexed by the fact that women still refrained from outdoor work when the domestic industries were 'utterly unremunerative and nearly extinct' at the end of the century:

> very few women do anything in the hayfield, and none in the harvest, I believe . . . . It struck me as very remarkable that I did not see a woman working in an allotment during my visit. . . . This is not to be regretted, as far as women who have families are concerned, as they have quite enough to do in attending to their house duties, but there are many who could well spare time to do occasional work on their husbands' or fathers' allotments. Women are not commonly even employed as dairymaids. Men do the milking and usually turn the churn, while farmers' wives or daughters generally make the butter.[143]

The rise in real wages for Bedfordshire male agricultural labourers alleviated the necessity for married women to work by this time. After the final collapse of wages for women engaged in handmade lace in the 1870s and making

---

[139] Grey, *Cottage Life*, p. 92.
[140] Sharpe, *Adapting to Capitalism*, p. 63.
[141] PP 1843, XIV, Report by Burns, p. 48.
[142] PP 1893–4, XXXV, Report by Bear, p. 20.
[143] Ibid., pp. 19–20.

straw-plait in the 1880s, single women looked to bonnet-making and service as substitutes. Older village women tentatively clung to work in the domestic industries, combining them with a range of other tasks such as charring and taking in washing. Such work represented women's appropriation of more informal means of eking out a living in nineteenth-century rural England. Chapter 6 will survey these informal channels of employment in more detail.

6

Survival strategies

Women, work and the informal economy

The preceding chapters have shown that women's work in the formal labour market was diminishing in many regions over the course of the nineteenth century. This decrease in female productivity was certainly not uniform, and different patterns of participation have been uncovered depending on region, local occupational structure and custom. Female labour was coming under pressure from a number of sectors. The wider use of agricultural technology in the nineteenth century – first the scythe, then the reaper and reaper-binder – undermined women's role in the harvest. Economic forces – agricultural boom followed by depression – opened up and then closed off avenues of other agricultural labour: by the late 1870s farmers were becoming increasingly unlikely to engage women to weed, pick stones and hoe crops as a cost-cutting device. For women who had traditionally worked in domestic industry, the death-knell was sealed in the 1870s and 1880s by another wave of cheap foreign imports. Ideologically women – especially married women – who worked outside the home were increasingly criticised for not conforming to the model of female propriety and dependency expected of the ideal Victorian woman. Simultaneously however, women themselves were becoming less willing to undertake low-paid, low-status, backbreaking labour – for the farmer, the farmer's wife or the local manufacturer. This is partly linked to the rise in real male wages in the latter decades of the nineteenth century, but also denotes a change in women's attitude towards their work. Joanna Bourke notes that the movement of women back into the home in the latter part of the century is 'generally assumed to be one of the great oppressive changes in history'.[1] Yet women did not necessarily perceive the move in this light, and were happy to be relieved of the monotony and degradation of hard physical labour. Bourke argues that many working-class women 'wholeheartedly' embraced their new identity as housewives, which they viewed as a good option, 'the best available'.[2]

---

[1] Joanna Bourke, 'Housewifery in working-class England, 1860–1914', in Pamela Sharpe, ed., *Women's Work: The English Experience, 1650–1914* (London, 1998), pp. 332–58 (p. 333). See also Joanna Bourke, *Working-Class Cultures in Britain, 1890–1960: Gender, Class and Ethnicity* (London, 1994), ch.3.
[2] Bourke, 'Housewifery', p. 334.

Care needs to be exercised when evaluating shifts in women's economic participation in rural England. It is clear that women's opportunities to find work in the formal labour market of many rural regions was becoming more and more restricted. There is also abundant evidence to confirm that male real wages rose across rural England after 1870, easing constraints on the family budget. But despite this, labouring family incomes remained extremely inflexible in the late nineteenth century. The ideal of the family wage – propagated by some prominent rural trade union organisations – remained just that: an ideal.[3] So, although it is important to acknowledge the desire and active route women took to withdraw from the formal labour market, any intermittent earnings women procured could still make a significant difference to an individual family's survival. Women may have been taking a less active role in the formal economy of the nineteenth-century countryside, but they did not become idle or isolated from productive functions. Women were fully involved in the informal economy across the whole century. Some women continued to move between the formal and informal markets as the state of their finances dictated. While it is difficult to probe the mechanisms of informal channels of work and exchange, an assessment of these is essential to a full understanding of female employment patterns in the nineteenth century. Indeed, the significance of the informal economy may have a direct bearing on the ways we approach the study of women's employment in the formal labour market. It is only when women's participation in the whole range of tasks in the informal and domestic economy is considered – and placed alongside trends in formal labour participation – that we can reach a fuller understanding of the economics of everyday life in the countryside.

Women's paid work for an employer tends to dominate the historiography of rural female labour patterns as most of the accessible sources relate to the management of the workforce on farms, estates, country houses and in manufacturing. But the published sources used in this book also hint at the importance of women's involvement in informal exchange. Chapter 2 highlighted the recognition by writers such as David Davies and Frederick Morton Eden of the remunerative value of the whole range of tasks undertaken by

---

[3] The National Agricultural Labourers Union (NALU), formed in 1872 under the leadership of Joseph Arch, argued that women should not be employed in agriculture on three grounds: it kept women from their domestic and motherly duties in the home; it depressed male agricultural wages as women were cheap labour, and it reduced the number of jobs available for male workers in agriculture. The NALU officially excluded women from their membership although this did not mean that women were absent from union strikes and activities. However, as Alun Howkins has pointed out, the preclusion of women may have reflected the growing belief among male agricultural trade unionists that 'respectable' women should not work in the fields. See Alun Howkins, *Reshaping Rural England: A Social History, 1850–1914* (London, 1991), p. 189; Karen Sayer, 'Field-faring women: The resistance of women who worked in the fields of nineteenth-century England', *Women's History Review*, 2 (1993), pp. 185–98.

women. Parliamentary reports also point to this hidden area of women's work. Respondents to the Poor Law Report were conscious that women could often make more money through taking in washing or charring than any other means in the early 1830s. Later Royal Commissions are also sensitive to the variety of options accessed by women: the positive gains from allotments, cultivating garden produce and keeping animals is a recurrent theme in much nineteenth-century printed literature. But whereas historians have been sensitive to the numerous ways women in urban society made ends meet, the astuteness of rural women in manipulating and controlling alternative means of income is less well understood. One avenue available to explore this issue is the rural autobiography. A huge number of these exist, and although they differ greatly in quality, such writing offers an alternative view of rural life that has yet to be fully exploited by historians. Rural autobiographies permit us a glimpse into the broader aspects of rural existence, and the devices women used to 'make shift'.

Defining the informal economy

Historians' appreciation of the less formal methods appropriated by the labouring poor to eke out a living has grown considerably in recent years. Following the pioneering research of Olwen Hufton, a number of terms have been employed to define these strategies. Hufton's study of eighteenth-century France exposed an environment where poor harvests, rising prices, increased population and industrial depression coalesced from the 1750s to produce a severe economic crisis. In such conditions, families found it increasingly difficult to support themselves and turned to an 'economy of makeshifts'. Hufton's definition of a makeshift economy embraced 'innumerable forms of subsidiary income' such as an additional job or seasonal migration to find work. But poverty drove labourers into more undesirable and criminal practices: smuggling, theft, vagrancy, extortion, prostitution, begging, abandonment of children and the elderly, even infanticide.[4] Hufton recognised that in periods of economic depression, women became central to the operation of the system. Mothers, she argues, became 'the pivotal force' of the economy of makeshifts, marshalling 'the family for the purposes of living on its wits', while unmarried women and widows – even more likely than their married counterparts to fall victim to the ravages of poverty – also relied on 'the economy of expedients . . . making shift as best they could'.[5]

---

[4] Olwen Hufton, *The Poor of Eighteenth-Century France, 1750–1789* (Oxford, 1974), p. 16.
[5] Olwen Hufton, 'Women and the family economy in eighteenth-century France', *French Historical Studies*, 9 (1975), pp. 1–22 (p. 19); Olwen Hufton, 'Women without men: Widows and spinsters in Britain and France in the eighteenth century', *Journal of Family History*, winter (1984), pp. 355–76 (pp. 363–4).

Numerous studies of women and the family in nineteenth- and early twentieth-century urban landscapes have drawn upon the idea of an informal economy. At the centre of many accounts stands the formidable and controlling figure of the matriarch. The centrality of the female figure is a common theme in working-class autobiography with Robert Roberts' being the classic description. 'Over our community the matriarchs stood guardians', he writes.[6] In turn-of-the-century Salford the idea of respectability – traded through gossip – underpinned the close-knit streets, defining the boundaries between acceptable and improper behaviour. The sense of neighbourly co-operation was vital:

> Many kindly families little better off than most came to the aid of neighbours in need without thought of reward, here or hereafter . . . not all assistance sprang from the heart: in a hard world one never knew what blows fate would deal; a little generosity among the distressed now could act as a form of social insurance against the future.[7]

These themes resonate through studies of urban communities. Carl Chinn develops the concept of a 'hidden matriarchy' in late nineteenth-century Birmingham, with a mother's duties being 'multi-functional'.[8] Ellen Ross's study of the East End of London reveals a similar pattern. Women were the dominant force in the neighbourhood and kin networks – separate from the material and cultural concerns of men – controlling a number of survival strategies and creating 'shared working class values and identities'.[9] In Ross's words:

> In most neighbourhoods, an 'intermediate' economy, constructed around neighbourhood exchange, scavenging, theft, and barter, and in which wives and children were particularly active, supplemented the (mostly male) wage-based economy. At all times wives' housekeeping skill and their neighbourhood activity, provides the difference between mere subsistence and a reasonable level of comfort.[10]

Reference to 'self-help', 'mutual aid', 'neighbourhood exchange' and 'reciprocal obligation' litter Ross's portrayal of London life.[11] Similarly, in

---

[6] Robert Roberts, *The Classic Slum: Salford Life in the First Quarter of the Century* (Manchester, 1971), p. 26.
[7] Roberts, *Classic Slum*, p. 26.
[8] Carl Chinn, *They Worked all Their Lives: Women of the Urban Poor in England, 1880–1939* (Manchester, 1988), p. 19.
[9] Ellen Ross, 'Survival networks: Women's neighbourhood sharing in London before World War One', *History Workshop Journal*, 15 (1983), pp. 4–27 (p. 5).
[10] Ross, 'Survival networks', p. 7.
[11] Ross, 'Survival networks'; Ellen Ross, 'Labour and love: Rediscovering London's working-class mothers, 1870–1918', in Jane Lewis, ed., *Labour and Love: Women's*

his study of the late nineteenth-century London neighbourhoods of Somers Town, Lisson Grove and Globe Town, Andrew August found women's 'ingenuity and resourcefulness determined the ability of their families to avoid the equivalent of bankruptcy, the workhouse'.[12] Anna Davin's depiction of childhood in the same city augments this portrayal: children often performed domestic and paid labour to contribute to the family purse, which was always controlled by the mother.[13] In late nineteenth-century Lancashire, women found 'alternative strategies' to bolster family incomes.[14] In Newcastle, women's 'resourcefulness' was apparent in the face of 'the never-ending task of making do'.[15] Integral to community life in inter-war Liverpool were 'reciprocity, redistribution, exchange and mutual aid'. There, according to Pat Ayres, 'the working-class family economy consisted of monetary and non-monetary, personal and impersonal, formal and informal, legal and illegal elements'.[16]

The activities falling under women's jurisdiction were extensive and overlapping. They took in lodgers (often kin, but also strangers), washing and sewing, as well as a range of other homeworking pursuits (painting toy soldiers, constructing Christmas crackers, making matchboxes) to earn money.[17] Again, the labour of children was expected in most of these practices. Women also performed household labour for the family – cooking, cleaning, making and mending -- and controlled the budget. The manipulation of credit facilities – predominately pawnbroking, but also pawn running (collecting and selling used clothes), shop credit and money lending – were crucial to women's ability to balance the weekly budget.[18] Close links

---

Experiences of Home and Family, 1850–1940 (Oxford, 1986), pp. 73–96; Ellen Ross, ' "Fierce questions and taunts": Married life in working-class London, 1870–1914', *Feminist Studies*, 8 (1982), pp. 575–602; Ellen Ross, *Love and Toil: Motherhood in Outcast London, 1870–1918* (Oxford, 1993).

[12] Andrew August, *Poor Women's Lives: Gender, Work, and Poverty in Late-Victorian London* (Cranbury, 1999), p. 71.

[13] Anna Davin, *Growing up Poor: Home, School and Street in London, 1870–1914* (London, 1996), ch. 9 and ch. 10.

[14] Elizabeth Roberts, *A Woman's Place: An Oral History of Working-Class Women, 1890–1940*, 1st edn 1984 (Oxford, 1995), p. 148.

[15] Jane Long, *Conversations in Cold Rooms: Women, Work and Poverty in Nineteenth-Century Northumberland* (Woodbridge, 1999), p. 211.

[16] Pat Ayres, 'The hidden economy of dockland families: Liverpool in the 1930s', in Pat Hudson and W. R. Lee, eds, *Women, Work and the Family Economy in Historical Perspective* (Manchester, 1990), pp. 271–90 (p. 287).

[17] For taking in lodgers see Leonore Davidoff, 'The separation of home and work? Landladies and lodgers in nineteenth and twentieth-century England', in Sandra Burman, ed., *Fit Work for Women* (London, 1979), pp. 64–97.

[18] Ayres, 'The hidden economy', p. 281. See also Melanie Tebbutt, *Making Ends Meet: Pawnbroking and Working-Class Credit* (Leicester, 1983); Paul Johnson, *Saving and Spending: The Working-Class Economy in Britain, 1870–1939* (Oxford, 1985).

between neighbours and kin allowed intricate exchanges of aid, time and money: children were minded; clothes, linen and money were lent; births, deaths and illnesses were supervised; errands were run; shelter was offered in times of violence or crisis; collections were made and official intrusion was blocked. Most of these services were based on reciprocal obligation and acted as an insurance policy against desperation. Reneging on this understanding could have disastrous consequences for a family's reputation and well-being. The informal economy, as Hufton shows, also comprised criminal activities, although these have tended to be seen as separate to the everyday operation of survival networks. Penny Lane suggests that this is erroneous. Deeds such as theft (from employers, shops, husbands), receiving and selling stolen goods, gaining relief and charity under false pretences, embezzlement and prostitution, should all be made integral to the definition of informal activities, and were 'seen by poor women as "legitimate" means of earning a living'.[19]

A consistent motif running through this literature implies that women could gain considerable power in their households and neighbourhoods through successful mastery of the domestic sphere. The division of duties within marriage was clearly demarcated, with men perceived as the main providers and women the managers. According to Bourke, although women's ability to make ends meet has often been demoted by historians, being seen as 'producing little intrinsic value', in fact women's skills in the household enhanced their status and bargaining power in the home, and afforded them respect and credibility as good wives.[20] Female networks also created distinct female spaces. Men's encroachment into kitchens, yards, streets and doorsteps was seen as an intrusive and unwelcome infringement into the woman's domain. Women's culture – because it focused on family, kin, home and street – often goes unrecognised. But while women were empowered by their involvement in informal strategies, this argument should not be pushed too far. The fragility of household incomes created tensions, between husbands and wives, parents and children, neighbours and kin.[21] When things went wrong, women were blamed for financial problems, for neglect of domestic responsibilities and breaching the marriage contract. Moreover, if women had to seek work in the formal labour market to augment the budget, she did so from a weak position: employers were able to extract the cheapest labour from married women because of their association with the home and childrearing.

---

[19] Penelope Lane, 'Work on the margins: Poor women and the informal economy of eighteenth and early nineteenth-century Leicestershire', *Midland History*, 22 (1997), pp. 85–99 (p. 96).
[20] Bourke, 'Housewifery', p. 334 and p. 343.
[21] See Ross, *Love and Toil*, ch.3; Pat Ayres and Jan Lambertz, 'Marriage relations, money and domestic violence in working-class Liverpool, 1919–1939', in Lewis, ed., *Labour and Love*, pp. 195–219.

How do the conclusions of these studies on urban districts translate into rural England? Were there comparable networks of lending and promise between women who lived in nineteenth-century villages? Historians are beginning to piece together evidence on the processes of informal economic relations. Mick Reed has unearthed a system of neighbourhood exchange and barter of goods, services and work, based not necessarily on cash and profit, but on obligation and trust, in his research on small producers. Although money transactions and the power of the market became more dominant towards the late nineteenth century, Reed contends that 'the ethics of neighbourhood exchange' persisted into the twentieth century.[22] Women's involvement in alternative cash-inducing activities is also emerging. Jane Humphries has examined women's participation in the exploitation of common rights in the late eighteenth and early nineteenth centuries. Grazing rights, gleaning, collecting fuel and food from commons and wastes were all valuable to labouring families' subsistence and were principally executed by women (with the assistance of children).[23] Humphries claims that enclosure eroded such non-wage sources of subsistence. As a result women and children became more available for exploitative waged labour in the countryside. In turn this 'led to changes in women's economic position within the family and more generally to increased dependence of whole families on wages and wage earners'.[24] Peter King has looked specifically at the value of gleaning to rural labouring family budgets, arguing that this form of common right became more important to women in some rural regions in the early nineteenth century as other forms of labour decreased.[25] Moreover, the doubling of acreage under wheat cultivation through enclosure possibly aided women in their efforts. King concludes that gleaning was 'not a marginal activity', and contributed 'a vital piece in the jigsaw of makeshifts that kept their household economies afloat'.[26] This chapter, then, will attempt to build on these studies and assess the participation of women in the

---

[22] Mick Reed, '"Gnawing it out": A new look at economic relations in nineteenth-century rural England', *Rural History*, 1 (1990), pp. 83–94 (p. 89).

[23] Jane Humphries, 'Enclosures, common rights and women: The proletarianisation of families in the late eighteenth and early nineteenth centuries', *Journal of Economic History*, L (1990), pp. 17–42. In a later article Humphries adopts the term 'self-provisioning' to describe products and services which were used by labouring families but did not pass through the market and were not monetised. In the period 1821 to 1840, Humphries argues that the use of self-provisioning by agricultural labouring families rose. After 1840 the importance of earnings grew. Jane Humphries, 'Female-headed households in early industrial Britain: The vanguard of the proletariat?', *Labour History Review*, 63 (1998), pp. 31–65 (p. 57).

[24] Humphries, 'Enclosure, common rights and women', p. 21.

[25] Peter King, 'Customary rights and women's earnings: The importance of gleaning to the rural labouring poor, 1750–1850', *Economic History Review*, XLIV (1991), pp. 461–76 (p. 462).

[26] King, 'Customary rights and women's earnings', p. 474.

informal economy and the range of activities open to them. How did contemporaries perceive the contribution of women? Were countrywomen afforded the same responsibility and recognition in the home and village, and did they have access to the same credit facilities, village and kin networks, as their urban counterparts?

Domestic labour and household management

It was a universal trend in rural labouring family households for women to be in charge of the domestic budget. Her efficiency and ingenuity in overseeing the household economy was vital to the survival of the family, a fact that is often recognised in autobiographies. In a pattern which parallels that of working-class, urban reminiscences, the skill and self-sacrifice of the mother is a central theme in rural writing. Looking back at their families' living circumstances, adult authors are often confounded by how their mothers managed to make ends meet; the secrecy surrounding family survival was guarded by women, and their ability to cope with unpromising resources is viewed with wonder and gratification. George Bourne, describing one of Lucy Bettesworth's Surrey neighbours, writes, 'How she contrives at all is a standing mystery. The economics seem impossible.'[27] David Barr's mother battled with 'poverty and the many difficulties involved in rearing a large family' in mid nineteenth-century Warwickshire, by exercising 'the most rigid thrift and economy'.[28] George Hardy recounts his mother's domestic accomplishments as 'the daily miracle'.[29] The language used by Lord Snell, who rose from humble beginnings in a Nottinghamshire agricultural village to the Cabinet, is illuminating, comparing the endeavour and contrivance of rural labouring women to the Chancellor:

> Even more striking than the patient endurance of the farm worker, was the constant industry and careful planning of his wife. She had to practice a financial austerity such as a British Chancellor of the Exchequer have long since forgotten. The expenditure of the family had to be kept within closely calculated limits, lest over-spending during one week should involve under-feeding throughout the next.[30]

Village women, most of whom lacked a decent, formal education, were certainly not fools when it came to understanding the worth of money and

---

[27] George Bourne, *Lucy Bettesworth* (London, 1913), p. 80.
[28] David Barr, *Climbing the Ladder: The Struggle and Successes of a Village Lad* (London, 1910), p. 19.
[29] George Hardy, *Those Stormy Years* (London, 1956), p. 11.
[30] Lord Snell, *Men, Movements and Myself* (London, 1936), p. 11.

dealing with tradespeople and shopkeepers. As Lucy Linnett, from Great Billing in Northamptonshire, puts it, 'Mother, who only had a fortnight at school, was as quick as any of the tradesmen to count how much change was due to her'.[31] Roger Langdon's portrayal is also interesting, not least because it implies the self-abnegation women withstood in order that their families had sufficient food:

> I know my mother had to struggle hard against wind and tide, as one might say, to keep us six great rollicking boys tidy, and how she did it as well as she did, with the scarcity of materials at her command, I really cannot conceive; but I do know that she many times went without food, so that we might have our fill.[32]

Food allocation in the nineteenth-century rural working-class household was unequal. In fact, this was a trend found in working-class households throughout Britain, and the lower nutritional and dietary intake of women is well documented.[33] Although women were in charge of household budgeting and consumption, they did not use this control to their own advantage. Women put themselves last in the apportionment of household food and self-denial was a familiar tale. The shoemaker's wife in Alfred Williams' village, for example, 'was most slavish in her attendance' of her harsh and often brutal husband, 'denying herself the necessities of life to procure things for his comfort'.[34]

Women's competence in domestic budgeting is widely appreciated in rural autobiographical writing, but this expertise did not necessarily strengthen their position in the household. Food allocation is one of the most visible manifestations of the inherent powerlessness of women. Moreover, women were reliant on their husbands to carry out their part of the marriage contract. Men could withhold money from their wives. Some spent their wages on alcohol and could become violent and disruptive. Lucy Bettesworth's father, Harding, was not an unaffectionate man, but was 'wont to get so violent with drink that his wife went in fear of her life, and never at any time was he one who decently cared for his family. Thus it fell to the girls and their mother to "keep home together".'[35] For those husbands who did fulfil their role as providers, they did not always recognise the lengths women went to to keep the family afloat. Once the weekly wage had been handed over – and the husband had therefore completed his duty to provide – his responsibility was

---

[31] Northamptonshire Record Office (hereafter NtRO), Village Memoirs, X2959a and X2960a. Great Billing by Lucy Linnett, p. 21.
[32] Roger Langdon, *The Life of Roger Langdon* (London, 1909), p. 18.
[33] Roberts, *A Woman's Place*, ch.4; August, *Poor Women's Lives*, p. 125.
[34] Michael Justin Davis, ed., *In a Wiltshire Village: Scenes from Rural Victorian Life*, 1st edn 1981 (Stroud, 1992), p. 91.
[35] Bourne, *Lucy Bettesworth*, p. 11.

surrendered to his wife, who was now culpable if the budget did not balance. Two excellent descriptions of the different perspectives held by men and women over the household income come from Flora Thompson and Richard Hillyer. Thompson outlines the pattern of pay-day in nineteenth-century Oxfordshire, whereby the husband handed his weekly wage over to his wife, who in return gave him back 1s as 'pocket money': 'That was the custom of the countryside. The men worked for the money and the woman had the spending of it. The men had the best of the bargain.'[36] Although Thompson acknowledges that men's labour was arduous, this was partly compensated for by the fact that they worked in company and shared interests and outlooks with their fellow workers. Women, on the other hand, with their childcare and household responsibilities, were 'kept close at home' and had 'the worry of ways and means on an insufficient income':

> Many husbands boasted that they never asked their wives what they did with the money. As long as there was food enough, clothes to cover everybody, and a roof over their heads, they were satisfied, they said, and they seemed to make a virtue of this and think what generous, trusting, fine-hearted fellows they were. If a wife got in debt or complained, she was told: 'You must larn to cut your coat accordin' to your cloth, my gal'. The coats not only needed expert cutting, but should have been made out of elastic.[37]

Hillyer's portrayal reinforces the division of responsibility in the labouring household. His family lived in Byfield, Northamptonshire. His father's understanding of his position in life was simple. Every Saturday he handed over his cowman's wage of 15s. His wife gave him back 1s, out of which he bought tobacco and garden seeds. His duty was accomplished and his indifference regarding how his wife managed the budget is striking. 'If he worked, and earned what money he could, Mother would see to the rest . . . [he] believed her capable of dealing with any crisis which might arise for any of us. Beyond that his thoughts did not go.'[38] The family were poor but Hillyer's father 'had no wish to assert himself against his circumstances'.[39] This made life for his mother very difficult, with the need to keep out of debt central to her conception of the respectability and independence of the family:

> The great fear of Mother's life – getting into debt – never troubled him at all. If he owed a little money, well he had to, he could trust to his own honesty to pay it, some time or other, and people could think what they liked. But for her it was torture to owe a penny. It seemed to put her in the power of those she owed it to, and it had been her passionate endeavour, all her life, to be free of other people's

---

[36] Flora Thompson, *Lark Rise to Candleford*, 1st edn 1939 (Harmondsworth, 1984), p. 62.
[37] Ibid.
[38] Richard Hillyer, *Country Boy* (London, 1966), p. 25.
[39] Ibid., p. 72.

impertinence, and scorn. Within her narrow circumstances no one should look down on her. For anyone to have found her house dirty, or her children's clothes unmended, to put herself within reach of any slight, was torture.[40]

Although Hillyer's mother associated debt with dishonour, for many poor labouring families the use of credit was unavoidable. For rural women there were fewer options available than in cities. Pawnbrokers were largely an urban phenomenon. According to Paul Johnson, in 1870 over four-fifths of pawnbrokers' shops were located in towns and cities. In a rural county such as Hereford, the ratio of pawnbrokers to population was 1:62,000, while the corresponding proportion in an industrial county such as Warwick was 1:2600.[41] In rural England then, there was only limited opportunity for women to raise money by pawning clothes and goods; instead, rural labourers relied more heavily on shop credit. Depictions of the accounting procedures maintained by rural shopkeepers reveal a system not necessarily based on cash, but on credit. Shop-owners acknowledged that some debts would never be settled. In Williams' Wiltshire village, the local dissenting parson Daniel Lewis and his wife managed the village shop and bakery stores. The couple were forced to live 'very simply, even severely', partly in accordance with their religious beliefs, but also because 'trade was bad at the shop, and scarcely anyone paid for what they had; he had not the heart to demand the debts'.[42] The reflections of C. Henry Warren on the nineteenth-century Kentish village of Fladmere tell a similar story. His father owned the village shop. A cubbyhole at the back of the premises served as an office, where defaulting customers, such as Polly Scarce, were taken to 'sort out business'. She came out of their meeting 'sniffling and red-eyed', resembling 'a frightened animal anxious only to escape'. His father shouted after Polly, calling her a ' real bad lot' and threatening her with the police, although this was a red herring: 'from what I have since learned, I have no doubt that when she was out of the way he went straight back to his desk, drew his scratchy pen through her accounts and sighed.'[43] Although not all shopkeepers would have been as lenient as these two examples, they highlight one use of credit in the nineteenth-century village. It was women who formed associations with rural traders and shopkeepers, who comprehended the movement in food prices and availability, and who manipulated this form of credit when they needed to balance the household income at the end of the week.

Other avenues of thrift employed by women were connected to the 'make-and-mend' economy of the rural household. For much of the nineteenth

---

[40] Ibid.
[41] Johnson, *Saving and Spending*, p. 170.
[42] Davis, ed., *In a Wiltshire Village*, p. 103.
[43] C. Henry Warren, *A Boy in Kent* (London, 1937), pp. 81–2.

century ready-made clothing was beyond the means of most labouring incomes. Women's proficiency with the needle was therefore indispensable. Being a good needlewoman (along with learning to brew, bake and 'put down a pig') was one of the 'accomplishments' that had been part of his grandmother's 'training', according to Allan Jobson.[44] Alfred Ireson argues that the 'tiny needle was the great industry of industry in the homes' of the rural labouring poor in the mid-nineteenth century.[45] Arthur Randall's mother made her family's shirts, 'getting the material for them once a year when the harvest wages came in'.[46] As a girl Gladys Otterspoon helped her mother knit her father's socks and sew his flannel shirts, all of which were 'too dear to buy'.[47] Women made clothes for all members of the family and waste was unheard of. The worn-out clothes of men and older children were cut down and remade for younger children.[48] Little had changed by the early twentieth century. One author recalls her mother knitting stockings from sheep wool collected from fences, pulling the raw material into one thread on a hand spindle and dying it with elderberries or blackberries. The stockings, after considerable wear, were unpicked and used for other items: 'Nothing was ever wasted; if Father's long pants were worn out, they'd be cut up to make warm knickers for me. She used every bit she could and she and Father often sat making rag rugs out of old clothes in the evenings.'[49] However, one innovation that did make its appearance in the late nineteenth-century cottage home was the sewing machine, although the initial outlay needed for the device meant affordability was not universal. Sewing machines reduced the burden of hand-stitching, but did not eliminate it. 'With the help of Jane's treadle sewing-machine in the front room – bought from Aunt Lizzie', Michael Home recalls his mother making 'many of our clothes', although 'there would be constant darning and mending' to do in addition.[50]

Women baked much of the family's food, pickled and preserved produce, as well as the household washing. None of these were easy tasks given the primitive nature of cottage homes in the nineteenth century. Indeed, autobiographical material highlights the physical environment of village life and how dilapidated housing, inadequate space and lack of running water in the home could affect women's efforts to maintain a respectable and efficient household. One American observer, touring the English countryside in 1899, noted that the 'average cottage interior is dismally shabby and its furnishings

---

[44] Allan Jobson, *An Hour-Glass on the Run* (London, 1959), p. 44.
[45] Quoted in John Burnett, ed,. *Destiny Obscure: Autobiographies of Childhood, Education and Family from the 1820s to the 1920s* (London, 1982), p. 83.
[46] Arthur Randall, *Sixty Years a Fenman* (London, 1966) p. 16.
[47] Mary Chamberlain, *Fenwomen: A Portrait of Women in an English Village* (London, 1975), p. 33.
[48] Snell, *Men*, p. 11.
[49] Sylvia Marlow, *Winifred: A Wiltshire Working Girl* (Bradford-on-Avon, 1991), p. 25.
[50] Michael Home, *Winter Harvest: A Norfolk Boyhood* (London, 1967), p. 37.

meagre. The rooms at the disposal of any one family are few and small, and you find in the best of them little beyond the bare necessities for housekeeping of the most primitive sort.'[51] The sheer physical burden placed on women by tasks such as washing, ironing and cooking was considerable. In most cases, water had to be carried some distance – from the village pump to the home – before work could begin. E. Ibbotson lived in late nineteenth-century Somerset and recollects that this task 'fell to the hard-pressed housewife during the day, with a yoke and two buckets. Such yokes were well made and fitted comfortably on the shoulders; even then it was a heavy job for mothers.'[52] Fires had to be lit and kept burning to boil the water. Clothes were rubbed using hard bars of soap, and after being boiled in the copper, they were taken out, rinsed in a tin or wooden tub, wrung out and hung out to dry (weather permitting).[53] One observer remembers washday as being 'intolerable, not only in the garden, but also in the house. . . . The dank smell of soapy linen permeated the house.'[54] Families often shared the use of washhouses and baking ovens with their neighbours, as their homes were not commodious enough to accommodate such contraptions. In Kate Taylor's Suffolk village four cottages shared the use of a 'backhouse', which contained a large washing copper and a brick oven. The cottage wives had to take it in turns to use these facilities, making it essential that neighbouring women co-operated with each other.[55] Mark Thurston also describes the principles which were followed in his Essex village: 'this communal bakehouse . . . was used by women in rotation, each woman having her appointed day or hour, and the baking taking place once a fortnight in winter and rather more in summer.'[56] Shared facilities could be a cause of tension between villagers. 'The cottagers have their feuds', one farmer noted, 'and the joint use of washhouses or bake-ovens between two or more adjoining cottages is a frequent source.'[57] To cook large Sunday dinners, women could also use the bakehouse attached to the village bakery. Mrs Sargeant of Rothwell, Northamptonshire argued that 'most people' in her village used the bakehouse 'for their Yorkshire Puddings and Pastries up to 1910'. She explains:

---

[51] Clifton Johnson, *Among English Hedgerows* (London, 1899), p. 7.
[52] E. M. H. Ibbotson, 'Ilmington in the nineteenth century: Reminiscences of an agricultural labourer', *The Local Historian*, 9 (1971), pp. 338–43 (p. 340).
[53] See Eve Hostettler, '"Making Do": Domestic life among East Anglian labourers, 1890–1910', in Leonore Davidoff and Belinda Westover, eds, *Our Work, Our Lives, Our Words: Women's History and Women's Work* (London, 1986), pp. 36–53 (p. 42) for a description of the washing process.
[54] Warren, *Boy in Kent*, pp. 111–12.
[55] Quoted in Burnett, ed., *Destiny Obscure*, p. 290.
[56] C. Henry Warren, *Happy Countryman* (London, 1946), p. 31. These are Warren's recordings of the memoirs of Mark Thurston of Larkfield, Essex, born in 1861.
[57] Arthur H. Savory, *Grain and Chaff from an English Manor* (Oxford, 1920), p. 71.

Roasting meat was placed in a large greased tin and the pudding batter poured around it. On Sundays we took this to the Bake-house on our way to Chapel, calling for it on our way home. The charge used to be 1½ but increased to 4d as wages increased.[58]

In contrast to official parliamentary reports of the nineteenth century, much of this evidence indicates that poor labouring women strove hard to maintain respectability in their households, despite the lack of domestic comforts. As Kate Edwards recollects:

The women did try hard to keep their houses clean and tidy and neat. They were proud o' what they had, even if it were only a few odd sticks of furniture and one bed. . . . They were forever making and mending and washing and ironing, and took a pride in doing it. They knowed very well that what they cou'n't or di'n't conjure up out o' bits and pieces, their families cou'n't have.[59]

Women not only deployed their domestic accomplishments for the benefit of the family inside the household; they sold their skills for money. This could involve taking work into their own homes, or going into other households to perform certain tasks. Arthur Tweedy recollects that his mother 'was never without a few lodgers who came to work in the parish, doing all kinds of work, such as fencing, draining, ditching'.[60] His mother clearly made money out of this enterprise, but for Mrs Loveland, who offered accommodation to a distant relative through marriage, the lodger added 'to the difficulties of the housekeeping', which were run under a tight budget.[61] Taking in lodgers required sufficient space and amenities. Crucially, a market for casual labour in the village also had to exist in order to attract itinerant workers in need of a bed. As a result, this means of making money was restricted in the nineteenth-century countryside. Instead, women were much more likely to take washing or dressmaking into the home in order to add to the family income. Mrs Stone had an invalid husband and 'kept home together' in late nineteenth-century Surrey, 'by such scanty laundry-work as could be brought to her'.[62] Fred Kitchen's widowed mother 'being a good needlewoman, soon found plenty of work from the big houses' in his late nineteenth-century South Yorkshire village.[63] Similarly, Joseph Arch's mother contributed to

---

[58] NtRO, Village Memories, Rothwell by Mrs G. Sargeant, p. 6.
[59] Sybil Marshall, *Fenland Chronicle: Recollections of William Henry and Kate Mary Edwards* (Cambridge, 1967), p. 225.
[60] Arthur Tweedy, 'Recollections of a farm worker. Part 1', *Bulletin of the Cleveland and Teesside Local History Society*, 21 (1973), pp. 1–6 (p. 1).
[61] Bourne, *Lucy Bettesworth*, pp. 79–80.
[62] Ibid., p. 65.
[63] Fred Kitchen, *Brother to the Ox: The Autobiography of a Farm Labourer* (Horsham, 1981), p. 36.

the 'common family fund' by washing. He writes: 'We should have been in a very bad way if my mother, by her laundry earnings, had not subsidised my father's wage.'[64] In Williams' late nineteenth-century Wiltshire village, the wife of the local shoemaker combined all three tasks to 'eke out enough to supplement her husband's earnings'. Thus she 'went out washing and charring, and did sewing as well; from early morning till late at night. She was toiling and toiling to earn an honest shilling.'[65] Meg Ladell remembers her mother taking in washing, as well as charring for the local butcher. 'If she hadn't', she contends, 'we would have starved and gone barefoot.'[66]

Scattered throughout the household accounts of many of the large estates are references to local women charring and washing. At Skipwith Hall in East Yorkshire, in 1849, as well as the regular indoor servants, Anne Roberts was paid for charring, brewing ale in the scullery and washing, earning £1 15s 4d between July and December.[67] The same references are found in the accounts of Burton Constable in Holderness. In 1872, for instance, Mrs Machlin and Mrs Thomson were employed on a casual basis as charwomen and for making beds; Mrs Thompson also earned 14s for 'dressing feathers'.[68] Cast-off clothes and food items were also administered as part payment for such tasks. These were often as valuable as cash payments. Albert Granger's mother earned 1s a day washing in Northamptonshire houses and was often given meat such as duck to take home 'by the ladies'.[69] Lucy Linnett's mother, who washed for the local butcher in Great Billing, was given 1s a day, 'her dinner and half a pint of stout for her lunch'.[70] Ladell's mother was paid 1s in meat for a day's work on Saturdays. This translated into 'a meal for the family on Sunday'.[71] Given the unvarying and predictable mealtime fare that could be afforded out of a poor labourer's wage, the addition of meat was a great benefit to the family diet.

Women's domestic labour used the children of the household. The care and supervision of children fell into the women's domain and from a young age the labour of children was expected: children were an integral part of the household economy in nineteenth-century rural England and they carried out specific and important functions to aid their parents. These were often apportioned along gendered lines. Tweedy's recollections reflect this division of labour. 'We all had jobs to do before and after school', he writes. 'My

---

[64] Joseph Arch, *Joseph Arch. The Story of His Life* (London, 1898), p. 31.
[65] Alfred Williams, *A Wiltshire Village* (London, 1912), p. 180.
[66] Chamberlain, *Fenwomen*, p. 41.
[67] Brynmor Jones Library, University of Hull, DDFA 37/23 Housekeeping book, Forbes Adams family of Skipwith Hall, 1845 to 1852.
[68] East Riding Record Office, DDCC (2) 19/7, Servants' wages and liveries book, Burton Constable, 1872.
[69] NtRO, Village Memories, Burton Latimer by Albert Granger, pp. 2–3.
[70] NtRO, Village Memories, Great Billing by Lucy Linnett, p. 4.
[71] Chamberlain, *Fenwomen*, p. 41.

job was gathering sticks for the fire and weeding the huge garden. My sisters had to clean the house and even bake.'[72] Children assisted with sewing and knitting of family clothes by unpicking. As a boy Joseph Millott Severn helped his mother 'run the steels in the tucks of crinolines', in addition to collecting water from the well when he 'was big and strong enough to wind up the monster bucket which held two large pails of water, it became one of my duties to fetch it'.[73] Ibbotson also fetched water, his job being to 'carry sufficient water on Saturday to supply us till Monday, and store it in a large glazed vessel holding several gallons'.[74] In situations where women went out to work, the eldest female child was usually expected to take over the running of the household in her mother's absence. This happened to Hillyer's mother, who was left at home while her mother, a widow, went out washing, cleaning and to work in the fields. At the age of 11 Hillyer's mother was 'left at home to bring up the rest. . . . She scrubbed, and washed, and cooked what food there was, for them all, and began as a child to carry the same sort of responsibilities she would struggle with all her days.'[75]

Children were also required to work for money. Davin argues that in late nineteenth-century London, parents took for granted the right of the labour of their children, and children in turn accepted the need for their work.[76] This situation was replicated in rural labouring families. Any money children gained was considered part of the mother's budget. As a young boy, Ibbotson began work for the local farmer bird-scaring – chasing rooks off the newly sown fields – earning 6d a day. The 6d he earned for Sunday work, his parents allowed him to keep. When he left school in 1891 he began work leading horses for 3s a week. That sum, he claims, 'was a lift to Mother's weekly budget'.[77] Mark Thurston was put out to work on several tasks as a boy in Essex in the 1860s and 1870s, including bird-scaring, milk rounds and minding sheep on the Commons. His wages were a boon to the family income and, as he aged, his economic value and status grew:

> Scanty as his wages were, they comprised a sufficient addition to the Thurston finances to be important. But if a boy from seven years to ten years was worth eighteenpence a week to the farmer, a boy of from ten years to thirteen was obviously worth something more. His parents, callused by necessity, would be quick to take advantage of this fact. And so, as Mark grew older and stronger, he became . . . a 'quarter-man' entitled to a quarter of an adult's wages. . . . Later

---

[72] Tweedy, 'Recollections', p. 2.
[73] Joseph Millott Severn, *My Village: Owd Codnor, Derbyshire* (Hove, 1935), p. 118 and p. 10.
[74] Ibbotson, 'Ilmington', p. 340.
[75] Hillyer, *Country Boy*, p. 74.
[76] Davin, *Growing Up Poor*, p. 165.
[77] Ibbotson, 'Ilmington', p. 341 and p. 339.

on, at an age determined by his degree of physical fitness, he would become a 'half-man' and then a 'three-quarters' man with wages to correspond.[78]

The importance of children's wages dominated rural households well into the twentieth century. Roberts claims that both parents and children recognised the value of these earnings, and parents' moral authority over their offspring ensured that the arrangement was not questioned.[79]

In rural areas after 1870, families could find themselves in confrontation with School Board attendance officers if they kept their younger children from school. This was one of the few occasions when official inspection bodies made an impact on village life. The level of surveillance and intrusion to which inner city families were subject in the late nineteenth century was much greater than in remoter rural regions.[80] Inspectors, though, were sometimes given short shrift, if the case of Sally Turner is representative. She had been employing her grandson to run errands and fetch water in connection to her laundry work when he should have been at school. She teased and 'chaffed' the inspector, demanding 'Will they send me to prison, then? If they do they'll have to keep me. And there won't be no washin' there, will there?' Her only concession was to 'send 'n when he got time. When she could spare 'n he should go.'[81]

Maintaining and gathering resources

The exploitation of commons and wastes by women and children was significantly curtailed by the onset of enclosure from the late eighteenth century. This meant that it became increasingly difficult – and uneconomical – for labouring families to keep cows, cut turf and collect other fuel. But this did not prevent women from appropriating other avenues of resource-gathering in the nineteenth century. The aid of children was again central to these activities, and indicates the importance of female and child collaboration in informal tasks. Scouring the country lanes for sticks, dead wood and almost anything else that could be used as domestic fuel was a primary pursuit. In Northamptonshire, women 'often went sticking too and would come down the lane with arms or aprons full of sticks'.[82] Edwin Grey claims that a 'good deal of fallen wood was also collected for the fires, for after a storm or gale, the women and children would go "wooding"'.[83] Even by the turn of the

---

[78] Warren, *Happy Countryman*, p. 36.
[79] Roberts, *A Woman's Place*, pp. 40–2.
[80] See Long, *Conversations in Cold Rooms*, ch.6.
[81] Bourne, *Lucy Bettesworth*, p. 68.
[82] NtRO, Village Memories, Easton Maudit by K. Essam, p. 21.
[83] Edwin Grey, *Cottage Life in a Hertfordshire Village* (St Albans, 1935), p. 54.

twentieth century, women were still observed scavenging the villages and fields for fuel. Bourne noted that in Surrey 'On the road . . . women were, and still are, frequently noticeable, bringing home on their backs faggots of dead wood, or sacks of fir-cones, picked up in the fir-woods a mile away or more'.[84]

A second activity, which remained a significant godsend to the dietary intake of poor rural families in the nineteenth century, was the collection of a whole range of foodstuffs. Fruits, berries and mushrooms all provided variety to the limited mealtime fare. They also ensured women were kept busy in the kitchen making jams, pickling and preserving. Blackberries, cowslips, elderberries, dandelions and other wild fruits and plants were also sought as ingredients for homemade wine, which, along with brewing, was still carried out by rural women in their cottage homes. In the childhood home of Miss Fauk 'large quantities of home made wine were made from cowslips, dandelions, sloes, potatoes, elderberries, plums etc. . . . When friends called a glass of wine was always offered.'[85] For those living in coastal villages, as Bob Cooper's Sussex family did, the assortment of food available for procurement also included 'prawns, winkles, shrimps and the odd lobster from the foreshore, each in their season'.[86] While such foodstuffs augmented the family larder, they were also sometimes intended for sale in the market place, thereby providing a further income-generating resource. Once more, any earnings gained by children through their gathering and selling activities were fed back into the maternal purse. In Barr's Warwickshire village, children made excursions for mushrooms, hazelnuts, cowslips and 'anything else that might be lawfully appropriated'. These goods were then sold at market 'and converted into cash, partly to help the maternal exchequer and partly as a perquisite for the children'.[87] Bowden similarly recalls being 'up in the dark' as a child in North Yorkshire at mushroom time, selling the load collected by him and his siblings at Masham before returning in time for school. Three to four shillings was made by this means.[88] The memoirs of Winifred Grace, who was born in Wiltshire in 1899, are interesting for several reasons. They indicate the predominance of the non-waged economy, the expectation of child labour and the vital subsistence provided by village resources, even in the early twentieth century:

> We worked and lived off the land; not off money but off everything around us, and making do. We had to do all kinds of things to keep going in the winter else we

---

[84] George Bourne, *Change in the Village*, 1st edn 1912 (London, 1955), p. 23.
[85] NtRO, Village Memories, Pottersbury by Miss Fauk, p. 8.
[86] Bob Cooper, *A Song for Every Season: A Hundred Years of a Sussex Farming Family* (London, 1971), p. 54.
[87] Barr, *Climbing the Ladder*, p. 20.
[88] Bowden, 'Recollections of a farm worker', p. 35.

would have starved. And children had to help, however young we were. When we came home from school in summer time there might be wild raspberries to pick around the Plain; if it was spring we'd be sent to hunt for plover's eggs.... These eggs were too valuable for the family to keep and they had to go to the Crown Hotel in Everleigh. The money we got for this went to Mother of course. Other eggs we could get were pigeons', and rooks'.... We never thought of raiding birds' nests in play; everything was serious and to do with work.[89]

An additional natural resource that was widely sought after was acorns. The autumn acorn harvest was useful for rural families as they could be used to fatten the cottage pig. Acorn loads were also sold to other members of the village community for the same purpose. The accepted price for a bushel of acorns in the second half of the nineteenth century was 1s.[90] William Clift claims that some families picked up to 100 bushels of the windfall, contributing a not inconsiderable sum to the family income in the mid-nineteenth century.[91] However, reciprocal transactions also took place. As a child Kate Taylor gathered acorns that were handed over to the miller for pig-feed. This, in turn, was regarded as payment for the family's corn to be ground when the gleaning season had finished. Thus, no money was formerly exchanged.[92]

The vital contribution made by gleaning is incontrovertible; women's and children's efforts in this activity could make a significant difference to the well-being of labouring families in the winter months following the harvest. Autobiographies reinforce the importance of gleaning time to village women and children, and this communal activity features frequently. The priority given to the depiction of the gleaning fields is interesting, pointing to the value rural labourers themselves invested in the task. Gleaning also represents an old village custom which had largely died out by the early twentieth century: authors are reminiscing about a traditional aspect of rural life which was undermined and finally destroyed by the onset of modern, mechanical farming.

In *Good Neighbours*, his portrait of village life in Buckinghamshire in the 1870s and 1880s, Walter Rose insists that it is 'impossible to over-estimate the value of that gleaned corn to the very poor'.[93] Wheat gleanings were by far the most profitable and were used to bake the family's bread. Gleanings from barley, beans, oats and peas could be fed to the cottage pig. The amount gleaned varied according to region, family size and age. Williams' Wiltshire family considered 'our harvest a poor one if it did not total fifteen or sixteen

---

[89] Marlow, *Winifred*, pp. 23–4.
[90] See for example Grey, *Cottage Life*, p. 93; Davis, ed., *In a Wiltshire Village*, p. 117.
[91] William Clift, *The Reminiscences of William Clift of Bramley* (Basingstoke, 1909), pp. 65–6.
[92] Quoted in Burnett, ed., *Destiny Obscure*, p. 290.
[93] Walter Rose, *Good Neighbours: Some Recollections of an English Village and Its People* (Cambridge, 1942), p. 30.

bushels of threshed grain',[94] while in Northamptonshire around thirteen or fourteen bushels was seen as a decent total.[95] However, Ralph Whitlock estimated that a gleaning load usually 'varied from two to six bushels a family',[96] and Mark Thurston believed that a good season's gleaning totalled 'to as much as two or three sackfuls a family'.[97] Bill Partridge argues that 'Some o' the women . . . used to git as much as a comb o' wheat' to grind into flour.[98] Mary Coe claims that her family's endeavours added up to 'our flour for the year', or if sold, enough to pay the annual rent,[99] yet Kate Taylor's family 'hoped to glean sufficient wheat for bread for the winter'.[100] In turn-of-the-century Suffolk, Bessie Harvey's gleanings were meagre compared to some of the other estimations, amounting to just 'enough for two or three bakings of bread on Fridays'.[101]

Such reminiscences allude to the significance of gleanings to rural families. Other nineteenth-century reports attempted to translate gleanings into monetary values. C. D. Brereton, writing in 1824, argued that the extension of land under wheat cultivation in early nineteenth-century Norfolk had proved favourable to labouring families, enabling women and children to glean between eight and sixteen bushels of wheat. 'The earnings of the women and children by this means', he wrote, 'have often amounted to more than the earnings of the labourer himself in harvest, when his wages are the highest'.[102] James Phillips Kay believed that the average gleanings of over 500 labouring families in Norfolk and Suffolk in the late 1830s amounted to the equivalent of £1 1s 10d, or 3 per cent of average annual incomes.[103] But this estimation may rather downplay the contribution made by gleanings to the poor of East Anglia, and falls into the minimum level of percentage contribution uncovered by King's research.[104] Between 1750 and 1850, King found that access to gleaning fields remained constant, and total gleanings represented between 3 or 4 per cent and 13 and 14 per cent of the average labouring family's annual income.[105] Gleanings were more significant to some

---

[94] Williams, *Wiltshire Village*, p. 270.
[95] NtRO, Village memories, Eye by J. W. Botterell, no page numbers.
[96] Ralph Whitlock, *Peasant's Heritage* (London, n.d.), p. 48.
[97] Warren, *Happy Countryman*, p. 28.
[98] Quoted in Charles Kightly, *Country Voices: Life and Lore in Farm and Village* (London, 1984), p. 19.
[99] Chamberlain, *Fenwomen*, p. 29.
[100] Quoted in Burnett, ed., *Destiny Obscure*, p. 290.
[101] Bessie Harvey, 'Youthful memories of my life in a Suffolk village', *The Suffolk Review*, 2 (1963), pp. 198–201 (p. 199).
[102] Revd C. D. Brereton, *A Practical Inquiry into the Number, Means of Employment and Wages of Agricultural Labourers* (Norwich, 1824), p. 49.
[103] James Phillips Kay, 'Earnings of agricultural labourers in Norfolk and Suffolk', *Journal of the Statistical Society*, 1 (1839), pp. 179–83 (p. 183).
[104] King, 'Customary rights and women's earnings', p. 473.
[105] Ibid., p. 474.

families: where incomes were generally low, if there were more children, in years of dearth and in female-headed households.[106] But access to gleaning was regionally specific, being more widespread in central and southern England. In areas of the north and west this customary right was virtually unknown.[107] Although gleaning remained an important aspect of the informal economy after 1850, the amount of gleanings left in the harvest fields was reduced by the more widespread adoption of machine technology, and therefore limited the contribution women and children could make to family subsistence.[108] The use of horse rakes, reaping machines and reaper-binders left cleaner harvest fields – and therefore fewer gleanings – a process outlined by David Smith, writing on late nineteenth-century Essex:

> The custom survived the first insufficient reapers, but with the introduction of the first modern binders, and the use of the horse rake to gather any corn left lying in the fields, the gleaners wandered disconsolate for a year or so, and then gave it up.[109]

But in attempting to assess the contribution made by gleaning, and the extent this altered over the course of the nineteenth century, we should not overlook the significance bestowed on rural women through their involvement in this customary task. The role played by women in leading and supervising children was crucial; the larger the family group, the more substantial the amount of gleaning possible, and the organisation of the family team ensured significant returns. 'As soon as a child could distinguish straw from wheat', Thurston recalls, 'he was pressed into this important annual labour; and when the size of the average cottager's family is borne in mind, it will readily be appreciated what a chattering, flickering crowd the gleaners made.'[110] Gleaners usually began their work, sometimes at the instruction of a bell, at eight o'clock in the morning, and continued until dusk. Village women fiercely guarded gleaning rights and disputes could arise. An altercation occurred between women of the neighbouring Northamptonshire villages of Yarwell and Nassington over land that had once been part of the former parish, but was awarded to the latter in 1880. At gleaning time, as Nassington women moved into the contested fields

---

[106] Ibid., pp. 464–6.
[107] Ibid., p. 474.
[108] David H. Morgan, 'The place of harvesters in nineteenth-century village life', in Raphael Samuel, ed., *Village Life and Labour* (London, 1975), pp. 29–72 (p. 65).
[109] David Smith, *No Rain in Those Clouds* (London, 1943), p. 41. Stephen Hussey argues that changes in harvest technology did not put an end to gleaning in Essex and that it survived until after the Second World War. Stephen Hussey, '"The last survivor of an ancient race": The changing face of Essex gleaning', *Agricultural History Review*, 45 (1997), pp. 61–72.
[110] Warren, *Happy Countryman*, p. 27.

to glean, the Yarwell women 'took the law into their own hands . . . claimed ancient rights and ordered the Nassington gleaners to depart'. The story is told by Lucy Lock:

> One stalwart Yarwell women took the chief aggressor from Nassington by her shoulders, and pushed her across a certain ditch, which was considered the boundary between the two parishes, telling the Nassington people that they should all return to Nassington where they belonged.[111]

Consequently 'for some years there was a grudge', but the rebuttal was firm enough to prevent further discord. Farmers themselves rarely attempted to prevent women and children from gleaning after the great gleaning court cases of the late eighteenth century, although certain regulation were followed.[112] Whitlock writes,

> No farmer in our district ever dreamt of turning away the gleaners from his fields. There was, however, an unwritten law that gleaners might not enter a field until every sheaf was taken to the rick. If they did so, they were told to get out and probably found it difficult to gain admission at the proper time.[113]

In the fields women and children gathered up small handfuls of wheat, which the women twisted into bundles, thrusting the ends under the bond and setting them down in the stubble with the ears pointing skywards. It was considered more profitable to glean in dull weather, when the crop could be spotted more easily. The day's gleanings were carted home in sacks, aprons, prams or any other convenient device. At home 'all the ears were cut off with a sharp knife or scissors, and then stored in sacks and kept indoors. The cottage was like a barn upstairs and down, too; you could scarcely move for the corn.'[114] Whitlock and his siblings 'lay in bed at night and listened to the mice nibbling and scampering beneath the sacks'.[115] Farmers usually allowed their labourers the use of a barn in which the family's gleanings could be threshed after work. If this was not possible – in a female-headed household for example – sums of around 6d were charged for the threshing.[116] The final process involved taking the threshed gleanings to the mill for grinding. Again,

---

[111] NtRO, Village Memories, Yarwell by Lucy Lock, p. 49.
[112] King, 'Customary rights and women's earnings', p. 472. See also Peter King, 'Gleaners, farmers and the failure of legal sanctions, 1750–1850', *Past and Present*, 125 (1989), pp. 117–50; Peter King, 'Legal change, customary right, and social conflict in late eighteenth-century England: The origins of the great gleaning case of 1788', *Law and History Review*, 10 (1992), pp. 1–31.
[113] Whitlock, *Peasant's Heritage*, p. 48.
[114] Davis, ed., *In a Wiltshire Village*, p. 127.
[115] Whitlock, *Peasant's Heritage*, p. 49.
[116] Ibid.

although some millers extracted cash payments for this service, in many villages no money changed hands. The transaction is outlined by Whitlock:

> Every week the miller from Aronchurch came to the village with flour for the shop and he took back with him for grinding what gleanings had been threshed. The following week he brought back the flour, but kept the bran and milling offal to pay for his work. If the cottager kept pigs and claimed all the coarser meals he had to pay the miller a small fee.[117]

If practicable, cottagers did keep pigs. 'Life without a pig', Rose maintains, 'was almost unthinkable. To have a sty in the garden . . . was as essential to the happiness of a newly married couple as a living room or a bedroom.'[118] Cottage gardens allowed labourers the space to produce and maintain food and animals. In fact, the two often went hand in hand, as did the labour of parents and children to maintain them. The mutuality of village life is conspicuous. Commenting on the state of the labouring poor in East Yorkshire in the early nineteenth century, H. E. Strickland pointed out that 'the greater part of labourers have gardens attached to their cottages for the growth of vegetables and are able to feed annually a bacon hog'.[119] The evidence of Thomas Jackson, who was born near Market Weighton in the 1780s, substantiates this. His family owned a garden amounting to half an acre of land 'of the richest soil, which produced a yearly supply of potatoes, sufficient for the use of the family, and the support of a pig'.[120] The rearing of pigs rose in popularity after enclosure made it unprofitable, or simply not possible, for labourers to keep cows.[121] Rural families often kept two pigs, one being killed for home consumption and the other sold at market. The proceeds would go on rent or towards purchasing the next two pigs. The task of feeding domestic animals often fell to the wife or older children, while men cleaned out the sties. The dung was used as manure on the garden or allotment. Gardens and animals therefore tended to sustain each other. But in certain regions the keeping of cows did not disappear, and was deemed so valuable to the well-being of labourers that farmers rented out land to employees for cow grazing. In Yorkshire in 1848, it was argued that the keeping of cows was 'so highly appreciated by both the labourers and their employers that efforts are now being generally made to facilitate this valuable acquisition to the poor man'.[122] It has been estimated that half the labourers on the Sledmere estate,

---

[117] Ibid., pp. 49–50.
[118] Rose, *Good Neighbours*, p. 58.
[119] H. E. Strickland, *General View of the Agriculture of the East Riding of Yorkshire* (York, 1812), p. 285.
[120] Thomas Jackson, *Recollections of my Own Life and Times* (London, 1874), p. 9.
[121] Humphries, 'Enclosures, common rights and women', p. 28.
[122] George Legard, 'Farming of East Yorkshire', *Journal of the Royal Agricultural Society*, 9 (1848), pp. 85–136 (pp. 125–6).

in the centre of the Yorkshire Wolds, rented cow pastures of around three acres in the early 1870s. The annual value of a cow at that time was put at £12.[123]

The responsibility women took in maintaining and using cottage gardens and animals was important to the family economy. The skill of the housewife was especially vital at pig-killing time. This was the 'great event in the domestic life of the year' according to Rose. 'All other duties were held over for it. No woman was ever heard to complain of the work it involved. It was accepted as a challenge, a decisive test of her position in the village as a capable wife.'[124] A woman's adeptness in the kitchen was on show at pig-killing time more than any other. Pig killing and dismembering were male tasks; after completion the pig was handed over to the woman to be 'put down'. The pig created hours of work for her – chopping, salting, curing and cooking – most of it in full view of her neighbours at this communal time. In their insightful investigation of the cottage pig, Robert Malcolmson and Stephanos Mastoris argue, 'Culinary reputations were at stake; comparisons were drawn; and cottage women took pride in producing food of quality, based on private recipes, in wasting nothing, and in achieving in their cooking some savoury refinements.'[125] The efforts of Miss Falk's mother certainly made an impression on her, and points to the range of produce that was created from the pig carcass:

> Pig killing days were red letter days to the owners and their friends. There were many tasty delicacies to put on the table such as black pudding, faggots, chitterlings, home made lard, bone puddings and bone pies. . . . The owners would sometimes canvas the village for orders for the home killed pork, or they would cure it for bacon. Huge sides of bacon and large hams could be seen hanging on the walls.[126]

Women were primarily in charge of other small domestic animals such as poultry, ducks and bees. All of these added to the family diet by providing eggs, meat and honey. This was recognised by a report into the state of Norfolk agriculture in the 1870s: 'where the daughters and wives look after the poultry', it stated, 'they'll never lose any money and they'll never starve.'[127] Income generated by the produce was also an important addition to the family budget. Duck-breeding for the London market was the motive

---

[123] M. G. Adams, 'Agricultural change in the East Riding of Yorkshire, 1850–1880: An economic and social history' (Ph.D. thesis, University of Hull, 1977), p. 391.
[124] Rose, *Good Neighbours*, p. 65.
[125] Robert Malcolmson and Stephanos Mastoris, *The English Pig: A History* (London, 1998), p. 115.
[126] NtRO, Village Memories, Pottersbury by Miss Falk, pp. 7–8.
[127] Various, *The Agricultural Crisis: The Condition, Prospects and Needs of Norfolk Agriculturists* (London, 1879), p. 23.

for labourers' wives in Rose's Buckinghamshire village, with sums amassed being quite considerable: 'some folks saved enough by it to buy their own cottages.'[128] Bee-keeping was similarly profitable. In early twentieth-century Gloucestershire, 'Many villagers kept bees.... The rent of a cottage was about £4 or £5 a year and the bees were kept to pay the rent.'[129] Jobson's grandmother probably had more pleasure from her exploitation of bees though. From the honey she made mead, 'strong stuff, enough to send home the bees themselves in a state, let alone the humans who took a full glass'.[130] Finally, the value of gardens and allotments was viewed as being beneficial to the rural labouring poor, not least because they provided what was seen as a suitable occupation for women. Allotments were linked to the home and aided the management of family budgets; social observers were therefore more likely to approve of female labour in cottage gardens and allotments than agricultural labour for the farmer. One commentator in the 1843 Report on the Employment of Women and Children in Agriculture drew this distinction:

> there are perhaps, 100 allotments here; the women and children invariably work on them. The good effects, in every respect, are beyond calculation. This system promotes happiness, contentment, industry, regularity of habits, and is duly appreciated by the poor themselves.[131]

In the 1890s, Arthur Wilson Fox found that allotment holders who rented one-eighth of an acre at 4s to 5s in west Norfolk could make up to £3 a year profit.[132]

The monetary value of gardens, allotments and animals was crucial to the nineteenth-century rural labouring poor. The contribution made by women, although difficult to assess in economic terms, enhanced family subsistence in significant ways. They added to the self-reliant ethos of nineteenth-century village life, as George Ewart Evans alludes to in this depiction of Pricilla Savage, an agricultural labourer's wife 'who had to bring up a large family on low wages':

> With so little money few things could be bought in the shops and people rarely went out to buy things in the town; the village was almost entirely self-supporting, most families living on what they grew or reared on their yards or allotments.[133]

---

[128] Rose, *Good Neighbours*, p. 73.
[129] Gloucestershire Federation of Women's Institutes, *'I Remember': Social Life in Gloucestershire Villages, 1850–1950* (Gloucester, 1961), p. 14.
[130] Jobson, *Hour-Glass*, p. 91.
[131] PP 1843, XII, Reports of Special Assistant Poor Law Commissioners on the Employment of Women and Children in Agriculture. Report by Stephen Denison on Norfolk, Suffolk and Lincolnshire, p. 260.
[132] PP 1893–4, XXXV, Royal Commission on Labour. The Agricultural Labourer. Report by Arthur Wilson Fox on the Poor Law Union of Swaffham, p. 71.
[133] George Ewart Evans, *Ask the Fellows who Cut the Hay* (London, 1956), p. 55.

Moreover, searching for resources in the country lanes, gleaning in the harvest fields or digging the family's garden gave women some freedom from the drudgery of housework:

> Some women of the village took great pride in doing things other than their everyday duties of cooking, mending washing and cleaning. Some gathered cowslips, dandelions or elderberries for wine . . . gleaning, doing odd jobs in the allotment park or garden.[134]

Village networks

Many of the non-monetary forms of labour undertaken by women suggest a self-sustaining and interconnected village economy. Women formed the backbone to this informal rural economy in that their domestic management and maintenance of scarce resources kept the family infrastructure afloat. The contribution made to household incomes through housework, making and mending, gleaning, berrying, nurturing and digging are almost impossible to quantify, although it is clear from autobiographical writing that they were important, and continued to be viewed as such even in the late nineteenth century. But alongside these contributions, another layer of female activities have to be placed, because a network of mutual-aid arrangements between friends, neighbours and kin also existed in most villages. These revolved around nursing the sick and elderly, delivering babies, minding children and running errands; deeds whose value are even more difficult to assess. The operation of these networks afforded women a chance to gossip, form close associations and friendships and carve out distinguishable female spaces in the village.

Many accounts of nineteenth-century rural life feature a role-call of women who acted as overseers of village health and welfare. These tended to be older women who no longer participated in the formal labour market but passed on their valuable experience in attending births, marriages and deaths. This is well illustrated by Richard Cobbold's depiction of Wortham in mid-nineteenth-century Suffolk. Women provided neighbourly assistance by carrying faggots from cottage to cottage, running errands to the shops, nursing and minding the sick and needy. Old Moll King, for example, wife of the village barber, was the 'active nurse of all the parish,'[135] while Lucy Rodwell, aged 72, was 'always on the trudge' between houses, being 'the active agent for many'.[136] In the Northamptonshire village of Stoke Albany

---

[134] NtRO, Village Memories, Easton Maudit, p. 21.
[135] Richard Fletcher, ed., *The Biography of a Victorian Village: Richard Cobbold's Account of Wortham, Suffolk* (London, 1977), p. 124.
[136] Ibid., p. 161.

there was 'Nanny Atkins, Mrs Dodson, Mrs Walls and many other kind neighbours who could bring the baby into the world, care for the mother, cope with the washing, cook for the husband and family and run their own homes in addition'.[137] In South Marston, Wiltshire, the role was filled by Granny Bowles, who in middle age had 'adopted the profession of mid-wife', ensuring doctors were rarely needed to attend births, and 'accidents were rare':

> She presided over births and deaths . . . at any time and all times, day or night, Sunday or week day, she was at everyone's beck and call. She left her own household to tend to the needs of others; did many and various acts of kindness and real self-sacrifice without ever knowing it or caring about it, for she was not covetous of people's favour.[138]

Kin and neighbourhood networks served other purposes. Family relations were called upon to assist with minding children when circumstances demanded it. Informal adoption also occurred. Allan Jobson's Suffolk parents sent their children away to be brought up for periods by close family relations as their 'family purse' was stretched 'to breaking-point' by the arrival of several children. Eliza, the eldest child, was sent to her grandmother; Rebecca, the next in age, went to live with a childless aunt and the youngest child remained at home. The grandmother's assistance was offered even though 'she was a poor widow who eked out a livelihood by repairing sacks at a few coppers a score, and whose earthly possessions . . . would go into a wheelbarrow'.[139] Hillyer's mother, so afraid of debt, never sent away a needy neighbour empty-handed. Her maxim was 'It's the poor must look after the poor'.[140] This notion of mutual support – even under the most adverse circumstances – was a shared understanding among neighbours and kin. Gifts of food and drink were also exchanged between houses. Fred Gresswell remembers that families provided each other with 'pig-cheer' after the annual pig killing. Pig's fry, which consisted of sweetbread, liver and pork, was sent round to relatives and friends 'who would repay the compliment in due course'.[141] Similarly at Milton in Northamptonshire, neighbours would save scraps of food to feed their friends' pigs and when killing time came 'the neighbours who had helped feed the pigs, would receive as their reward, a nice plate of fry'.[142]

But networks also gave women a common interest, a chance to share news and gossip. Lucy Bettesworth did not find herself isolated after marriage took

---

[137] NtRO, Village Memories, Stoke Albany by G. Deacon, p. 25.
[138] Davis, ed., *Wiltshire Village*, p. 88.
[139] Jobson, *Hour-Glass*, p. 28.
[140] Hillyer, *Country Boy*, p. 104.
[141] Fred Gresswell, *Bright Boots: An Autobiography* (Newton Abbott, 1956), p. 74.
[142] NtRO, Village Memories, Milton by Mrs Florence Turner, p. 8.

THE INFORMAL ECONOMY

her away from the family home. She 'could hardly have been lonely amongst her own people. There was her mother's house across the land; a little higher up lived now her elder sister . . . The other neighbours were all old friends, if the young wife wanted a gossip.'[143] In Byfield, Old Eliza, who presided over the village births and deaths, was considered 'a very privileged person in her way' as she was party to the entire village news and gossip, which she could then pass on.[144] The tradition of separate rural women's leisure or cultural pursuits is not strong in rural autobiographical writing. This stands in contrast to urban neighbourhoods, where women were integrated into the street and pub culture of cities such as London and Newcastle.[145] The reflections of this Northamptonshire inhabitant reveal some of the restrictions in women's movements in village life:

> By comparison with the more varied life of their men folk the village women were deprived of society other than a gossip with a neighbour. The Women's Institute had not arrived to relieve the monotony. Washing, mending clothes, darning socks and catering for numerous children must have seemed to them a humdrum system. Excluded from bar parlours, women who needed the stimulus of ale, had to convey it homewards from the Lion or the Griffin in mugs and jugs.[146]

Williams also argues that a change in women's relations with each other had occurred when women withdrew from the agricultural day labour force. When women worked in the fields, helped with the hay and corn harvests, and gleaned, he attests, women were given a common purpose and outlook. In his words 'they were thrown in healthier contact with each other . . . they entered into each other's lives and occupations more, and understood one another better.'[147] However, these are male perspectives and tend to ignore or downplay women's involvement in village life through a network of exchange. The operation of these networks, and the value they gave to women's lives, is hidden from some observers. There were times when women's informal activities offered them a break from the daily grind of survival and these should not be dismissed or overlooked as worthless.

Small sums of money did occasionally pass hands in exchange for services rendered. Eliza Freeston remembers that her family owned one of the few large wooden mangles in her Northamptonshire village in the late nineteenth century. So 'other villagers brought their clean washing and

---

[143] Bourne, *Lucy Bettesworth*, p. 13.
[144] Hillyer, *Country Boy*, p. 24.
[145] August, *Poor Women's Lives*, p. 128; Ross, 'Survival networks', pp. 10–11; Long, *Conversations in Cold Rooms*, pp. 210–12. August suggests that women's pub culture was firmly established, but women's claims to leisure were more restricted than men's: women forfeited leisure activities because they lacked the time and money.
[146] NtRO, Village Memories, Boughton by G. E. Kimball, no page numbers.
[147] Davis, ed., *In a Wiltshire Village*, pp. 131–2.

mother allowed them to use the mangle for a small charge of I believe 1d'.[148] According to Grey, women who nursed their neighbours during confinement in Harpenden charged from 2s 6d to 6s for their time.[149] However, these monetary transactions were the exception; most evidence confirms that exchange networks were based on reciprocity. Although Granny Bowles did not expect anything in return for her midwifery services in South Marston, neighbourly assistance was underpinned by the unspoken rule of obligation. And in Harpenden, while some women charged for their midwifery skills, 'now and again they got nothing but a promise'.[150] This system is neatly outlined by the following passages. Mabel Ashby's grandmother earned money in the harvest fields, but most of her income was generated by

> using her skill and intelligence in others' emergencies. She wrote letters for her neighbours, helped them to cut out shirts, to whitewash ceilings. Sometimes she would sit up at night with the sick. Little money passed but her services were meticulously paid for. Her garden was dug, vegetable and rabbits brought, faggots of wood were stacked against her wall.[151]

Mark Thurston's explanation of childbirth is no less illuminating:

> Same as if there's a woman living in a row of cottages. Let's say, and her time's come. A neighbour goes in and gives a hand, and maybe she's five or six months gone herself. She goes home and then presently the time comes for *her* to have her baby; and then the woman she 'friended comes in and helps her. That's how it was, and that's how it ought to be.[152]

This examination of informal channels of exchange has not exhausted the range of coping mechanisms exploited by rural labouring families. Strategies such as poaching, theft and prostitution also existed. Thurston poses the following question in his memoirs: 'And what could you expect from such a hungry, growing boy but that sometimes he should try to compensate himself for such a hard lack by minor thefts?'[153] However, acknowledgement of involvement in illegal pursuits is rare in rural autobiographical literature, particularly female association with crime. This does not mean they were absent from village life. But we should not be surprised that authors are reluctant to describe the more illicit aspects of the village economy because,

---

[148] NtRO, Village Memories, Blisworth by Eliza Freestone, no page numbers.
[149] Grey, *Cottage Life*, pp. 162–3.
[150] Ibid., p. 163.
[151] M. K. Ashby, *Joseph Ashby of Tysoe, 1859–1919: A Study of English Village Life* (Cambridge, 1961), p. 5.
[152] Warren, *Happy Countryman*, p. 54.
[153] Ibid., p. 19.

as John Burnett contends, many writers were concerned with representing the ideal of working-class respectability in their memoirs.[154]

Conclusion: blurring village divisions

Two images drawn by male authors in the 1870s shed light on the status of rural labouring women in the late nineteenth century. In 1873 one contributor to the *Labourers Union Chronicle*, the mouthpiece of the National Agricultural Labourers Union, was looking forward to the day

> when clothing clubs will be things of the past, because each labourer's wife, being no longer a drudge in the fields, but a managing, economical housewife, will be enabled by her husband's earnings to provide all that is necessary in clothing and otherwise for decency and comfort.[155]

Augustus Jessopp, the vicar of Scarning in Norfolk, writing just four years later, believed that the aspiration of the first commentator had come to fruition. According to Jessopp, one manifestation of the amelioration of agricultural workers' conditions was a change in the position of the labourer's wife. She was 'no longer the poor drudge she almost invariably came after her fourth or fifth child', being interested in literature and taking pride in the ownership of material possessions such as perambulators and sewing machines. As a consequence she had 'almost passed out of the labour market'.[156] These observations disregard the whole range of ventures women entered into to secure the maintenance of the family. Activities such as housework, garden cultivation, gathering food and fuel supplies and assisting neighbours do not accord with a market definition of work. But even though such pursuits were not necessarily reimbursed with monetary gains, they all supplemented the family budget. Ross's research on pre-1914 London suggests that the relationships women formed with neighbours, kin, shopkeepers and charity workers 'could do as much as husbands' wages to determine how comfortably their families lived'.[157] Evidence from autobiographical literature indicates that the same argument should be applied to women living in village communities in the nineteenth century.

The work women undertook in the informal economy should not be considered as peripheral or immaterial to the family's well-being. Although the male wage – closely followed by child earnings – formed the crux of family

---

[154] Burnett, ed., *Destiny Obscure*, p. 58.
[155] Quoted in Karen Sayer, *Women of the Fields: Representations of Rural Women in the Nineteenth Century* (Manchester, 1995), pp. 125–6.
[156] Augustus Jessopp, *Arcady. For Better for Worse* (London, 1877), p. 18.
[157] Ross, 'Survival networks', p. 4.

income in the nineteenth century, these were bolstered by the numerous vital but incalculable tasks performed by women. Women were central to many forms of informal barter and exchange, and an examination of these reveals the extent to which women were still active participants in the nineteenth-century economy. The need for women to eke out an existence from a patchwork of resources was perhaps more vital in low-wage agricultural counties, where it was not possible to sustain a family from one wage source alone. It is also evident that women moved between the formal and informal economies at different times of the year, and different stages of the lifecycle, depending on their familial circumstances. Where the male wage could not be stretched to feed the whole family, if men withheld part of their wages or when there was no male wage coming into the household at all, women were forced to seek work on farms or in country houses, and to combine these earnings with transactions in the informal, household economy. Bourne's description of Mrs Loveland encapsulates this multifaceted nature of women's labour. She was a 'full-fleshed bundle of contradictions, that tender-hearted mother and resolute pig-butcher, that clever seamstress and toilsome field-worker and patient sick-nurse in one.'[158] A typical day's work would find Mrs Loveland in the fields, but as 'she trims Swedes for the sheep, or picks up potatoes . . . she will be planning . . . her evening duties – some miraculous patching of trousers for her husband, some inexpensive cookery for her invalid son'.[159] Women used a combination of strategies to subsist; they were resilient, adaptable and responsive to difficult circumstances. Women's methods of 'gnawing it out' have usually been overlooked or dismissed in studies which concentrate on men's working lives, but it is clear that they should be taken into account in any assessment of living standards and employment patterns in the nineteenth-century countryside.

The informal village economy operated within a complex web of barter, credit and exchange networks. Although the maternal figure is often eulogised, men's, women's and children's roles were all interrelated. Men were the prime monetary providers and women the managers. Women were the supervisors of children, who secured resources and earnings for the maternal exchequer. The whole family had a hand in tending cottage gardens, allotments and animals: their tasks operated in conjunction with one another and were inter-reliant. Pigs were ministered and slaughtered by the men; after the killing the pigs were 'put away' by women. Women's and children's role in the gleaning fields was a complement to men's labour in the harvest fields, and often decisive. There was a gender distinction in role designation. Men's contribution to the rural household was dominated by wages gained through employment in the labour market, while women's main respon-

---

[158] Bourne, *Lucy Bettesworth*, p. 72.
[159] Ibid., pp. 75–6.

sibilities – even if they worked outside the home – were connected to domestic and childcare functions. Yet for women in particular, the division between the formal and informal, the public and the private, was not strictly demarcated. Women moved between these spheres throughout the nineteenth century and boundaries of economic activity were blurred. Female involvement in these aspects of village life has yet to be fully comprehended by historians, and has implications for traditional accounts of rural England.

Conclusion

Assessing women's work

It is difficult to pinpoint the experience of the 'typical' or 'average' woman worker. The economies of different rural regions both constricted and unlocked opportunities for women to work at different times in the nineteenth century. Patterns of female labour participation do not correspond easily to general categorisation. Continuity and change, formal and informal, public and private, all had some resonance, but depended on a number of factors: where a woman lived, how old she was, her marital status, whether or not she had children, the age of any children she did have, the occupation of her husband and the attitudes of local employers. We have to understand the interrelation between economic change, the lifecycle dimension and ideological shifts, how these affected women's employment at the local level and the generalised trends that emerge from regional analysis to build up a nationwide picture of women's work. By assessing both national printed documentary material and archival evidence at the local level, it has been shown that the model of rural women's labour in the nineteenth century was not as straightforward as some historians have suggested.

No reliable statistics on female labour participation exist for the early nineteenth century. However, printed and non-printed sources reveal several changes in the extent of female employment in the period c1795 to 1850. In some regions and sectors the desirability of female labour grew. Increased arable cultivation led to more women being employed for manual tasks such as hoeing, weeding, stone-picking, and the planting and picking of root crops. But this trend was not universal across arable areas: in parts of East Anglia, for example, the level of female labour was shrinking over the first three decades of the century. Moreover, at the same time, the likelihood of women being engaged as year-round farm servants across most parts of southern England was rapidly diminishing. In the labour-intensive, hand-manufactured domestic industries, women's labour was at a premium during the French Revolutionary Wars. Yet, correspondingly, hand spinning, once the mainstay of rural female productivity, virtually disappeared from the countryside. Mechanisation and foreign imports threatened women's livelihoods in the lace, straw, button and glove trades after 1815, although female employment levels remained significant in these occupations – particularly lace and straw – until the second half of the century. Underlying all these movements one trend endured: women's earnings, although not central to the family income, remained important.

CONCLUSION

After the mid-nineteenth century, the representation of women's work is dominated by the notion of decline. Census returns, parliamentary investigators and other commentators advance the withdrawal of women from the rural workforce. Census material is clearly limited: many women who worked on farms were given no job designation by enumerators, as their seasonal labour was not regarded as an occupation. However, farm records do largely reinforce the diminution of the female labour force. Women were progressively less likely to work on farms as both day labourers and servants. The census cannot be seen as an accurate statement of the number of women working in agriculture, but the decline proposed by census figures is suggestive of the actual trend on many farms. This argument should not be overstated though. Careful reading of printed evidence denotes the continued presence of female workers in certain circumstances, a pattern again confirmed by non-printed sources. Regional diversity is the key to understanding rural women's work throughout the century. Moreover, using a broad definition of employment to include involvement in informal networks of exchange, the economic participation of women in nineteenth-century village life was still very much in evidence after 1850.

How far did rural women have control over their labour force participation? In the nineteenth-century countryside 'opportunities' or 'choices' about when and where women could enter the workforce were constricted. Women workers were faced with a number of barriers. As we have seen, some of these were related to economic and regional factors. Others, though, were explicitly gendered. The sexual division of labour was well established in agriculture by the beginning of the century. Much evidence points to the persistence of task allocation throughout the nineteenth century, but women's labour became increasingly marginal to certain agricultural operations. As new technologies – first hand and later mechanised innovations – were introduced into nineteenth-century agriculture, men monopolised their use. Women, meanwhile, continued to be engaged in manual tasks. Female agricultural workers were sought for their nimble fingers and their ability to quietly tolerate tedious and unrewarding jobs. The same argument was applied to women who were employed in domestic industries such as handmade pillow lace and straw-plaiting. These abilities were not regarded as skilled in their own right and women workers were generally assigned a lowly status. This, in turn, legitimised the payment of low wages to women, as did the assumption that their main duties were connected to the home and family. This supposition was somewhat misplaced. In 1871, for example, only one-third of all women living in England and Wales between the ages of 20 and 24, and two-thirds of all women aged between 24 and 35 were married. In addition, for every three women aged 20 and over who were married, there were two who were widows.[1] Future research on these

---

[1] Patricia Hollis, *Women in Public: The Women's Movement 1850–1900* (London, 1979), p. 33.

groups of women and their place in the nineteenth-century rural workforce in needed. The ideological convictions that placed significant limitations on female opportunities are encapsulated in the following quote. Here Arthur Savory is describing the women who worked on his 300-acre mixed farm in the Vale of Evesham at the end of the nineteenth century:

> Women are splendid at all kinds of light farm work whenever deftness and gentle touch are required, such as hop-tying and picking or gathering small fruit like currants, raspberries and strawberries; but I do not consider them in the least capable of taking the place of men in outwork which demands muscular strength and endurance and the ability to withstand severe heat or bitter cold or wet ground underfoot, through all the varying seasons. Village women have, too, their home duties to attend to, and it is most important that their men-folk should be suitably fed and their houses kept clean and attractive.[2]

Ideological and economic forces coalesced to circumscribe women's involvement in the rural labour force. But this did not necessarily mean that female workers were always held back by oppressive forces over which they had no control. At certain stages in the nineteenth century, the rural woman worker emerges from the shadows of her urban equivalent, often provoking moral panic in the process. In early nineteenth-century Bedfordshire, the wages earned by women engaged in domestic industries were so high that they threatened to overturn traditional family hierarchies. Female farm servants in northern England were also viewed as subversive, displaying behaviour that no decorous, model Victorian woman should: independence, mobility and brute strength. That such women were found working in mixed company, and were often hired at fairs which were synonymous with immorality and promiscuity, further appalled Victorian onlookers. But rural women workers did not always emerge into the spotlight from a position of strength. The gang system, which operated in mid-nineteenth-century eastern England, is the most obvious example of this. In that case, parliamentary investigators were shocked that exploitative systems of labour were not unique to urban-based manufacturers and that forms of subcontracting operated in rural regions. This prompted the only government legislation aimed specifically at curtailing the employment of women (and children) in the nineteenth-century countryside. Karen Sayer has posited that the Gangs Act of 1867 had a significant effect on female labour.[3] Indeed, the role of the state, according to Sayer, was decisive in reducing women's work in agriculture. 'By 1900 women had largely passed from view as casual farm labourers', she argues. 'The state had intervened, they had been disciplined.'[4]

---

[2] Arthur H. Savory, *Grain and Chaff from an English Manor* (Oxford, 1920), pp. 75–6.
[3] Karen Sayer, *Women of the Fields: Representations of Rural Women in the Nineteenth Century* (Manchester, 1995), p. 68.
[4] Sayer, *Women of the Fields*, p. 137.

CONCLUSION

This claim is problematic, overstating the strength of government legislation and downplaying the wider economic and ideological factors which were operating in the nineteenth century. Moreover, the agency of women themselves is lost. Although women's ability to make conscious, individualistic decisions about the nature of their labour was limited, we should not discount the possibility that women did have some options over when to withdraw from the formal labour market in the later decades of the century.

Autobiographical material indicates that housewifery skills were central to rural labouring families' conception of respectability in the late nineteenth century.[5] Alfred Ireson, who was born in Oundle in 1856, argues that 'trial and difficulty' characterised village life in his childhood. Although labourers toiled for long hours, the recompense was 'barely enough to keep body and soul together'. As a result 'everything depended on the skill and character of the mother. . . . The struggle for respectability!'[6] Flora Thompson maintains that 'Victorian ideas . . . had penetrated to some extent' into her Oxfordshire village, 'and any work outside the home was considered unwomanly'.[7] The decline in married women's labour participation may be partly attributable to choice: as real wages rose, women were presented with an opening to withdraw from poorly paid work in the formal labour market. Single women engaged as farm servants in counties such as East Yorkshire, displayed an increasing desire to be employed in domestic service in local towns, and evidence from labouring women also indicates that they wanted their daughters to work as servants rather than agricultural labourers. George Bourne was also sensitive to a change in the outward appearance of many rural women in turn-of-the-century Surrey. Twenty years earlier, Bourne insisted, housework had been neglected by working women, who had 'become merely the "hands" or employees of farmers, struggling to make up money enough every week for a wretched shopping'.[8] Mothers had little chance of teaching their daughters domestic skills and 'the home became a place to sleep in, to feed in; not a place in which to try to live well'.[9] Nor could women take time to consider their own plight and comprehend how 'squalid' and 'neglected' their lives had become. By 1900 this situation had altered:

> Field-work, which fostered a blowsy carelessness, has declined, and at the same time the arrival of 'residents' has greatly increased the demand for charwomen and

---

[5] John Burnett, ed., *Destiny Obscure: Autobiographies of Childhood, Education and Family from the 1820s to the 1920s* (London, 1982), p. 58; David Vincent, *Bread, Knowledge and Freedom: A Study of Nineteenth-Century Working Class Autobiography* (London, 1981), p. 55.
[6] Quoted in Burnett, ed., *Destiny Obscure*, p. 83.
[7] Flora Thompson, *Lark Rise to Candleford*, 1st edn 1939 (Harmondsworth, 1984), p. 114.
[8] George Bourne, *Change in the Village*, 1st edn 1912 (London, 1955), p. 159.
[9] Ibid., p. 158.

washerwomen. The women, therefore, find it worthwhile to cultivate a certain tidiness in their persons, which extends to their homes . . . perhaps middle-class ideas of decent house-work are at last coming in, to fill the place left empty by the obsolete peasant ideas.[10]

However, Bourne was a perceptive observer. While he noted that middle-class notions of domesticity had taken hold among the women of the rural labouring poor, the outcomes were not all beneficial for labouring women. In the past Bourne believed that poor women's drudgery had been an 'organic part' of the community in which they lived, and the character and ability which resulted from their position enabled them to hold their heads up high and 'look with complacency upon women bred in other ways'.[11] But the household drudgery they experienced under the umbrella of middle-class domesticity was more restrictive. 'The truth is that middle-class domesticity, instead of setting cottage women on the road to middle-class culture of mind and body, has side-tracked them – has made of them charwomen and laundresses, so that other women may shirk these duties and be "cultured".'[12] Women continued to work throughout the century when the family budget dictated: any aspirations held by rural labouring men and women to emulate an urban, middle-class lifestyle of gentility and domesticity were severely undermined by the realities of continuing poverty and struggle in the nineteenth-century countryside.

---

[10] Ibid., p. 159–60.
[11] Ibid., p. 160.
[12] Ibid.

Bibliography

Manuscript sources

Bedfordshire and Luton Archives and Records Service, Bedford

OR 1370–81, Farm and estate accounts of Richard Orlebar, Podington, 1792 to 1888.
BS 2094, Letter from William Lee Antoine to Lawer, 20 August 1797.
R3 2114/264–316, Woburn estate accounts. Park Farm, Priestly Farm and Speedwell Farm, daily diaries of work, 1806 to 1808.
X 297/81, Farm accounts, Birchfield farm, Howbury estate, 1817–1819.
X 159/1–3, Wages books of the Long family, Manor Farm, Upper Stondon, 1817 to 1887.
MIC 85, J. Newman's account books, Cardington, 1839 to 1848 and Duck End Farm, Wilstead, 1875 to 1891.
Z 600/2, Farm accounts of William Barber of Rameridge End farm, Luton, August 1833 to August 1837.
R3 3772, Correspondence of the Russell estate. Duke of Bedford's Steward's correspondence. Thomas Bennett, August 1833.
X 52/70, Labour books, Chalgrave Manor Farm, 1847 to 1857.
R3 4739, Correspondence of the Russell estate. Duke of Bedford's Steward's correspondence. Thomas Bennett to C. Haedy, 1843.
FAC 129, The autobiography of Joseph Bell of Turvey. The story of twelve years in the life of a village orphan, 1846 to 1858, told by himself.
Census enumerators book, Podington, 1851.
Census enumerators book, Upper Stondon, 1861.
Z 512/1, Chawston Manor Farm, Labour books of John Wilkinson of Roxtow, 1868 to 1885.
M 15/32–4, Statement of affairs and list of creditors of Willis Brothers, straw hat and bonnet manufacturers of Luton, 1873.
X 117/22, Farm account book, Manor Farm, Stevington, 1875 to 1876.
M 15/35, List of creditors and accounts of John Eyres, straw-plait manufacturer, Luton, 1879.
X 259/1–4, Pillow lace books and photographs of Mrs Rachael Read, Pillow lace manufacturer, Cranfield, 1886.
X 230/6, Parsonage Farm, Shillington, Accounts, 1893 to 1898.
CRT 150/121, 'The good old times', *Bedfordshire Times*, April 1910.
X 342/5, Willington Nursery records, 1910.

BIBLIOGRAPHY

East Riding Record Office, Beverley

DDSA 1203/1–6, Farming receipts and expenses, Saltmarshe, 1801 to 1846.
DDSA 1219/1–2, Women's labour journals, Saltmarshe, 1818 to 1822 and 1835 to 1841.
DDSA 1198, Saltmarshe, MSS, History of the village and family written in 1894.
DDCC (2) 19/7, Servants' wages and liveries book, Burton Constable, 1872.
DDSA 1067, Labour journals of Laxton Manor Farm, May 1882 to January 1884.

East Yorkshire Local Studies Library, Beverley

Census enumerators book, Laxton, Saltmarshe, Kilpin and Yorkfleet, 1841.
Census enumerators book, Laxton parish, 1881.
Memoirs of Margaret Moate, born Cottingham, 1879.

Hull University, Brynmor Jones Library

DDLA 34/8, Langdale family of Holme-on-Spalding-Moor, Accounts, 1792–1799.
DDJL 5/1–4, Farm account books of John Lockwood, Beverley, 1817 to 1820 and 1824 to 1825.
DDLG 43/5–15, Farm and private accounts, Lloyd-Greame family of Sewerby, 1821 to 1893.
DDFA 37/23, Housekeeping book, Forbes Adams family of Skipwith Hall, 1845 to 1852.
DDEV 56/331–5, Farm account books, Breeks Farm, Seaton Ross, 1851 to 1858.

Luton Museum and Art Gallery

M8/6–8, Account books of Henry Horn, plait dealer, Dunstable, 1870s.

Newton and Cowper Museum, Olney

Proceedings of the Committee of Lace Manufacturers for the Counties of Buckingham, Bedford and Northampton, 1814 to 1815.

BIBLIOGRAPHY

Norfolk Record Office, Norwich

MEA 3/27–51, Farm accounts of Meade of Earsham, 1807 to 1838.
MS 21593/2, Haymaking accounts, Beauchamp-Proctor, Langley estate, 1824 to 1828.
MC 3/89, 400x, Stody Hall Farm accounts, 1827 to 1829.
MC 299/28, Farm account book of Betts of Forncett, Tibenham and elsewhere, including farm labour book, 1880 to 1902.

Norfolk Local Studies Library, Norwich

Census enumerators book, Flitcham, 1851 and 1871.
Census enumerators book, Ashmanhaugh, Beeston St Laurence, Belaugh, Horning, Hoverton St Peter and Neatishead, 1871, 1881 and 1891.

Northamptonshire Record Office, Northampton

X2959a–X2960a, Village Memories.

University of Reading Library, Reading

BED P245/1, Farm accounts, Eversholt, 1802 to 1817.
NORF P429/1–4, Farm records of Flitcham Hall farm, Flitcham, including labour account books, August 1847 to July 1852 and February 1871 to October 1873.
NORF 11/4/1, Labour book, Wereham, 1855 to 1868.
NORF 9.1/1–75, Farm account books, Neatishead, 1859 to 1938.

Parliamentary papers and government publications

PP 1821, IX, Select Committee on Petitions complaining of Depressed State of Agriculture of UK.
PP 1824, VI, Select Committee on Agricultural Wages, and the Condition and Morals of Labourers in that Employment.
PP 1833, V, Select Committee on State of Agriculture in UK.
PP 1834, XXX, Report from His Majesty's Commissioners for Inquiring into the Administration and Practical Operation of the Poor Laws. Appendix (B.1). Answers to Rural Queries in Five Parts. Part 1.
Annual Reports of the Poor Law Commissioners for England and Wales, 1835 to 1847
PP 1836, VIII, Select Committee on the State of Agriculture.

PP 1843, XII, Reports of Special Assistant Poor Law Commissioners on the Employment of Women and Children in Agriculture.
PP 1843, XIV, Children's Employment Commission (Trades and Manufacturers).
Annual Reports of the Poor Law Board, 1848 to 1871
PP 1863, XVII, First Report of the Children's Employment Commission.
PP 1864, XXII, Second Report of the Children's Employment Commission.
PP 1867, XVI, Sixth Report of the Children's Employment Commission.
PP 1867–8, XVII, First Report from the Commissioners on the Employment of Children, Young Persons and Women in Agriculture.
PP 1868–9, XIII, Second Report from the Commissioners on the Employment of Children, Young Persons and Women in Agriculture.
PP 1881, XVI, Royal Commission on Depressed Condition of Agricultural Interests. Reports of Assistant Commissioners.
PP 1882, XV, Royal Commission on Depressed Condition of Agricultural Interests. Reports of Assistant Commissioners.
PP 1893–4, XXXV, Royal Commission on Labour. The Agricultural Labourer. Reports from the Assistant Agriculture Commissioners.
PP 1893–4, XXXVII, Royal Commission on Labour. The Employment of Women.
PP 1900, LXXXII, Report by Mr Wilson Fox on the Wages and Earnings of Agricultural Labourers in the UK.

Census Reports of Great Britain: Population Tables
PP 1841, XXVII, Occupation Abstract (1844).
PP 1851, LXXXVIII, Ages and Occupations, vol. 1 (1852–3).
PP 1861, LIII, Abstracts of Ages, Occupations and Birthplaces of People, vol. 2 (1863).
PP 1871, LXXI, Ages, Civil Condition, Occupations, and Birthplaces, vol. 3 (1873).
PP 1881, LXXX, Ages, Condition as to Marriage, Occupations and Birthplaces, vol. 3 (1883).
PP 1891, CVI, Ages, Condition as to Marriage, Occupations and Birthplaces, vol. 3 (1893–4).
PP 1901, CVIII, Ages, Condition as to Marriage, Occupations, and Birthplaces, vol 1. (1904).

Newspapers

Beverley Guardian
Driffield Times
Eastern Counties Herald
Hull Advertiser

BIBLIOGRAPHY

Pre-1900 printed books, articles and pamphlets

Almack, Barugh, 'On the agriculture of Norfolk', *Journal of the Royal Agricultural Society*, 5 (1845), pp. 307–58.

Anon, 'Suggestions for improving the moral character of the agricultural labourers, etc', *Farmers Magazine*, 1 (1835), pp. 8–9.

Anon, 'The life of a farm labourer', *Cornhill Magazine*, 9 (1864), pp. 178–86.

Anon, 'Agricultural gangs', *Quarterly Review*, 123 (1867), pp. 173–90.

Arch, Joseph, *Joseph Arch. The Story of His Life* (London, 1898).

Austin, Thomas, *The Straw-Plaiting and Straw Hat and Bonnet Trade* (Luton, 1871).

'T.B.' and Young, Arthur, 'On spinning among the poor', *Annals of Agriculture*, 5 (1786), pp. 417–22.

Bacon, R. N., *The Report on the Agriculture of Norfolk* (London, 1844).

Bailey, J., *General View of the Agriculture of the County of Durham* (London, 1810).

Bailey, John and Culley, George, *General View of the Agriculture of the County of Cumberland* (London, 1794).

Bailey, John and Culley, George, *General View of the Agriculture of the County of Northumberland* (London, 1794).

Bailey, John and Culley, George, *General View of the Agriculture of the County of Cumberland*, 3rd edn (London, 1813).

Bailey, John and Culley, George, *General View of the Agriculture of the County of Northumberland*, 3rd edn (London, 1813).

Barugh, William, *Master and Man: A Reply to the Agricultural Labourer As He Really Is* (Driffield, 1854).

Batchelor, Thomas, *General View of the Agriculture of the County of Bedford* (London, 1808).

Bennett, William, 'The farming of Bedfordshire', *Journal of the Royal Agricultural Society*, 18 (1857), pp. 1–29.

Bernard, Thomas, 'Extract of an account of the introduction of straw platt at Avebury', *Report of the Society for Bettering the Condition and Increasing the Comforts of the Poor*, vol. 4 (1805), pp. 90–111.

Bernard, Thomas, 'Extract from an account of the ladies committee for promoting the education and employment of the female poor', *Report of the Society for Bettering the Condition and Increasing the Comforts of the Poor*, vol. 4 (1805), pp. 181–92.

Billingsley, John, *General View of the Agriculture of the County of Somerset* (London, 1794).

Bishton, J., *General View of the Agriculture of the County of Salop* (London, 1794).

Bowlby, A. L., 'The statistics of wages in the UK during the last hundred years (part 1). Agricultural wages', *Journal of the Statistical Society*, 61 (1898), pp. 702–22.

Boys, John, *General View of the Agriculture of the County of Kent* (Brentford, 1794).
Boys, John, *General View of the Agriculture of the County of Kent*, 2nd edn (London, 1813).
Brereton, Revd C. D., *A Practical Enquiry into the Number, Means of Employment and Wages of Agricultural Labourers* (Norwich, 1824).
Brown, R., *General View of the Agriculture of the West Riding of Yorkshire* (London, 1799).
Brown, Thomas, *General View of the Agriculture of the County of Derby* (London, 1794).
'F. C', 'Agricultural labour', *Farmers Magazine*, 2 (1835), p. 114.
Caird, James, *English Agriculture in 1850–51* (London, 1852).
Chester, G. John, *Statute Fairs: Their Evils and their Remedy* (York, 1856).
Claridge, John, *General View of the Agriculture of the County of Dorset* (London, 1793).
Clark, John, *General View of the Agriculture of the County of Hereford* (London, 1794).
Cobbett, William, *Cottage Economy*, 1st edn 1822 (Oxford, 1979).
Cobbett, William, *Rural Rides*, 1st edn 1830 (Harmondsworth, 1985).
Davies, David, *The Case of Labourers in Husbandry, Stated and Considered* (London, 1795).
Davis, Thomas, *General View of the Agriculture of the County of Wiltshire* (London, 1794).
Davis, Thomas, *General View of the Agriculture of the County of Wiltshire* (London, 1811).
Defoe, Daniel, *A Tour Through the Whole Island of Great Britain*, 2 vols, 1st edn 1726 (London, 1962).
Dent, J., 'The present condition of the English agricultural labourer', *Journal of the Royal Agricultural Society*, 2nd ser., 7 (1871), pp. 343–65.
Dickson, R. W., *General View of the Agriculture of the County of Lancashire* (London, 1815).
Donaldson, James, *General View of the Agriculture of the County of Northampton* (London, 1794).
Driver, Abraham, and Driver, William, *General View of the Agriculture of the County of Hampshire* (London, 1794).
Dryden, Alice, 'Pillow lace in the Midlands', *Pall Mall Magazine*, 8 (1896), pp. 379–91.
Duncumb, J., *General View of the Agriculture of the County of Hereford* (London, 1815).
Durham, Bishop of, 'Extract from an account of three cottagers keeping cows and renting land in Rutlandshire', *Report of the Society for Bettering the Condition and Increasing the Comforts of the Poor*, vol. 1 (1798), pp. 116–19.
Eddowes, Revd J., *Martinmas Musing: Or Thoughts About the Hiring Day* (Driffield, 1854).

BIBLIOGRAPHY

Eddowes, Revd J., *The Agricultural Labourer as He Really Is, or Village Morals in 1854* (Driffield, 1854).

Eden, Sir Frederick Morton, *The State of the Poor*, 3 vols (London, 1797).

Estcourt, Thomas, 'Provisions for the poor', *Annals of Agriculture*, 34 (1800), pp. 145–50.

Estcourt, Thomas, 'An account of the result of an effort to better the condition of the poor in a country village', *Annals of Agriculture*, 43 (1805), pp. 1–9 and pp. 289–99.

Farey, J., *General View of the Agriculture and Minerals of Derbyshire*, 3 vols (London, 1811, 1813 and 1817).

Foot, Peter, *General View of the Agriculture of the County of Middlesex* (London, 1794).

Fraser, Robert, *General View of the County of Cornwall* (London, 1794).

Fraser, Robert, *General View of the County of Devon* (London, 1794).

Garnier, Russell M., *Annals of the British Peasantry* (London, 1895).

Glasse, Revd Dr, 'Extract from an account of the advantage of a cottager keeping a pig', *Report of the Society for Bettering the Condition and Increasing the Comforts of the Poor*, vol. 1 (1798), pp. 193–6.

Glasse, Revd Dr, 'Extract from an account of the superior advantages of dibbling wheat, or setting it by hand', *Report of the Society for Bettering the Condition and Improving the Comforts of the Poor*, vol. 3 (1802), pp. 85–92.

Gooch, Revd, *General View of the Agriculture of the County of Cambridge* (London, 1813).

Granger, Joseph, *General View of the Agriculture of the County of Durham* (London, 1794).

Griggs, Mr, *General View of the Agriculture of the County of Essex* (London, 1794).

Harries, E., 'Land for cottagers', *Annals of Agriculture*, 36 (1801), pp. 355–9.

Hasbach, William, *A History of the English Agricultural Labourer*, 1st edn 1894 (London, 1966).

Heath, Richard, *The Victorian Peasant*, 1st edn 1893 (Gloucester, 1989).

Holland, H., *General View of the Agriculture of the County of Cheshire* (London, 1808).

Holt, John, *General View of the Agriculture of the County of Lancaster* (London, 1794).

Howitt, William, *The Rural Life of England*, 1st edn 1838 (Shannon, 1971).

Howlett, Revd John, 'The different quantity and expense of agricultural labour in different years', *Annals of Agriculture*, 18 (1792), pp. 566–72.

Jackson, Thomas, *Recollections of my Own Life and Times* (London, 1874).

James, William and Malcolm, Jacob, *General View of the Agriculture of the County of Buckinghamshire* (London, 1794).

James, William and Malcolm, Jacob, *General View of the Agriculture of the County of Surrey* (London, 1794).

BIBLIOGRAPHY

Jefferies, Richard, *Hodge and His Masters*, 1st edn 1880 (Stroud, 1992).
Jessopp, Augustus, *Arcady. For Better for Worse* (London, 1877).
Johnson, Clifton, *Among English Hedgerows* (London, 1899).
Kent, Nathaniel, *General View of the Agriculture of the County of Norfolk* (London, 1794).
Leatham, Issac, *General View of the Agriculture of the East Riding of Yorkshire* (London, 1794).
Legard, Revd F. D., ed., *More About Farm Lads* (London, 1865).
Legard, George, 'Farming of the East Riding of Yorkshire', *Journal of the Royal Agricultural Society*, 9 (1848), pp. 85–136.
Little, H. J., 'The agricultural labourer', *Journal of the Royal Agricultural Society*, 2nd ser., 9 (1878), pp. 763–802.
Lowe, John, *General View of the Agriculture of the County of Nottingham* (London, 1798).
Marshall, William, *Rural Economy of Yorkshire*, 2 vols (London, 1788).
Mavor, William, *General View of the Agriculture of Berkshire* (London, 1809).
Maxwell, George, *General View of the Agriculture of the County of Huntingdon* (London, 1793).
Middleton, John, *General View of the Agriculture of the County of Middlesex* (London, 1813).
Monk, John, *General View of the Agriculture of the County of Leicester* (London, 1794).
Morris, Revd F. O., *The Present System of Hiring Farm Servants in the East Riding of Yorkshire With Suggestions for its Improvement* (Driffield, 1854).
Murray, A., *General View of the Agriculture of the County of Warwick* (London, 1813).
Nichols, George, 'On the condition of the agricultural labourer', *Journal of the Royal Agricultural Society*, 7 (1846), pp. 1–30.
Palliser, Mrs Bury, *A History of Lace* (London, 1875).
Parkinson, Richard, *General View of the Agriculture of the County of Rutland* (London, 1808).
Pearce, William, *General View of the Agriculture of the County of Berkshire* (London, 1794).
Phillips, Kay James, 'Earnings of agricultural labourers in Norfolk and Suffolk', *Journal of the Statistical Society*, 1 (1839), pp. 179–83.
Pitt, William, *General View of the Agriculture of the County of Stafford* (London, 1794).
Pitt, William, *General View of the Agriculture of the County of Leicester* (London, 1809).
Pitt, William, *General View of the Agriculture of the County of Northampton* (London, 1813).
Pitt, William, *General View of the Agriculture of the County of Worcester* (London, 1813).
Plymley, Joseph, *General View of the Agriculture of the County of Shropshire* (London, 1803).

Polleroy, William Thomas, *General View of the Agriculture of the County of Worcester* (London, 1794).
Priest, Revd St John, *General View of the Agriculture of Buckinghamshire* (London, 1813).
Pringle, Andrew, *General View of the Agriculture of the County of Westmoreland* (Edinburgh, 1794).
Pringle, Andrew, *General View of the Agriculture of the County of Westmoreland*, 3rd edn (London, 1813).
Purdy, Frederick, 'On the earnings of agricultural labourers in England and Wales, 1860', *Journal of the Statistical Society*, 24 (1861), pp. 328–73.
Rennie, Mr, Brown, Mr and Shirreff, Mr, *General View of the Agriculture of the West Riding of Yorkshire* (London, 1794).
Rudge, T., *General View of the Agriculture of the County of Gloucester* (London, 1813).
Simpson, Mary, 'The life and training of a farm boy', in Legard, ed., *More About Farm Lads*, pp. 75–100.
Simpson, Mary, *Ploughing and Sowing; Or Annals of an Evening School in a Yorkshire Village* (London, 1861).
Simpson, Mary, *Gleanings: Being a Sequel to Ploughing and Sowing* (London, 1876).
Sinclair, Sir John, 'Observations on the means of enabling a cottager to keep a cow', *Annals of Agriculture*, 37 (1801), pp. 225–45.
Skinner, Revd J., *Facts and Opinions Concerning Statute Hirings, Respectfully Addressed to the Landowners, Clergy, Farmers and Tradesmen of the East Riding of Yorkshire* (London, 1861).
Stevenson, Revd Nash, *On the Rise and Progress of the Movement for the Abolition of Statutes, Mops or Feeing Markets* (London, 1861).
Stevenson, W., *General View of the Agriculture of the County of Surrey* (London, 1809).
Stevenson, W., *General View of the Agriculture of the County of Dorset* (London, 1812).
Stone, Thomas, *General View of the Agriculture of the County of Huntingdon* (London, 1793).
Stone, Thomas, *General View of the Agriculture of the County of Lincoln* (London, 1794).
Stone, Thomas, *General View of the Agriculture of the County of Bedford* (London, 1794).
Strickland, H. E., *General View of the Agriculture of the East Riding of Yorkshire* (York, 1812).
Tansley, A. J., 'On the straw plait trade', *Journal of the Society of Arts*, 9 (1860), pp. 69–77.
Tuckett, J. D., *A History of the Past and Present State of the Labouring Population including the Progress of Agriculture, Manufactures and Commerce*, 2 vols, 1st edn 1846 (Shannon, 1971).

BIBLIOGRAPHY

Tuke, Mr, *General View of the Agriculture of the North Riding of Yorkshire* (London, 1794).

Turner, George, *General View of the Agriculture of the County of Gloucester* (London, 1794).

Vancouver, Charles, *General View of the Agriculture in the County of Cambridge* (London, 1794).

Vancouver, Charles, *General View of the Agriculture of the County of Essex* (London, 1795).

Vancouver, Charles, *General View of the Agriculture of the County of Devon* (London, 1808).

Vancouver, Charles, *General View of the Agriculture of Hampshire including the Isle of Wight* (London, 1810).

Various, 'Replies to the editors circular letter', *Annals of Agriculture*, 24 (1795), pp. 239–93 and pp. 297–348; continued in *Annals of Agriculture*, 25 (1796), pp. 473–506 and pp. 599–642; and *Annals of Agriculture*, 26 (1796), pp. 1–26 and pp. 115–58.

Various, *The Agricultural Crisis: The Condition, Prospects and Needs of Norfolk Agriculturists* (London, 1879).

Walker, D., *General View of the Agriculture of the County of Hertford* (London, 1795).

Wedge, John, *General View of the Agriculture of the County of Warwick* (London, 1794).

Wedge, Thomas, *General View of the Agriculture of the County Palatine of Chester* (London, 1794).

Whitehead, Charles, *Agricultural Labourers* (London, 1870).

Winchelsea, Earl of, 'Extract from an account of the advantages of cottagers renting land', *Report of the Society for Bettering the Condition and Improving the Comforts of the Poor*, vol. 1 (1798), pp. 129–39.

Worgan, G. B., *General View of the Agriculture of the County of Cornwall* (London, 1811).

Young, Arthur, *General View of the Agriculture of the County of Suffolk* (London, 1794).

Young, Arthur, 'On the price of wool, and state of spinning at present in England', *Annals of Agriculture*, 9 (1788), pp. 266–345.

Young, Arthur, 'Lace making', *Annals of Agriculture*, 37 (1801), pp. 448–50.

Young, Arthur, *General View of the Agriculture of the County of Hertfordshire* (London, 1804).

Young, Arthur, *General View of the Agriculture of the County of Norfolk* (London, 1804).

Young, Arthur, *General View of the Agriculture of the County of Lincoln* (London, 1813).

Young, Arthur, *General View of the Agriculture of Oxfordshire* (London, 1813).

Young, Arthur, *General View of the Agriculture of the County of Essex*, 2 vols (London, 1813).

Young, Revd A., *General View of the Agriculture of the County of Sussex* (London, 1813).

Post-1900 printed books, articles and pamphlets

Agar, Nigel, 'The Bedfordshire farmworker in the nineteenth century', *Bedfordshire Historical Record Society*, 60 (1981).
Alexander, Sally, 'Women's work in nineteenth-century London: A study of the years 1820–1850', in Mitchell and Oakley, eds, *The Rights and Wrongs of Women*, pp. 59–111.
Alexander, Sally, Davin, Anna and Hostettler, Eve, 'Labouring women: A reply to Eric Hobsbawn', *History Workshop Journal*, 8 (1979), pp. 174–82.
Allen, R. C., *Enclosure and the Yeoman: The Agricultural Development of the South Midlands, 1450–1850* (Oxford, 1992).
Allison, K. J., *The East Riding of Yorkshire Landscape* (London, 1976).
Anderson, Michael, *Family Structure in Nineteenth-Century Lancashire* (Cambridge, 1971).
Anthony, Richard, 'Farm servant vs. agricultural labourer, 1870–1914: A commentary on Howkins', *Agricultural History Review*, 43 (1995), pp. 61–4.
Apfel, William and Dunkley, Peter, 'English rural society and the new poor law: Bedfordshire, 1834–1847', *Social History*, 10 (1985), pp. 37–68.
Archer, John, *'By a Flash and a Scare': Incendiarism, Animal Maiming and Poaching in East Anglia, 1815–1870* (Oxford, 1990).
Armstrong, W. A., *Farmworkers: A Social and Economic History, 1770–1980* (London, 1988).
Armstrong, W. A., 'Labour 1: Rural population growth, systems of employment, and incomes', in Mingay, ed., *Agrarian History of England and Wales*, vol. VI, pp. 641–728.
Ashby, M. K., *Joseph Ashby of Tysoe, 1859–1919: A Study of English Village Life* (Cambridge, 1961).
August, Andrew, *Poor Women's Lives: Gender, Work and Poverty in Late-Victorian London* (Cranbury, 1999).
Ayres, Pat and Lambertz, Jan, 'Marriage relations, money and domestic violence in working-class Liverpool, 1919–1939', in Lewis, ed., *Labour and Love*, pp. 195–219.
Ayres, Pat, 'The hidden economy of dockland families: Liverpool in the 1930s', in Hudson and Lee, eds, *Women, Work and the Family Economy*, pp. 271–90.
Baldry, George, *The Rabbit Skin Cap: A Tale of a Norfolk Countryman's Youth*, 1st edn 1939 (Norwich, 1974).
Banks, Sarah, 'Nineteenth-century scandal or twentieth-century model? A new look at "open" and "close" parishes', *Economic History Review*, XLI (1988), pp. 51–73.

BIBLIOGRAPHY

Barber, Jill, '"Stolen goods": The sexual harassment of female servants in west Wales during the nineteenth century', *Rural History*, 4 (1993), pp. 123–36.

Baker, David, 'The inhabitants of Cardington in 1782', *Bedfordshire Historical Record Society*, 52 (1973).

Barr, David, *Climbing the Ladder: The Struggles and Successes of a Village Lad* (London, 1910).

Barrett, Michele *Women's Oppression Today* (London, 1980).

Barrett, Michele, and McIntosh, Mary, 'The "family wage"', in Whitelegg et al., eds, *The Changing Experience of Women*, pp. 71–87.

Beavington, F., 'The development of market gardening in Bedfordshire, 1799–1939', *Agricultural History Review*, 23 (1975), pp. 23–48.

Beckett, J. V., *The Agricultural Revolution* (Oxford, 1990).

Bedfordshire Federation of Women's Institutes, *Bedfordshire Within Living Memory* (Newbury, 1992).

Beechey, Veronica, 'On patriarchy', *Feminist Review*, 3 (1979), pp. 66–82.

Benenson, Harold, 'The "family wage" and working women's consciousness in Britain, 1880–1914', *Politics and Society*, 19 (1991), pp. 71–108.

Bennett, Judith, 'Women's history: A study in continuity and change', *Women's History Review*, 2 (1993), pp. 173–84.

Berg, Maxine, 'Women's work, mechanisation and the early phases of industrialisation in England', in Joyce., ed., *Historical Meanings of Work*, pp. 64–98.

Berg, Maxine, 'What difference did women's work make to the industrial revolution?', *History Workshop Journal*, 35 (1993), pp. 22–44.

Berg, Maxine, *The Age of Manufactures, 1700–1820: Industry, Innovation and Work in Britain* (London, 1994).

Berg, Maxine and Hudson, Pat, 'Rehabilitating the industrial revolution', *Economic History Review*, XLV (1992), pp. 24–50.

Beverstock, Revd A. H., *The English Agricultural Labourer* (London, 1912).

Blaug, Mark, 'The poor law report re-examined', *Journal of Economic History*, XXIV (1964), pp. 229–45.

Bouquet, Mary, *Family, Servants and Visitors: The Farm Household in Nineteenth and Twentieth-Century Devon* (Norwich, 1985).

Bourke, Joanna, '"I was always fond of my pillow": The handmade lace industry in the United Kingdom, 1870–1914', *Rural History*, 5 (1994), pp. 155–69.

Bourke, Joanna, *Working-Class Cultures in Britain, 1890–1960: Gender, Class and Ethnicity* (London, 1994).

Bourke, Joanna, 'Housewifery in working-class England, 1860–1914' in Sharpe, ed., *Women's Work*, pp. 332–58.

Bourne, George, *Change in the Village*, 1st edn 1912 (London, 1955).

Bourne, George, *Lucy Bettesworth* (London, 1913).

Bowden, Jack, 'Recollections of a farm worker', *Journal of the North Yorkshire County Record Office*, 1 (1975), pp. 35–9.

Boyer, George R., *An Economic History of the English Poor Law, 1750–1850* (Cambridge, 1990).
Bradley, Harriet, *Men's Work, Women's Work: A Sociological History of the Sexual Division of Labour in Employment* (Cambridge, 1989).
Buck, Anne, 'The teaching of lacemaking in the east Midlands', *Folk Life*, 4 (1966), pp. 39–50.
Buck, Anne, 'Middlemen in the Bedfordshire lace industry', *Bedfordshire Historical Record Society*, 57 (1978), pp. 32–58.
Burman, Sandra, ed., *Fit Work for Women* (London, 1979).
Burnett, John, ed., *Destiny Obscure: Autobiographies of Childhood, Education and Family from the 1820s to the 1920s* (London, 1982).
Burnett, John, ed., *Useful Toil: Autobiographies of Working People from the 1820s to the 1920s*, 1st edn 1974 (London, 1994).
Burnett, John, Vincent, David and Mayall, David, eds, *The Autobiography of the Working Class: An Annotated, Critical Bibliography, vol. 1, 1790–1900* (Brighton, 1984).
Burnette, Joyce, 'An investigation of the female–male wage gap during the industrial revolution in Britain', *Economic History Review*, L (1997), pp. 257–81.
Burnette, Joyce, 'Labourers at the Oakes. Changes in the demand for female day-labourers near Sheffield during the Agricultural Revolution', *Journal of Economic History*, LIX (1999), pp. 41–67.
Burrows, Mrs, 'A childhood in the fens about 1850–60', in Davies, ed., *Life As We Have Known It*, pp. 109–14.
Bushby, David, 'The Bedfordshire schoolchild', *Bedfordshire Historical Record Society*, 67 (1988).
Bythell, Duncan, *The Sweated Trades: Outwork in Nineteenth-Century Britain* (London, 1978).
Cannadine, David, 'The past and the present in the English industrial revolution, 1880–1980', *Past and Present*, 103 (1984), pp. 149–58.
Carter, Paul, 'Enclosure, waged labour and the formation of class consciousness: Rural Middlesex c.1700–1835', *Labour History Review*, 66 (2001), pp. 269–93.
Caunce, Stephen, 'East Riding hiring fairs', *Oral History*, 3 (1975), pp. 45–52.
Caunce, Stephen, 'Twentieth-century farm servants: The horselads of the East Riding of Yorkshire', *Agricultural History Review*, 39 (1991), pp. 143–66.
Caunce, Stephen, *Amongst Farm Horses: The Horselads of East Yorkshire* (Stroud, 1991).
Caunce, Stephen, 'Farm servants and the development of capitalism in English agriculture', *Agricultural History Review*, 45 (1997), pp. 49–60.
Chamberlain, Mary, *Fenwomen: A Portrait of Women in an English Village* (London, 1975).
Chambers, J. D., 'Enclosure and labour supply in the industrial revolution', *Economic History Review*, V (1953), pp. 319–43.

Chambers, J. D., and Mingay, G. E., *The Agricultural Revolution, 1750–1880* (London, 1966).

Channer, C. and Roberts, M. E., *Lacemaking in the Midlands* (London, 1900).

Charlesworth, Andrew, 'The development of the English rural proletariat and social protest, 1700–1850: A comment', *Journal of Peasant Studies*, 8 (1980), pp. 101–11.

Charlesworth, Andrew, *An Atlas of Rural Protest in Britain, 1548–1900* (London, 1983).

Chinn, Carl, *They Worked all Their Lives: Women of the Urban Poor in England, 1880–1939* (Manchester, 1988).

Cirket, A. F., 'The 1830 riots in Bedfordshire: Background and events', *Bedfordshire Historical Record Society*, 57 (1978), pp. 75–112.

Clark, Alice, *Working Life of Women in the Seventeenth Century*, 1st edn 1919 (London, 1982).

Clark, Anna, *The Struggle for the Breeches: Gender and the Making of the British Working Class* (London, 1995).

Clarkson, L. A., *Proto-Industrialisation: The First Phase of Industrialisation?* (London, 1985).

Clift, William, *The Reminiscences of William Clift of Bramley* (Basingstoke, 1909).

Cockburn, Cynthia, *Brothers: Male Dominance and Technical Change* (London, 1983).

Coleman, D. C., 'Proto-industrialisation: A concept too many', *Economic History Review*, XXXVI (1983), pp. 435–48.

Collins, E. J. T., 'Historical farm records', *Archives*, 35 (1966), pp. 143–49.

Collins, E. J. T., 'Harvest technology and labour supply in Britain, 1790–1870', *Economic History Review*, XXII (1969), pp. 453–73.

Collins, E. J. T., ed., *The Agrarian History of England and Wales, vol. VII, 1850–1914* (Cambridge, 2000).

Colyer, R. J., 'The uses of estate home farm accounts as sources for nineteenth-century agricultural history', *The Local Historian*, 11 (1975), pp. 406–13.

Cooper, Bob, *A Song for Every Season: A Hundred Years of a Sussex Farming Family* (London, 1971).

Cunningham, Hugh, 'The employment and unemployment of children in England, c.1680–1851', *Past and Present*, 126 (1990), pp. 115–50.

Cunningham, Hugh, *The Children of the Poor: Representations of Childhood since the Seventeenth Century* (Oxford, 1991).

Davidoff, Leonore, *Worlds Between: Historical Perspectives on Gender and Class* (Cambridge, 1995).

Davidoff, Leonore, 'The separation of home and work? Landladies and lodgers in nineteenth and twentieth-century England', in Burman, ed., *Fit Work for Women*, pp. 64–97.

Davidoff, Leonore and Westover, Belinda, eds, *Our Work, Our Lives, Our World: Women's History and Women's Work* (London, 1986).

BIBLIOGRAPHY

Davidoff, Leonore and Hall, Catherine, *Family Fortunes: Men and Women of the English Middle Class, 1780–1850* (London, 1987).
Davies, Margaret Llewelyn, ed., *Life as we have Known It*, 1st edn 1931 (London, 1977).
Davin, Anna, *Growing Up Poor: Home, School and Street in London, 1870–1914* (London, 1996).
Davis, Michael Justin, ed., *In a Wiltshire Village: Scenes from Rural Village Life*, 1st edn 1981 (Stroud, 1992).
Digby, Anne, *Pauper Palaces* (London, 1978).
Dony, John G., *A History of the Straw Hat Industry* (Luton, 1942).
Dunbabin, J. P. D., 'The "revolt of the field": The agricultural labourers movement in the 1870s', *Past and Present*, 26 (1963), pp. 68–97.
Dunbabin, J. P. D., 'The incidence and organisation of agricultural trade unionism in the 1870s', *Agricultural History Review*, 16 (1968), pp. 114–41.
Dunbabin, J. P. D., *Rural Discontent in Nineteenth-Century Britain* (London, 1974).
Dunn, Richard S. and Dunn, Mary Maples, eds, *The World of William Penn* (Philadelphia, 1986).
Earle, Peter, 'The female labour market in London in the late seventeenth and early eighteenth centuries', *Economic History Review*, XLII (1989), pp. 328–53.
English, Barbara, *The Great Landowners of East Yorkshire, 1530–1910* (Hemel Hempstead, 1990).
Ernle, Lord, *English Farming Past and Present*, 1st edn 1912 (London, 1961).
Evans, Ewart George, *Ask the Fellows Who Cut the Hay* (London, 1956).
Evans, Ewart George, *The Farm and the Village* (London, 1969).
Evans, Ewart George, *Where Beards Wag All: The Relevance of the Oral Tradition* (London, 1970).
Fischer, F. J., ed., *Essays in the Economic and Social History of Tudor and Stuart England* (Cambridge, 1961).
Fletcher, Richard, ed., *The Biography of a Victorian Village: Richard Cobbold's Account of Wortham, Suffolk* (London, 1977).
Fordham, Montague and Fordham, T. R., *The English Agricultural Labourer, 1300–1925* (London, 1925).
Fores, Michael, 'The myth of a British industrial revolution', *History*, 66 (1981), pp. 181–98.
Fraser-Newstead, Brenda, *Bedford Yesteryears: The Rural Scene* (Dunstable, 1994).
Freeman, Charles, *Luton and the Hat Industry* (Luton, 1953).
Freeman, Charles, *Pillow Lace in the East Midlands* (Luton, 1958).
Freeman, Mark, 'Rider Haggard and Rural England: Methods of social enquiry in the English countryside', *Social History*, 26 (2001), pp. 209–16.
Gamarnikow, Eva et al., eds, *Gender, Class and Work* (London, 1983).
Gerard, Jessica, 'Invisible servants: The country house and the local community', *Bulletin of the Institute of Historical Research*, 57 (1986), pp. 178–88.

Gerard, Jessica, *Country House Life: Family and Servants, 1815–1914* (Oxford, 1994).
Gilboy, Mrs Elizabeth, 'Labour at Thornborough: An eighteenth-century estate', *Economic History Review*, 1st ser., III (1932), pp. 388–98.
Gittins, Diana, 'Marital status, work and kinship, 1850–1930', in Lewis, ed., *Labour and Love*, pp. 249–65.
Gloucestershire Federation of Women's Institutes, *'I Remember': Social Life in Gloucestershire Villages, 1850–1950* (Gloucester, 1961).
Godber, Joyce, *History of Bedfordshire, 1066–1888* (Bedford, 1969).
Goddard, Nicholas, 'The development and influence of agricultural periodicals and newspapers, 1780–1880', *Agricultural History Review*, 31 (1981), pp. 116–31.
Goose, Nigel, *Population, Economy and Family Structure in Hertfordshire in 1851: The Berkhamsted Region* (Hatfield, 1996).
Green, F. E., *A History of the English Agricultural Labourer, 1870–1920* (London, 1920).
Green, J. A. S., 'A survey of domestic service', *Lincolnshire History and Archaeology*, 17 (1982), pp. 65–9.
Gresswell, Fred, *Bright Boots: An Autobiography* (Newton Abbot, 1956).
Grey, Edwin, *Cottage Life in a Hertfordshire Village* (St Albans, 1935).
Gritt, Andrew, 'The census and the servant: A reassessment of the decline and distribution of farm service in early nineteenth-century England', *Economic History Review*, LIII (2000), pp. 84–106.
Gróf, László L., *Children of Straw: The Story of a Vanished Craft and Industry in Bucks, Herts, Beds and Essex* (Buckingham, 1988).
Haggard, Henry Rider, *Rural England: Being an Account of Agricultural and Social Researches Carried out in the Years 1901 and 1902*, 2 vols (London, 1902).
Haggard, Lilias Rider, ed., *'I Walked by Night': By the King of the Norfolk Poachers*, 1st edn 1935 (Oxford, 1982).
Hall, Catherine, 'The early formation of Victorian domestic ideology', in Burman, ed., *Fit Work for Women*, pp. 15–32.
Hall, Catherine, 'The home turned upside down? The working class family in cotton textiles', in Whitelegg et al., eds, *The Changing Experience of Women*, pp. 17–29.
Hall, Catherine, *White, Male and Middle Class: Explorations in Feminism and History* (Cambridge, 1992).
Hammond, J. L. and Hammond, Barbara, *The Village Labourer* (London, 1911).
Hardy, George, *Those Stormy Years* (London, 1956).
Hartwell, R. M., *The Industrial Revolution and Economic Growth* (London, 1971).
Harvey, Bessie, 'Youthful memories of my life in a Suffolk village', *The Suffolk Review*, 2 (1963), pp. 198–201.
Hassell Smith, A., 'Labourers in late sixteenth-century England: A case

study from north Norfolk [Part 1]', *Continuity and Change*, 4 (1989), pp. 11–52.
Hassell Smith, A., 'Labourers in late sixteenth-century England: A case study from north Norfolk [Part 2]', *Continuity and Change*, 4 (1989), pp. 367–94.
Hayfield, Colin, 'Farm servants' accommodation on the Yorkshire Wolds', *Folk Life*, 33 (1994–5), pp. 7–28.
Higgs, Edward, 'Women, occupations and work in the nineteenth-century censuses', *History Workshop Journal*, 23 (1987), pp. 59–82.
Higgs, Edward, 'Occupational censuses and the agricultural workforce in Victorian England and Wales', *Economic History Review*, XLVIII (1995), pp. 700–16.
Hill, Bridget, 'Women, work and the census: A problem for historians of women', *History Workshop Journal*, 35 (1993), pp. 78–94.
Hill, Bridget, 'Women's history: A study in change, continuity or standing still?', *Women's History Review*, 2 (1993), pp. 5–22.
Hill, Bridget, *Women, Work and Sexual Politics in Eighteenth-Century England*, 1st edn 1989 (London, 1994).
Hillyer, Richard, *Country Boy* (London, 1966).
Hobsbawn, E. J. and Rudé, G. E., *Captain Swing* (London, 1969).
Hollis, Patricia, *Women in Public: The Women's Movement, 1850–1900* (London, 1979).
Home, Michael, *Winter Harvest: A Norfolk Boyhood* (London, 1967).
Honeyman, Katrina, *Women, Gender and Industrialisation in England, 1700–1870* (Basingstoke, 2000).
Hooson, D. J. M., 'The straw industry of the Chilterns in the nineteenth century', *East Midland Geographer*, 4 (1968), pp. 342–50.
Horn, C. A. and Horn, P., 'The social structure of an "industrial" community: Ivinghoe in Buckinghamshire in 1871', *Local Population Studies*, 31 (1983), pp. 9–20.
Horn, Pamela, 'Pillow lacemaking in Victorian England: The experience of Oxfordshire', *Textile History*, 3 (1972), pp. 100–15.
Horn, Pamela, 'Child workers in the pillow lace and straw plait trades of Victorian Buckinghamshire and Bedfordshire', *Historical Journal*, 17 (1974), pp. 779–96.
Horn, Pamela, *Labouring Life in the Victorian Countryside* (London, 1976).
Horn, Pamela, *The Rural World, 1780–1850: Social Change in the English Countryside* (London, 1980).
Horn, Pamela, 'Women's cottage industries', in Mingay, ed., *Victorian Countryside*, vol. 1, pp. 341–52.
Horn, Pamela, *The Changing Countryside in Victorian and Edwardian England and Wales* (London, 1984).
Horn, Pamela, *Life and Labour in Rural England, 1760–1850* (London, 1987).
Horn, Pamela, *Victorian Countrywomen* (Oxford, 1991).
Horrell, Sara and Humphries, Jane, 'Women's labour force participation and

the transition to the male breadwinner family', *Economic History Review*, XLVIII (1995), pp. 89–117.

Horrell, Sara and Humphries, Jane, '"The exploitation of little children": Child labour and the family economy in the Industrial Revolution', *Explorations in Economic History*, 32 (1995), pp. 485–516.

Hostettler, Eve, 'Gourlay Steell and the sexual division of labour', *History Workshop Journal*, 4 (1977), pp. 95–100.

Hostettler, Eve, '"Making do": Domestic life among East Anglian labourers, 1890–1910', in Davidoff and Westover, eds, *Our Work, Our Lives, Our World*, pp. 36–53.

Houston, Rab and Snell, K. D. M., 'Proto-industrialisation? Cottage industry, social change and industrial revolution', *Historical Journal*, 27 (1984), pp. 473–92.

Howkins, Alun, '"In the sweat of thy face: The labourer and work', in Mingay, ed., *Victorian Countryside*, vol. 2, pp. 506–20.

Howkins, Alun, *Poor Labouring Men: Rural Radicalism in Norfolk, 1870–1923* (London, 1985).

Howkins, Alun, 'Labour history and the rural poor, 1850–1980', *Rural History*, 1 (1990), pp. 113–22.

Howkins, Alun, 'Peasants, servants and labourers: The marginal workforce in British agriculture, 1870–1914', *Agricultural History Review*, 42 (1991), pp. 49–62.

Howkins, Alun, *Reshaping Rural England: A Social History, 1850–1925* (London, 1991).

Hudson, Pat, ed., *Regions and Industries: A Perspective on the Industrial Revolution in Britain* (Cambridge, 1989).

Hudson, Pat, *The Industrial Revolution* (London, 1992).

Hudson, Pat, 'Women and industrialisation', in Purvis, ed., *Women's History*, pp. 23–50.

Hudson, Pat and Lee, W. R., eds, *Women's Work and the Family Economy in Historical Perspective* (Manchester, 1990).

Hufton, Olwen, *The Poor of Eighteenth-Century France, 1750–1789* (Oxford, 1974).

Hufton, Olwen, 'Women and the family economy in eighteenth-century France', *French Historical Studies*, 9 (1975), pp. 1–22.

Hufton, Olwen, 'Women without men: Widows and spinsters in Britain and France in the eighteenth century', *Journal of Family History*, Winter (1984), pp. 355–76.

Humphries, Jane, 'Protective legislation, the capitalist state and working class men: The case of the 1842 mines regulation act', *Feminist Review*, 7 (1981), pp. 1–33.

Humphries, Jane, '". . . the most free from objection . . .". The sexual division of labour and women's work in nineteenth-century England', *Journal of Economic History*, XLVII (1987), pp. 929–48.

Humphries, Jane, 'Enclosures, common rights and women: The proletarian-

isation of families in the late eighteenth and early nineteenth centuries', *Journal of Economic History*, L (1990), pp. 17–42.
Humphries, Jane, '"Lurking in the wings...": Women in the historiography of the industrial revolution', *Business and Economic History*, 20 (1991), pp. 32–44.
Humphries, Jane, 'Female-headed households in early industrial Britain: The vanguard of the proletariat?', *Labour History Review*, 63 (1998), pp. 31–65.
Hunt, E. H., 'Industrialisation and regional inequality: Wages in Britain, 1760–1914', *Journal of Economic History*, XLVI (1986), pp. 935–66.
Hussey, Stephen, '"The last survivor of an ancient race": The changing face of Essex gleaning', *Agricultural History Review*, 45 (1997), pp. 61–72.
Ibbotson, E. M. H., 'Ilmington in the nineteenth century: Reminiscences of an agricultural labourer', *The Local Historian*, 9 (1971), pp. 338–43.
Jobson, Allan, *An Hour-Glass on the Run* (London, 1959).
John, Angela V., *By the Sweat of their Brow: Women Workers at Victorian Coalmines* (London, 1980).
John, Angela V., ed., *Unequal Opportunities: Women's Employment in England, 1800–1918* (Oxford, 1986).
Johnson, Paul, *Saving and Spending: The Working-Class Economy in Britain, 1870–1939* (Oxford, 1985).
Jones, E. L., *The Development of English Agriculture, 1815–1873* (London, 1968).
Jones, E. L., *Agriculture and the Industrial Revolution* (London, 1974).
Jordan, Ellen, 'The exclusion of women from industry in nineteenth-century Britain', *Comparative Studies in Society and History*, 31 (1989), pp. 273–96.
Joyce, Patrick, ed., *The Historical Meanings of Work* (Cambridge, 1987).
Kebble, T. E., *The Agricultural Labourer: A Summary of His Position*, 1st edn 1870 (London, 1907).
Kennett, David H., 'Lacemaking by Bedfordshire paupers', *Textile History*, 5 (1975), pp. 111–18.
Kerridge, Eric, *The Agricultural Revolution* (London, 1967).
Kightly, Charles, *Country Voices: Life and Lore in Farm and Village* (London, 1984).
King, Peter, 'Gleaners, farmers and the failure of legal sanctions, 1750–1850', *Past and Present*, 125 (1989), pp. 117–50.
King, Peter, 'Customary rights and women's earnings: The importance of gleaning to the rural labouring poor, 1750–1850', *Economic History Review*, XLIV (1991), pp. 461–76.
King, Peter, 'Legal change, customary rights, and social conflict in late eighteenth-century England: The origins of the great gleaning case of 1788', *Law and History Review*, 10 (1992), pp. 1–31.
Kitchen, Fred, *Brother to the Ox: The Autobiography of a Farm Labourer* (Horsham, 1981).

Kitteringham, Jennie, 'Country work girls in nineteenth-century England', in Samuel, ed., *Village Life and Labour*, pp. 73–138.
Kussmaul, Ann, *Servants in Husbandry in Early Modern England* (Cambridge, 1981).
Land, Hilary, 'The family wage', *Feminist Review*, 6 (1980), pp. 55–77.
Lane, Penelope, 'Work on the margins: Poor women and the informal economy of eighteenth and early nineteenth-century Leicestershire', *Midland History*, 22 (1997), pp. 85–99.
Langdon, Roger, *The Life of Roger Langdon* (London, 1909).
Law, C. M., 'Luton and the hat industry', *East Midland Geographer*, 4 (1968), pp. 329–41.
Lazonick, William., 'Industrial relations and technological change: The case of the self-acting mule', *Cambridge Journal of Economics*, 3 (1979), pp. 231–62.
Lewis, Jane, ed., *Labour and Love: Women's Experiences of Home and Family, 1850–1940* (Oxford, 1986).
Lindert, Peter H. and Williamson, Jeffrey G., 'English workers' living standards during the industrial revolution: A new look', *Economic History Review*, XXXVI (1983), pp. 1–25.
Long, Jane, *Conversations in Cold Rooms: Women, Work and Poverty in Nineteenth-Century Northumberland* (Woodbridge, 1999).
Lown, Judith, 'Not much a factory, more a form of patriarchy: Gender and class during industrialisation', in Gamarnikow et al. eds, *Gender, Class and Work*, pp. 28–45.
Lown, Judith, *Women and Industrialisation: Gender at Work in Nineteenth-Century England* (Oxford, 1990).
McKendrick, Neil, 'Home demand and economic growth: A new view of the role of women and children in the industrial revolution', in McKendrick, Neil, ed., *Historical Perspectives in English Thought and Society in Honour of J. H. Plumb* (London, 1974), pp. 152–210.
McMurry, Sally, 'Women's work in agriculture: Divergent trends in England and America, 1800–1930', *Comparative Studies in Society and History*, 34 (1997), pp. 248–70.
Mager, Wolfgang, 'Proto-industrialisation and proto-industry: The uses and drawbacks of two concepts', *Continuity and Change*, 8 (1993), pp. 181–215.
Malcolmson, Robert *Life and Labour in England, 1700–1780* (London, 1981).
Malcolmson, Robert, and Mastoris, Stephanos, *The English Pig: A History* (London, 1998).
Markham, Alice M., *Back of Beyond: Reminiscences of Little Humber Farm, 1903–1925* (North Ferriby, 1979).
Marlow, Sylvia, *Winifred: A Wiltshire Working Girl* (Bradford-on-Avon, 1991).
Marshall, Sybil, *Fenland Chronicle: Recollections of William Henry and Kate Mary Edwards* (Cambridge, 1967).

Megginson, Irene, 'To be a farmer's boy in East Yorkshire', *The Dalesman*, 39 (1977), pp. 524–7.
Mendels, Franklin F., 'Proto-industrialisation: The first phase of the industrial process', *Journal of Economic History*, XXXII (1972), pp. 241–61.
Miller, Celia, 'The hidden workforce: Female fieldworkers in Gloucestershire, 1870–1901', *Southern History*, 6 (1984), pp. 139–61.
Mincoff Elizabeth, and Marriage, Margaret S., *A History of Hand-made Lace* (London, 1900).
Mingay, G. E., *Enclosure and the Small Farmers in the Age of the Industrial Revolution* (London, 1968).
Mingay, G. E., ed., *The Agricultural State of the Kingdom in 1816* (Bath, 1970).
Mingay, G. E., *Rural Life in Victorian England* (London, 1976).
Mingay, G. E., ed., *The Victorian Countryside*, 2 vols (London, 1981).
Mingay, G. E., ed., *The Agrarian History of England and Wales, vol. VI, 1750–1850* (Cambridge, 1989).
Mingay, G. E., *A Social History of the English Countryside* (London, 1990).
Mitchell, Juliet and Oakley, Ann, eds, *The Rights and Wrongs of Women* (Harmondsworth, 1976).
Morgan, David H., 'The place of harvesters in nineteenth-century village life', in Samuel, ed., *Village Life and Labour*, pp. 29–72.
Morgan, David H., *Harvesters and Harvesting, 1840–1900: A Study of the Rural Proletariat* (London, 1982).
Morris, Revd M. C. F., *Yorkshire Reminiscences* (London, 1922).
Morris, Revd M. C. F., *The British Workman Past and Present* (London, 1928).
Moses, Gary, '"Rude and rustic": Hiring fairs and their critics in East Yorkshire, c.1850–75', *Rural History*, 7 (1996), pp. 151–75.
Moses, Gary, 'Proletarian labourers? East Riding farm servants, c.1850–1875', *Agricultural History Review*, 47 (1999), pp. 78–94.
Muskett, Paul, 'The East Anglian agrarian riots of 1822', *Agricultural History Review*, 32 (1984), pp. 1–13.
Mutch, Alistair, 'The "farming ladder" in north Lancashire, 1840–1914: Myth or reality?', *Northern History*, 27 (1991), pp. 162–83.
Neave, Susan and Ellis, Stephen, eds, *An Historical Atlas of East Yorkshire* (Hull, 1996).
Neeson, J. M., *Commoners: Common Right, Enclosure and Social Change in England, 1700–1820* (Cambridge, 1993).
Newby, Howard, *The Deferential Worker* (Harmondsworth, 1977).
Newby, Howard, *Country Life: A Social History of Rural England* (London, 1987).
Orwin, C. S. and Whetham, E. H., *A History of British Agriculture, 1846–1914* (London, 1964).
Osterud, Grey Nancy, 'Gender divisions and the organisation of work in the Leicester hosiery industry', in John, ed., *Unequal Opportunities*, pp. 45–70.
Overton, Mark, *Agricultural Revolution in England: The Transformation of the Agrarian Economy, 1500–1850* (Cambridge, 1996).

BIBLIOGRAPHY

Pahl, R. E., *Divisions of Labour* (Oxford, 1984).

Pahl, R. E., ed., *On Work: Historical, Comparative and Theoretical Approaches* (Oxford, 1988).

Parrott, Susan, 'The decline of hiring fairs in the East Riding of Yorkshire: Driffield, c.1874–1939', *Journal of Regional and Local Studies*, 16 (1996), pp. 19–31.

Peacock, A. J., *Bread or Blood: A Study of the Agrarian Riots in East Anglia in 1816* (London, 1965).

Pennington, Shelley and Westover, Belinda, *Homeworkers in England, 1850–1985* (Basingstoke, 1989).

Perkins, J. A., 'Harvest technology and labour supply in Lincolnshire and the East Riding of Yorkshire, 1750–1850', *Tools and Tillage*, 3 (1976), pp. 47–58.

Phillips, Anne and Taylor, Barbara, 'Sex and skill: Notes towards a feminist economics', *Feminist Review*, 6 (1980), pp. 79–88.

Pierenkemper, Toni, ed., *Zur Ökonomie des Privaten Havshalts* (Frankfurt, 1991).

Pinchbeck, Ivy, *Women Workers and the Industrial Revolution, 1750–1850*, 1st edn 1930 (London, 1981).

Purvis, June, ed., *Women's History: Britain, 1850–1945. An Introduction* (London, 1995).

Randall, Arthur, *Sixty Years A Fenman* (London, 1966).

Reay, Barry, *The Last Rising of the Agricultural Labourers: Rural Life and Protest in Nineteenth-Century England* (Oxford, 1990).

Reay, Barry, *Microhistories: Demography, Society and Culture in Rural England, 1800–1930* (Cambridge, 1996).

Reed, Mick, 'Indoor farm service in nineteenth-century Sussex: Some criticisms of a critique', *Sussex Archaeological Collections*, 123 (1985), pp. 225–41.

Reed, Mick, '"Gnawing it out": A new look at economic relations in nineteenth-century rural England', *Rural History*, 1 (1990), pp. 83–94.

Reed, Mick and Wells, Roger, eds, *Class Conflict and Protest in the English Countryside, 1700–1880* (London, 1990).

Rendall, Jane, *Women in an Industrialising Society: England, 1750–1880* (Oxford, 1990).

Richards, Eric, 'Women in the British economy since about 1700', *History*, 59 (1974), pp. 337–57.

Roberts, Elizabeth, *Women's Work, 1840–1940* (London, 1988).

Roberts, Elizabeth, *A Woman's Place: An Oral History of Working Class Women, 1890–1940*, 1st edn 1984 (Oxford, 1995).

Roberts, Michael, 'Sickles and scythes: Women's work and men's work at harvest time', *History Workshop Journal*, 7 (1979), pp. 3–28.

Roberts, Michael, '"Waiting upon chance": English hiring fairs and their meanings from the fourteenth to the twentieth century', *Journal of Historical Sociology*, 1 (1988), pp. 119–60.

Roberts, Robert, *The Classic Slum: Salford Life in the First Quarter of the Century* (Manchester, 1971).
Rose, Sonya, '"Gender at work": Sex, class and industrial capitalism', *History Workshop Journal*, 21 (1986), pp. 113–31.
Rose, Sonya, 'Gender antagonism and class conflict: Exclusionary strategies of male trade unions in nineteenth-century Britain', *Social History*, 13 (1988), pp. 191–208.
Rose, Sonya, 'Proto-industry, women's work and the household economy in the transition to industrial capitalism', *Journal of Family History*, 13 (1988), pp. 181–93.
Rose, Walter, *Good Neighbours: Some Recollections of an English Village and Its People* (Cambridge, 1942).
Ross, Ellen, '"Fierce questions and taunts": Married life in working-class London, 1870–1914', *Feminist Studies*, 8 (1982), pp. 572–602.
Ross, Ellen, 'Survival networks: Women's neighbourhood sharing in London before World War 1', *History Workshop Journal*, 15 (1983), pp. 4–27.
Ross, Ellen, 'Labour and love: Rediscovering London's working-class mothers, 1870–1918', in Lewis, ed., *Labour and Love*, pp. 73–96.
Ross, Ellen, *Love and Toil: Motherhood in Outcast London, 1870–1918* (Oxford, 1993).
Rule, John, *The Labouring Classes in Early Industrial England, 1750–1850* (London, 1986).
Rule, John and Wells, Roger, *Crime, Protest and Popular Politics in Southern England, 1740–1850* (London, 1997).
Saito, Osamu, 'Who worked when: Life-time profiles of labour force participation in Cardington and Corfe Castle in the late eighteenth and mid nineteenth centuries', *Local Population Studies*, 22 (1979), pp. 14–29.
Samuel, Raphael, ed., *Village Life and Labour* (London, 1975).
Savory, Arthur H., *Grain and Chaff from an English Manor* (Oxford, 1920).
Sayer, Karen, 'Field-faring women: The resistance of women who worked in the fields of nineteenth-century England', *Women's History Review*, 2 (1993), pp. 185–98.
Sayer, Karen, *Women of the Fields: Representations of Rural Women in the Nineteenth Century* (Manchester, 1995).
Schmiechen, James A., *Sweated Industries and Sweated Labour: The London Clothing Trades* (Urbana, 1984).
Scofield, R.S., 'Age-specific mobility in an eighteenth-century rural English parish', *Annals de Démographic Historiqué* (1970), pp. 261–74.
Seccombe, Wally, 'Patriarchy stabilised: The construction of the male breadwinner wage norm in nineteenth-century Britain', *Social History*, 11 (1986), pp. 53–76.
Severn, Joseph Millott, *My Village: Owd Condor, Derbyshire* (Hove, 1935).
Shammas, Carole, 'The world women knew: Women workers in the north of England during the seventeenth century', in Dunn and Dunn, eds, *The World of William Penn*, pp. 99–114.

Sharpe, Pamela, 'The women's harvest: Straw-plaiting and the representation of labouring women's employment, c.1793–1885', *Rural History*, 5 (1994), pp. 129–42.

Sharpe, Pamela, 'Time and wages of west country workfolks in the seventeenth and eighteenth centuries', *Local Population Studies*, 55 (1995), pp. 66–9.

Sharpe, Pamela, 'Continuity and change: Women's history and economic history in Britain', *Economic History Review*, XLVIII (1995), pp. 353–69.

Sharpe, Pamela, *Adapting to Capitalism: Women Working in the English Economy, 1700–1850* (Basingstoke, 1996).

Sharpe, Pamela, 'The organisation of the lace industry in England and Ireland', in Devonshire, Anne and Wood, Barbara, eds, *Women in Industry and Technology* (London, 1996), pp. 179–83.

Sharpe, Pamela, ed., *Women's Work: The English Experience, 1650–1914* (London, 1998).

Sharpe, Pamela, 'The female labour market in English agriculture during the Industrial Revolution: Expansion or contraction?', *Agricultural History Review*, 47 (1999), pp. 161–81.

Shaw-Taylor, Leigh, 'Labourers, cows, common rights and parliamentary enclosure: The evidence of contemporary comment c.1760–1810', *Past and Present*, 171 (2001), pp. 95–126.

Shaw-Taylor, Leigh, 'Parliamentary enclosure and the emergence of an English agricultural proletariat', *Journal of Economic History*, LXI (2001), pp. 640–62.

Sheppard, June A., 'East Yorkshire's agricultural labour force in the mid nineteenth century', *Agricultural History Review*, 9 (1961), pp. 43–54.

Shoemaker, Robert B., *Gender in English Society, 1650–1850: The Emergence of Separate Spheres?* (Harlow, 1998).

Short, Brian, 'The decline of living-in service in the transition to capitalist farming: A critique of the Sussex evidence', *Sussex Archaeological Collections*, 122 (1984), pp. 147–64.

Shorter, Edward, *The Making of the Modern Family* (London, 1976).

Smith, Christine, ed., *Stotford Reflections* (Baldock, 1993).

Smith, David, *No Rain in Those Clouds* (London, 1943).

Snell, K. D. M., *Annals of the Labouring Poor: Social Change and Agrarian England, 1660–1900* (Cambridge, 1985).

Snell, Lord, *Men, Movements and Myself* (London, 1936).

Sokoll, Thomas, 'Early attempts at accounting the unaccountable: Davies' and Eden's budgets of agricultural labouring families in late eighteenth-century England', in Pierenkemper, ed., *Zur Ökonomic des Privaten Havshalts*, pp. 34–58.

Sokoll, Thomas, *Household and Family Among the Poor: The Case of Two Essex Communities in the Late Eighteenth and Early Nineteenth Centuries* (Bochum, 1993).

Spencerley, G. F. R., 'The lace associations: Philanthropic movements to preserve the production of handmade lace in late Victorian and Edwardian times', *Victorian Studies*, 16 (1973), pp. 433–52.

Spencerley, G. F. R., 'The origins of the English pillow lace industry', *Agricultural History Review*, 21 (1973), pp. 81–93.

Spencerley, G. F. R., 'The health and disciplining of children in the pillow lace industry in the nineteenth century', *Textile History*, 7 (1976), pp. 154–71.

Spencerley, G. F. R., 'The English pillow lace industry, 1840–1880: A rural industry in competition with machinery', *Business History*, 19 (1977), pp. 68–87.

Stephens, W. B., *Sources for English Local History*, 1st edn 1981 (Chichester, 1994).

Styles, John, 'Clothing the north: The supply of non-elite clothing in the eighteenth-century north of England', *Textile History*, 25 (1994), pp. 139–66.

Tate, W. E., *The English Village Community and the Enclosure Movement* (London, 1967).

Tebbutt, Melanie, *Making Ends Meet: Pawnbroking and Working-Class Credit* (Leicester, 1983).

Thirsk, Joan, 'Industries in the countryside', in Fischer, ed., *Essays*, pp. 70–88.

Thirsk, Joan, *Alternative Agriculture: A History from the Black Death to the Present Day* (Oxford, 1997).

Thomas, Janet, 'Women and capitalism: Oppression or emancipation? A review article', *Comparative Studies in Society and History*, 30 (1988), pp. 534–49.

Thompson, Flora, *Lark Rise to Candleford*, 1st edn 1939 (Harmondsworth, 1984).

Thorburn, Dave, 'Gender, work and schooling in the plaiting villages', *The Local Historian*, 19 (1989), pp. 107–13.

Tilly, Louise and Scott, Joan, *Women, Work and Family*, 1st edn 1978 (London, 1987).

Turner, M. E., *English Parliamentary Enclosure: Its Historical Geography and Economic History* (Folkestone, 1980).

Turner, M. E., Beckett, J. V. and Afton, B., 'Taking stock: Farmers, farm records and agricultural output in England, 1700–1850', *Agricultural History Review*, 44 (1996), pp. 21–34.

Turner, M. E., Beckett, J. V. and Afton, B., *Farm Production in England, 1700–1914* (Oxford, 2001).

Tweedy, Arthur, 'Recollections of a farm worker. Part 1', *Bulletin of the Cleveland and Teesside Local History Society*, 21 (1973), pp. 1–6.

Valenze, Deborah, *The First Industrial Woman* (Oxford, 1995).

Verdon, Nicola, 'The employment of women and children in agriculture: A reassessment of agricultural gangs in nineteenth-century Norfolk', *Agricultural History Review*, 49 (2001), pp. 41–55.

Verdon, Nicola, '"... a much neglected historical source": The uses and limitations of farm account books to historians of rural women's work', *Women's History Notebooks*, 8 (2001), pp. 5–12.

Verdon, Nicola, 'The rural labour market in the early nineteenth century:

Women's and children's employment, family income and the 1834 Poor Law Report', *Economic History Review*, LV (2002), pp. 298–322.
Vickery, Amanda, 'Golden age to separate spheres? A review of the categories and chronology of English women's history', *Historical Journal*, 36 (1993), pp. 383–414.
Vincent, David, *Bread, Knowledge and Freedom: A Study of Nineteenth-Century Working Class Autobiography* (London, 1981).
Wade Martins, Susanna, *A Great Estate at Work: The Holkham Estate and Its Inhabitants in the Nineteenth Century* (Cambridge, 1980).
Wade Martins, Susanna and Williamson, Tom, 'Labour and improvement: Agricultural change in East Anglia, circa 1750–1870', *Labour History Review*, 62, 3 (1997), pp. 275–95.
Wardle, Patricia, *Victorian Lace* (London, 1968).
Warren, C. Henry, *A Boy in Kent* (London, 1937).
Warren, C. Henry, *Happy Countryman* (London, 1946).
Wells, Roger, 'The development of the English rural proletariat and social protest, 1700–1850', *Journal of Peasant Studies*, 6 (1979), pp. 115–39.
Wells, Roger, 'Social conflict and protest in the English countryside in the early nineteenth century: A rejoinder', *Journal of Peasant Studies*, 8 (1981), pp. 514–30.
Whitelegg, Elizabeth, et al. eds. *The Changing Experience of Women* (Oxford, 1982).
Whitlock, Ralph, *Peasant's Heritage* (London, n.d.).
Williams, Alfred, *A Wiltshire Village* (London, 1912).
Wilson Fox, Arthur, 'Agricultural wages on England and Wales during the last fifty years', *Journal of the Statistical Society*, 66 (1903), pp. 273–348.
Woodward, Donald, ed., *The Farming and Memorandum Books of Henry Best of Elmswell, 1642*, British Academy of Social and Economic History, no. 8 (1984).
Woodward, Donald, 'Early modern servants in husbandry revisited', *Agricultural History Review*, 48 (2000), pp. 141–50.
Wright, Thomas, *The Romance of the Lace Pillow* (London, 1900).
Yelling, J. A., *Common Field and Enclosure in England, 1450–1850* (London, 1977).

Theses

Adams, M. G., 'Agricultural change in the East Riding of Yorkshire, 1850–1880: An economic and social history' (Ph.D. thesis, University of Hull, 1977).
Gielgud, Judy, 'Nineteenth-century farm women in Northumberland and Cumbria: The neglected workforce' (D.Phil. thesis, University of Sussex, 1992).

Miller, Celia, 'Farm work and farm workers in Victorian Gloucestershire' (Ph.D. thesis, University of Bristol, 1980).

Sayer, Karen, '"Girls into demons": Nineteenth-century representations of English working class women employed in agriculture' (Ph.D. thesis, University of Sussex, 1991).

Speechley, Helen V., 'Female and child agricultural day labourers in Somerset, c.1685–1870' (Ph.D. thesis, University of Exeter, 1999).

Verdon, Nicola, 'Changing patterns of female employment in rural England, c.1790–1890' (Ph.D. thesis, University of Leicester, 1999).

Index

agricultural labour: during Napoleonic Wars, 47–9, 99–100, 142–3; female day labourers, 2–3, 21–9, 47–9, 55–61, 64–5, 67–72, 73–5, 98–106, 114–21, 196–7; harvest technology, 24–5, 27; in Bedfordshire, 141–3, 149–52, 158–63; in East Yorkshire, 102–4, 115–19, 128–31; in Gloucestershire, 29, 119; in Norfolk, 99–102, 115–16, 120–1, 128; in Northumberland, 28, 104–5, 116; in Somerset, 29, 105, 116, 119, 128; in South Yorkshire, 28, 105–6; sexual division of tasks, 121–4, 197. *See also* bondager system, child labour, dairying, farm labour and account books, farm service, gang labour, gleaning, market gardening, wages

agriculture: agricultural revolution, 18–19; common rights, 30, 42, 170, 180; depression, 51, 115, 164; enclosure, 19–20, 42; mechanisation of, 25, 73, 164, 197; trade unions, 21, 165

Alexander, Sally, 12, 22
allotments, 62, 66, 186, 188
animals, maintenance of, 45, 62, 187–8
Ashby, Mabel, 192
Austin, Alfred, 64, 65, 66
autobiographical literature, 37–9, 166

Batchelor, Thomas, 140, 144, 148
Bear, William, 132, 139, 159, 162
Bedfordshire, 47, 50, 53, 54, 55, 62, 132–63
Bell, Joseph, 146
Bennett, William, 132
Berg, Maxine, 10, 134, 136
Bettesworth, Lucy, 172, 190
Beverley, 96
bondager system, 67, 97
Bouquet, Mary, 2, 28, 82
Bourne, George, 171, 194, 199–200
Boyle, Robert, 70
Bridlington, 86, 92, 95, 96
Buckinghamshire, 47, 49, 53, 55, 136, 138, 144, 145

budget, management of, 171–4
Burnette, Joyce, 2, 28, 29, 105–6, 126, 128
button-making, 53, 65, 67, 133, 196

Caddington, 150
Caird, James, 34
Cambridgeshire, 55, 67, 107
Cardington, 155, 156
Castle Acre, 72, 107, 108–9
Caunce, Stephen, 81, 83, 85, 87, 91
census records, 31–3, 73–5, 82, 96, 117–19, 197
Chester, 55
child labour, 5; in agriculture, 55–61, 67, 84, 100–3, 115, 116, 120–1, 127, 129, 141, 151–2, 179; contribution of earnings, 43–4, 61–3; in domestic industries, 53, 62, 134, 155; in gangs, 108–14; gathering resources, 180–6; in household labour, 168, 178–80; in manufacturing, 10, 62
Children's Employment Commission: Trades and Manufacturers (1843), 137, 139; First Report (1863), 137, 146, 153–4, 157–8; Second Report (1864), 137; Sixth Report (1867), 67, 109–11, 113–14
Cobbett, William, 34, 51, 133, 149
Cornwall, 62
cottage gardens, 45, 62, 66, 70, 186–7, 194
credit, 168, 174
Cumberland, 43, 49, 70, 116

dairying, 64, 95, 123–4, 147
Davidoff, Leonore, 12
Davies, David 34, 40, 41–5, 61, 128, 165
Davin, Anna, 22, 168
Denison, Stephen, 64, 66, 72, 108–9
Derbyshire, 53, 55
Devon, 28, 46, 65, 70, 80, 82, 133, 138
domestic ideology, 15, 24
domestic industries, 3, 22, 23, 43, 47, 53–5, 196, 198. *See also* button-making, glove-making, lace-making, spinning, straw-plaiting

229

INDEX

domestic service, 26, 81–2, 157, 199
Dorset, 47, 49, 53, 55, 65, 70, 80, 133
Doyle, Sir Francis, 64
dressmaking, 65
Driffield, 86, 93, 94, 95
Durham, 49, 55, 67, 80, 128

Earsham, 99–102, 122
East Riding of Yorkshire, 49, 55, 57, 77, 123, 125, 155, 186. *See also* agricultural labour, farm service, wages
Eden, Frederick, 34, 40, 41–5, 61, 132, 165
Essex, 26, 47, 61, 99, 123, 133, 136, 146, 184
Evans, George Ewart, 188
Eversholt, 142–3

family hiring, 67, 80
family income, 43–4, 61–3, 66, 129–31, 165, 179–80, 188, 193–5, 196
family wage, 14–15, 165
farm labour and account books, 36–7, 106, 197
farm service, 77–81, 149, 198; decline of female service, 94–7, 196; definition of female farm servants, 81–2; depiction of servants, 92, 198; harassment of women, 90; hiring fairs, 84–7; hiring of women, 83–4; lodgings, 90; servants' wages, 49–51, 92–4; supervision of servants, 91; work patterns, 87–90. *See also* bondager system, family hiring
Fox, Arthur Wilson, 73, 188
Fraser, James, 71, 111–14, 127
fruit picking, 62

gang labour, 67, 107–14, 198
Gangs Act (1867), 110, 113, 198–9
gathering fuel, 180–1
General Views of Agriculture, 45–52
Gielgud, Judy, 2, 28, 77, 82, 85, 88, 104, 116, 123
gleaning, 30, 45, 57, 62, 64, 70, 123, 159, 170, 182–6
Gloucestershire, 29, 46, 119, 125
glove-making, 53, 65, 67, 133, 196
gossiping, 190–1
Grey, Edwin, 145, 148, 156, 158, 162, 180, 192

Hammond, J. L. and Barbara, 19
Hasbach, William, 19, 40
Hassell Smith, A., 122
Hedon, 95

Henley, Joseph, 72
Hertfordshire, 47, 49, 155–6
Hillyer, Richard, 173, 190
Home, Michael, 175
Horn, Pamela, 22, 136
Horrell, Sara, and Humphries, Jane, 10, 11, 17, 30, 61
housework, 164, 169, 175–6, 199–200
Hoverton St Peter, 115, 128
Howden, 86, 93, 96
Howkins, Alun, 23, 80, 81, 107
Hudson, Pat, 10
Hufton, Olwen, 166, 169
Huntingdon, 55

industrialisation: factory production, 11, 13; female labour force participation, 16–17; proto-industry, 10–11, 13; separation of home and workplace, 12; textile workers, 11, 14. *See also* domestic ideology, family wage, protective legislation, skilled labour, spinning
informal economy, 30, 165–71. *See also* allotments, animals, budget, cottage gardens, credit, gleaning, housework, kin networks, lodgers, neighbourhood networks, nursing, pig keeping, sewing, washing

Jefferies, Richard, 96
Jobson, Allan, 175, 188, 190

Kent, 55, 57, 64, 65, 66, 67, 75, 79, 80, 174
kin networks, 169, 189
King, Peter, 30, 57, 170
Kussmaul, Ann, 77, 78, 81

lace-making, 43, 53, 65, 67, 196; census figures for Bedfordshire, 153–5; condemnation of workers, 147–9; decline in, 157–8, 162; history of, 132–9; lace dealers, 144, 145; lifecycle, 156; skill and status, 162, 197; wages in, 143–4, 149, 150, 152–3, 157
Lancashire, 55, 80
Laxton, 117–19, 125, 129–31
Leicestershire, 53
lifecycle, 33, 43–4, 62, 84, 127–31, 196–8
Lincolnshire, 43, 55, 65, 66, 67, 71, 74, 80, 82, 107
lodgers, taking in, 45, 62, 168, 177

INDEX

male labourers, 5; in agriculture, 24, 74, 99–102, 104, 115–16, 121–4, 141–3, 149–52; in domestic industries, 147–8, 153; in farm service, 90–1, 95; keeping pigs, 186–7; in manufacturing, 13–14; tending allotments, 188
male wages, 11, 24–5, 44, 48, 50, 61–2, 70, 92–4, 126–7, 143, 146–7, 172–3
Malton, 95
market gardening, 75, 159–61
Market Weighton, 95
Markham, Alice, 88
Marshall, William, 46
Middlesex, 49, 55
Midlands Lace Association, 139
Miller, Celia, 2, 29, 119
Moate, Margaret, 88
Morris, Reverend, 87, 88, 89

neighbourhood networks, 169, 170, 189–93
Norfolk, 42, 49, 53, 55, 63, 65, 75, 107, 119, 125, 188. *See also* agricultural labour, Castle Acre, Earsham, gang labour, gleaning, wages
North Yorkshire, 55, 57, 123, 181
Northamptonshire, 43, 47, 53, 55, 134, 136, 138, 139, 172, 173, 176, 178, 180, 184–5, 189, 190, 191
Northumberland, 55, 57, 65, 72, 75, 123. *See also* agricultural labour, bondager system, wages
Nottinghamshire, 53, 55, 67, 74, 80, 171
nursing, 62

Oxfordshire, 97, 130, 133, 173, 199

Parliamentary Papers, 34–5, 40, 63–75. *See also* Children's Employment Commission, Poor Law Report (1834), Report on the Employment of Women and Children in Agriculture (1843), Royal Commission on the Employment of Children, Young Persons and Women in Agriculture (1867–70), Royal Commission on Labour (1893–4)
patriarchy, 15–16
Patrington, 96
pawnbroking, 168
pig keeping, 186–7, 194
Pinchbeck, Ivy, 9, 23–4, 40, 46, 47, 98–9, 105, 106, 107, 135, 147
Podington, 142–3, 151, 152, 154–5, 156

Poor Law, 41
Poor Law Report (1834), 52–63, 128, 135, 141, 152, 166
Portman, Edwin, 71, 91
protective legislation, 15. *See also* Gangs Act (1867)
Purdy, Frederick, 67

Randall, Arthur, 120, 175
Report on the Employment of Women and Children in Agriculture (1843), 63–6, 72–3, 108–9, 188
Roberts, Elizabeth, 15
Rose, Walter, 182, 188
Ross, Ellen, 167, 193
Royal Commission on the Employment of Children, Young Persons and Women in Agriculture (1867–70), 67–73, 91, 110–14, 120, 126, 127, 150, 151, 153
Royal Commission on Labour (1893–4), 74–5, 132, 139, 162, 188

Saltmarshe, 102–4, 117, 125, 128
Savory, Arthur, 130
Sayer, Karen, 35, 40, 63, 198
Sewerby, 115–16, 125
sewing, 168, 175
Sharpe, Pamela, 2, 3, 18, 26–7, 30, 99, 123, 136, 144, 146
shopkeepers, 174
Simpson, Mary, 85, 86, 91
skilled labour, definition of, 13–14, 197
Snell, K. D. M., 22–7, 55, 57, 79, 81, 98–9, 102, 106, 121
Somerset, 53, 55, 65, 70, 124. *See also* agricultural labour, wages
Speechley, Helen, 2, 29, 105, 116, 124, 126, 128
spinning, 11–12, 42–3, 46, 53, 66, 133, 196
Staffordshire, 55, 62
Stanhope, Edward, 71, 126
straw-plaiting, 43, 47, 53, 67, 196; census figures for Bedfordshire, 153–5; condemnation of workers, 147–9; dealers, 145–6; decline of, 157–8, 162; history of, 139–41; lifecycle, 156; seasonal fluctuations, 145; wages in, 143–4, 147, 149–50, 153, 157
Strickland, H. E., 92, 186
Suffolk, 42, 55, 61, 62, 65, 67, 183, 189
Surrey, 63, 65
Sussex, 55, 57, 65, 79, 80, 181
Swaffham, 111–12

INDEX

Thirsk, Joan, 133
Thompson, Flora, 97, 130, 173, 199
Thurston, Mark, 176, 179, 183, 192
Tremenheere, Henry, 71

Upper Stondon, 152, 155

Valenze, Deborah, 26, 135
Vaughan, Henry, 64, 66

wages: agricultural day rates, 29–30, 43–5, 48–9, 65–6, 67, 70, 124–5; wage-gap, 43, 49–50, 70, 94, 126–7. *See also* child labour, family income, farm servants, lace-making, male wages, straw-plaiting
Warwickshire, 62, 171, 181

washing, 45, 62–3, 168, 176, 177–8
Wereham, 120
West Yorkshire, 55
Westmorland, 49, 55, 57, 70
Williams, Alfred, 172, 174, 178, 182, 191
Wiltshire, 46, 62, 65, 70. *See also* Williams, Alfred
Winfarthing, 120
women workers, depiction of, 63, 66, 71–3, 76, 164, 197–8. *See also* farm servants, lace-making, straw-plaiting
Worcestershire, 62

Yorkshire, 65, 80, 105–6
Young, Arthur, 42, 47, 138